ORGANIZATION⟷COMMUNICATION

EMERGING PERSPECTIVES II

PEOPLE, COMMUNICATION, ORGANIZATION

LEE THAYER, Series Editor

University of Wisconsin, Parkside

Associate Editors

Charles Conrad

University of North Carolina, Chapel Hill

Gerald M. Goldhaber

State University of New York, Buffalo

W. Charles Redding

Purdue University

Organization⟵⟶Communication: Emerging Perspectives I, edited by
Lee Thayer

in preparation

Metaphor and Organization: An Ideological Analysis, by Stephen R. Axley

Responsive Institutions: A Communication Order without Control, by Joseph
Pilotta, John W. Murphy, Tricia Jones, and Elizabeth Wilson

Power and Politics in Organizational Culture, by Dennis K. Mumby

Studying Human Communication: Evaluating Method and Data, edited by
Nancy J. Wyatt and Gerald M. Phillips

Television and Organizational Life, edited by Nick Trujillo and Leah R.
Ekdom

Organization⟷Communication
Emerging Perspectives II

Lee Thayer, Editor

University of Wisconsin, Parkside

ABLEX PUBLISHING CORPORATION
Norwood, New Jersey

Library of Congress Cataloging-in-Publication Data
(Revised for vol. 2)

Organization—communication.

  (People, communication, organization)
  Includes bibliographies and indexes.
  1. Organization. 2. Communication in organizations.
I. Thayer, Lee O.
HD31.0727   1986   302.3'5   85-6159
ISBN 0-89391-274-3 (v. 1)
ISBN 0-89391-425-8 (v. 2)

Ablex Publishing Corporation
355 Chestnut Street
Norwood, New Jersey 07648

Contents

v

The Contributors

DAVID A. BEDNAR is Associate Professor of Management, University of Arkansas-Fayetteville. His publications have appeared in *Labor and Industrial Relations Review, National Productivity Review, Journal of Business Communication, Journal of Business Education,* and others. He is co-author (with Donald D. White) of *Organizational Behavior* (1986) and (with Grant T. Savage) of *Managerial Communication* (forthcoming).

HENRI BROMS is Adjunct Professor of Iranology and Linguistics at the University of Helsinki; he is also Chief Librarian, Helsinki School of Economics and Business Administration. He has ten monographs on cross-cultural and semiotic subjects, among them *Mythology in Management Culture* (1982) and *An Introduction to Semiotics of Culture* (in press).

JIB FOWLES, Professor in the School of Human Sciences and Humanities at the University of Houston-Clear Lake, teaches courses on communications and social change. His books include *Mass Advertising as Social Forecast* and *Television Viewers vs. Media Snobs.*

HENRIK GAHMBERG is Associate Professor of Organization at the Swedish School of Economics and Business Administration in Helsinki. His current research interests include the role of human values in strategic decisions and corporate culture. His publications include *Communication and Learning in Organizations* (1980).

JILL J. MCMILLAN is Assistant Professor of Speech Communication at Wake Forest University. Since receiving her Ph.D. in 1982, she has been interested in exploring the message-making of organizational members, as it occurs both individually and collectively, and in organizational culture and power in organizations.

ALICE SAPIENZA teaches strategic planning in the Graduate School of Public Health, having been awarded a DBA from Harvard Business School after degrees in chemistry and English. She brings to her research seven years of general management experience of her own, which now focuses upon the interaction of culture and strategy in a range of institutions.

GRANT T. SAVAGE is Assistant Professor of Management at Texas Tech University. A graduate of Ohio State University, he has published articles in *Communication Monographs* and the *International Journal of Small Group Research.* He is co-author (with David A. Bednar) of *Managerial Communication* (forthcoming).

EDWARD C. STEWART is an experimental psychologist who was born in São Paulo, Brazil. He has taught at Pittsburgh, Delaware, Minnesota, and The George Washington University, moving to International Christian University in Tokyo in 1980, where his research has concentrated on the cultural base of the Japanese management of technology.

NICK TRUJILLO teaches organizational communication and public relations as Assistant Professor, Center for Communication Arts, Southern Methodist University. His publications have appeared in *Communication Monographs* and *Critical Studies in Mass Communication*. He is currently studying the dramatization of organizational life on prime-time television.

FREDRIK ULFHIELM is a graduate of Stockholm University, where he studied business administration, psychology, and Japanology. He is currently lecturer in business administration, sharing his time between the Åbo Swedish University (Åbo Akademi) in Åbo, Finland, and the Royal Institute of Technology in Stockholm, Sweden.

JOANNE YATES teaches communication at MIT's Sloan School of Management, where she developed the Sloan Communication Program. She is currently at work on *Control through Communication:* The Origins of Internal Communication in American Firms, 1850–1920, and is co-founder of the *Journal of Management Communication*.

Introduction to the Series

The main engine of Western civilization, as we know it, is at once the most indispensable and the least celebrated. It is not money, nor technology, nor even number. It is not science as such, nor ideology as such, nor even "industrialization" or "development" as such. Yet no aspect of Western civilization, as we know it, would be possible without it.

It is *organization*. Or better, perhaps the *idea* of organization.

All human civilization, as we know it, hinges upon some sort of "arrangement" between two or more people as to what role each will play in the pursuit of the larger good. The idea of kinship as central to all human civilization—as argued by Lévi-Strauss—is one example. A love relationship is another. Every business and every institution and every voluntary human enterprise is another. As the popular American song has it, "You do the cookin' honey/I'll pay the rent." Feminists or modernists may argue against *this* sort of arrangement; but they simply want to organize things in some *other* way.

Manifestiations of a given society's *ideas* of and about organization are so ubiquitous as to go unnoticed. Every society believes its way of organizing itself is "natural" or "God-given" or at least "right." To the members of every culture, the arrangements that exist for carrying out human enterprises in *other* cultures—from the domestic to the spiritual—may seem odd, or even bizarre. The main pretext for war, at least as we know it, has been that those odd and alien arrangements for doing things in other cultures were seen as a threat.

Human existence, as we know it, and the life of any society, as we know it, would be impossible without *some* idea as to how every human enterprise that involves two or more people is to be *organized*. Every mind emerges in the way it is trained to organize its grasp and its "understanding" of the world. We cannot exist apart from *some* way of organizing ourselves and the world in which we live.

Yet we know precious little about where our ideas about organizing ourselves and our world come from. We know still less, it would seem, about the *efficacy* of one way of organizing ourselves and our world vs. another (witness the never-ending quest, in our age, for the "best" or the ultimate way of organizing or managing a business enterprise, or of organizing the relationship between male and female). And we know still less, perhaps, about the long-range (or even the short-range) human *consequences* of this way or that way of organizing ourselves and the world in which we live—economically, politically, spiritually. The Navajo said, "Let it be done in beauty." Western man says, "Let it be done rationally." The consequences, even for our physical environment, are radically different.

We know so little about such matters of such great consequence to us, it may be, because any attempt to understand how we organize ourselves and our worlds is at the same time an attempt to understand how we understand. Trying to understand such things as make us human may be, as Alan Watts once suggested, a little like trying to bite one's own teeth.

But the ultimate "frontier" is not space. It is the way we come to be human, and all of the human artifacts we create and utilize to endow us with whatever humanity we may realize in our sojourn on earth. Of these, none is more central to our lives than the ways we have come to organize ourselves—whether for an affair or a space mission. It is those taken-for-granted arrangements between and among people engaged in one or another human enterprise that enable our lives and the life of our society. To understand them is to understand ourselves better. And to understand ourselves better is the only ground upon which we can stand to make better the conditions of our lives, now and for generations following, for us and for all of the peoples of the world.

To speak of organization is to speak of communication. The two may be more than merely coterminous. They may perhaps be two aspects of the same thing.

For if what another says is to have any meaning at all, one must have *some* sense of the nature of the human enterprise in which one is engaged with the other. And one must have *some* sense of the role one plays in that enterprise as that role relates to the role of the other. To "understand" what is going on and to participate in it in some way, one must already have understood how it is organized—whether it is a game, a conversation, a trip across town, or a board meeting. It is *that* understanding, that sense one has of how things are organized and how one fits into them, that makes human communication possible. And conversely. Wherever and whenever there has been evidence of the one, there has been evidence of the other. Paradoxically, to the Western mind, each is the precondition of the other. Each is interdependent with the other.

And thus the sense of the title of this book series: PEOPLE, COMMUNICATION, ORGANIZATION. Together, they comprise the enabling *system*, the inescapable *system*, which undergirds all human enterprise. As components of that system which undergirds *all* human enterprise, they are inextricably intertwined. To understand one is to understand the other. To be concerned about one necessarily invokes the other. Ultimately, we cannot understand people without taking into account how they communicate and the nature of the human organizations they get themselves into. We cannot understand human communication without taking into account the organized structures within which it occurs, and the nature of the people who assume or induce those social arrangements. And our understanding of human organization and of organizational life is going to be no better than our understanding of how people make each other, and how they are made, in communication. For it is *in* communication that we energize and give sense to the structures and the conditions of everyday life, those of human existence and of organizational life.

We *say* the structures and arrangements of our world into existence. And we have our lives, both within and without organizations, in the consequences of our saying-so. If there be defects or shortcomings, it is not to our enterprises and institutions to which we must look. If the arrangements by which we conduct the work and play of the world are not as we would have them, then we must look to the origin of those arrangements. We must look to the way in which we recreate them moment to moment, day to day, in what we say of them and think of them. They come into existence and evolve as they do because we *mind* them as we do. It is only as we come to mind them differently that "they" change. If one's marriage is not all that one had hoped; if one's business enterprise does not return all that it was expected to return; if the legal or other institutions of this society are not functioning as they "should"— then we must look to our ways of minding them—to *how* we understand them and speak of them.

Such social arrangements as bring us together in twos or eights or thousands are not born of necessity. They are born of human imagination—of *how* we can and do speak of the world, and of how we take it into account.

PEOPLE, COMMUNICATION, ORGANIZATION, each enables and constrains the other. How? What are the consequences of enabling ourselves in one way rather than another? Of minding the world one way rather than another? Of organizing ourselves one way rather than another? Of creating and practicing our humanity *in* communication in one form of organization rather than another? Of creating and practicing our humanity *in* organizations that constrain our ways of saying and seeing the world in one way rather than another? Of believing that any one is independent of the other?

This, then, is the charter for this series of books: To address the way we organize ourselves and our enterprises and our institutions as a result of the way we communicate with one another. And to address the way we communicate with one another as a result of how we have organized ourselves and our enterprises and our institutions. And what the human consequences are, or may be.

In doing so, we will want to speak to the thoughtful "practitioner" as much as to the grounded "philosopher," to the practical as much as to the abstract, to the layman as much as to the expert. For there is nothing esoteric about the subject; no one's life falls outside of the intellectual concerns which will guide us here. In this arena of life, unless all gain in understanding, no one does. That is in the nature of what we join here to think about and explore.

Lee Thayer
Series Editor

Editor's Preface

In this series of books on Organization ↔ Communication, we intend to bring together periodically a set of essays that explores the leading edge of theory and thought about how communication affects organizational life and performance, and how the structure and functioning of organizations affects communication within and about organizations. This second volume in the series does just that.

Taken together, the essays in this volume provide a provocative cross-section of such emerging thought and theory. They do not provide a complete cross-section; they were not intended to do so. There are topics or genres of thought and theory that are not represented in this volume. They will be given voice in a subsequent volume in the series—in order to provide adequate space for each, and to ensure the richest possible mix of voices on each occasion.

It would, however, also be misleading to attempt to review systematically every aspect of concern and interest in this growing field as if they were all developing steadily and equally, and not, as growth occurs, in spurts. So we have in this volume, as we did in the first volume in this series, attempted to address certain perspectives that seem to us to be of focal concern at this time—in this case: (a) how image-making and reality construction in and about organizations occur, and how a better understanding of these basic processes may aid in the design and governance, and the evaluation, of organizations; (b) how information and communication technologies have evolved, and how their deployment has affected the dynamics of organizations, and their "management"; (c) how the broader cultures within which organizations operate affect the internal "cultures" of those organizations, and the kinds of differences this makes for analyzing and understanding the dynamics of organizational life; and (d) how teaching about and learning about organizations in the classroom or from "experience" may interact with the paradigmatic philosophies of organization "management" and control that we have come to take for granted, and which may therefore be a part of the "problems" of organizational performance and organizational life.

So, in Part I, *Alice Sapienza* suggests that the image-making that occurs within and about organizations constitutes the underlying "strategy" or thrust of a given organization. *Jill McMillan* would have us "return to the basics," and look at the rhetorical postures and processes that establish the constraints and possibilities within which every kind of organization must function. And *Nick Trujillo* recaps the emergence and present condition of the "interpretive" approach, and how this affects (or perhaps should have affected) our own perception both of how to do research on organizations and how more fruitfully to function within organizations.

We know very little about how innovative communications and information technologies got folded into organizational life, and how these enfoldments affected organizational life and organizational performance. In Part II, *Jib Fowles* reviews "how we got to" the present state-of-affairs with respect to organizational communications technologies. And *JoAnne Yates* reviews intensively, as an example of how organizational communications technologies might be assessed, the effects of the evolutionary development of one such technology—"duplicating"—in American firms from their first appearance to the present. All communication is *mediated,* if only by the voice or the gestures of (or one's relationship to) another. How various forms of mediation affect the conditions of social enterprise, and affect how things get done in social enterprises of all sorts, is (or perhaps "should" be) of fundamental concern to all students of organization and communication, whatever their home port discipline.

In Part III, another very basic question is addressed. We've heard much in recent years—and much of it pop and trivial—about organizational "cultures." What we haven't heard much about is how the larger culture, in which every organization must function and upon which it must draw, affects the "cultures" of the organizations within it. Since there has been so much interest in the differences between the Japanese and the "Western" way of running organizations, two of our authors take a studied look at how those differences might best be accounted for, and how the larger culture bears upon such differences as there may be. *Fredrik Ulfhielm* examines the ways in which language itself may affect work group dynamics, leadership, and decision-making. And *Edward C. Stewart* proposes that we may be misreading the Japanese culture in our pop versions of it, and offers a more grounded view. His is a lengthy paper. But we felt that a voice wanting to set some matters straight (in his view) deserved the space, and will reward the reading.

The last section of this volume clusters around the notion of "competence," and what a modified understanding of competence in communication might mean for the teaching and practice of communication in organizations. *David T. Bednar & Grant T. Savage* raise a number of useful questions about what communication competence has to do with the teaching and learning of communication for performance in the modern world. And *Henri Broms & Henrik Gahmberg* ask us to imagine some

alternative functions of one of the most common and yet most sophisticated communication rituals in organizations—that of "planning."

There is much more about so much more to be said. But we believe
that what has been assayed in the following pages will profit all of those
who have some interest either in organizations, or in communication, or
in what the one may have to do with the other.

Lee Thayer

Sydney, Australia
September, 1986

PART I

Image, Persona, and Interpretation:
Changing Points of Departure

1

Image-Making as a Strategic Function: On the Language of Organizational Strategy

Alice M. Sapienza

INTRODUCTION

Words lead such interesting lives! "Strategy," for example, began as a Greek word for the "office of a general." It then became the "science and art of employing the political, economic, psychological, and military forces of a nation . . . to afford the maximum support to adopted policies," especially in wartime (Merriam-Webster's *Third International Dictionary*, 1966, p. 2256). Only a few decades ago, a comparatively short time for many words, "strategy" began to take up residence in the boardroom as well as on the battleground. Perhaps because of this word's relative newness in the vocabularies of managers and organizational theorists, we are still struggling with its connotations. That large and growing body of popular and academic literature on *organizational* strategy appears to contain as many perspectives as there are meanings of this word.

Recently, Pennings (1985) divided this literature into three categories. The first category included authors for whom "strategy" meant a "*statement of intent* that constrains or directs subsequent activities"—a connotation close to the military origins of the word (p. 2, emphasis added). The second category included authors for whom "strategy" meant, not an articulated statement, but an *inference* drawn by observers of "an [organizational] action of major impact that constrains or directs subsequent activities" (p. 3).

The third category, becoming "increasingly in vogue," included authors for whom "strategy or the specific activities attached to it . . . [constitute] a *social construction of reality*. . . . " (p. 3, emphasis added). That is, as Pennings explained: "[Organizations] consist of people whose collective experience leads them to convictions that represent their image of the organization and its strategy" (p. 3). For these authors, "strategy" meant the shared sense of organizational mission and direction that resided in the minds of managers and was projected (i.e., inferable by observers) through their language and organizational behavior.

In Pennings' third category, authors described the environment with which managers' strategy attempted to grapple, not as *objective* ("out there"), but as *enacted*. For them, environment was an intersubjective reality ("in our heads"), formed "through the social interaction processes of key organizational participants. . . . Organizations and environments [and strategies] are convenient labels for patterns of activity" (Smircich & Stubbart, 1985, p. 726; see also Mintzberg, 1978).

I should like to point out that the above connotations of "strategy" really reflect the assumptions these authors make about human rationality. In Pennings's first and second categories, authors assume that organizational decision-makers act according to *bounded rationality*. Bounded rationality is what decision theorists and economists mean by "rational" action: managers choose the most appropriate means (strategy) for a given end (goal)—and this choice is based on clear and consistent preferences (cf. Harsanyi, 1977; see also Thompson, 1967). Rational choice is bounded or limited, of course, by the limitations of humans as information processors. (Managers never have perfect knowledge of the future consequences of their action.)

In Pennings's third category, authors assume that decision-makers act according to an *alternative rationality*. For authors of this persuasion, the logic of managers' strategy is not factual but social—what makes sense/is rational depends on the history of the organization and its culture. This different kind of intelligence ("alternative rationality") is based on Karl Marx' proposition that human consciousness is determined by the human social context (cf. "sociology of knowledge," Berger & Luckmann, 1966; Mead, 1934).

March (1978, pp. 592-93) gives this example of alternative rationality:

> Suppose we imagine that knowledge, in the form of precepts of behavior, evolves over time within a system and accumulates across time, people, and organizations without complete current consciousness of its history. Then sensible action is taken by actors without comprehension of its full justification. . . . [Choice, then,] is not understood as following from a calculation of consequences in terms of prior objectives.

In my view, no matter what their assumption about human rationality, all authors in this body of strategy literature—and managers—agree that "strategy" involves a *response* to some *stimulus*. Beyond this common ground, disagreement arises over (a) whether strategy is articulated by organizational decision-makers or inferred by observers of organizational action, (b) whether managers' strategic intent precedes or follows strategic action, and (c) whether the so-called strategic stimulus resides in an objective or enacted environment (and whether such a distinction between "objective" and "enacted" really exists!).

Let me propose the following synthesis of perspectives. Stimuli are "objective," but they are processed by managers in accord with an alternative rationality. That is, managers' shared organizational culture influences how they make sense of their "objective" world—how they move from data, the stuff of perceptions, to information, the stuff of decisions. The environment "out there" is *perceived* by managers and thus enacted ("in their heads"). Once perceived, the stimulus ceases to be anything other than an intersubjective reality—a reality constructed in accord with an alternative rationality.

I propose that the language with which managers communicate is key, particularly the imagery with which they communicate aspects of the stimulus. I further propose that managers' response to the intersubjective reality they create is in accord with bounded rationality. There is no conflict between the two rationalities; one is not better than the other, although some decision theorists might argue this point (again, see March, 1978). As human information processors, managers move with facility between alternative and bounded rationalities, resolving apparent contradictions within the *mediating* processes (i.e., the perceptual processes) between the stimulus and the response. As culturally bound decision-makers, managers are incapable (like all of us) of perceiving a stimulus "objectively." But that does not imply that their strategic response to the stimulus is not rational in the "bounded" sense of the word. In short, let me put the rationality issue to rest: it is not a case of either/or, but of both.

In this exploration of the language of organizational strategy, I begin by reviewing briefly the evolution of models of learning and the relationship between learning and culture in organizations. This review will clarify the importance of language in the strategic processes, particularly the importance of images with which aspects of the stimulus are communicated. I then present empirical research that illuminates how *imagery* (part of the intersubjective reality) is often the *stimulus* to which managers respond strategically.

First, I should like to present two key definitions. In this discussion, "strategy" means an heuristic, or general rule towards a general (and, most often, unknown) goal (e.g., Beer, 1981). Remember the earlier definition of military strategy referred to at the beginning of this essay: the mustering of a group's strengths to ensure adherence to its policies and goals. Strategic decisions resulting in strategic actions place or maintain the organization on its trajectory towards such goals.

"Image" is a mental construct (spatial and quasi-pictorial as well as verbal) that is *symbolic of a basic attitude* towards some thing (e.g., Kosslyn,

1978). For example, the image of the largest U.S. hospital chains as "supermeds" conjures up a picture of larger-than-life medical corporations, on a par with other industrial giants, outcompeting the traditional community hospital for market share. Depending on your ideology regarding delivery of health care, "supermeds" may symbolize one of two basic attitudes: efficient, economical providers of care; or callous, profit-dominated ogres.

The next section starts with the bioecological origins of learning theories, and moves to my own culture/cognition model of organizational learning that, I hope, will be the major contribution of this essay to the theory and practice of organizational strategy.

LEARNING: THE OPERANT CONDITIONING PARADIGM

Individual Learning

Darwin's (1854) theory of natural selection can be viewed as species "learning" by phylogenetic adaptation (response) to environmental characteristics (stimuli). For example, individual members of a plant species that have thicker leaves can survive longer periods of drought. Over time, given prolonged drought conditions in our imaginary environment, this species of plant could be said (anthropomorphically) to have learned to grow fleshier leaves in order to store water. Drought (as a stimulus) selected out fleshier leaves (as a response).

In a later model of learning, called "classical conditioning," Pavlov (Rachlin, 1976) proposed that an organism learns when it associates a reflex action (e.g., a hungry dog salivating at the smell of food) with *another* stimulus (e.g., lights or bells prior to the arrival of food). In this case, the reflex is said to be "conditioned."

In the "operant conditioning" model [cf. B. F. Skinner (Rachlin, 1976)], an organism is said to learn when it associates the means of satisfying a drive (e.g., hunger) with the action (operant) by which success is achieved (e.g., pecking a red key). This model is not concerned with involuntary or reflex action but with spontaneous behavior ("thrashing around") that is rewarded/reinforced and then associated with the desired outcome under similar conditions in the future (Rachlin, 1976). A child learns to say "mama" by associating this vocalization (operant) with the effect of mama's attention, praise, love, etc. Successful behaviors (including language and syntax) become part of our behavioral repertoire. We learn, in fact, what enables us to survive in our enacted world.

In the early decades of the twentieth century, there was a theoretical and empirical camp that sought to broaden the model of operant conditioning. It included cognitive, as distinct from behavioral, psychologists for whom human learning was complicated by cognitive (mental, or thinking) structures that "stood between"—that is, mediated—stimulus and response. Also called *interpretive schemata* or *frame of reference*, cognitive structures are simply mental constructs (like norms or rules or beliefs) that both organize and process data (Schroeder, Driver, & Streufert, 1967; Abelson, 1976). Cognitive structures are derived from culturally rewarded experience, and stored in memory using "culturally produced sign systems" or language (Vygotsky, 1978, p. 23; see also Mead, 1934).

For example, one simple cognitive structure is the multiplication table. We have memorized a rule that goes something like "two times two is four" and so on. When we see "2 × 2," that stimulus cues our multiplication table/cognitive structure, and we then respond with "4" (e.g., Newell & Simon, 1972). These structures are discovered by observing and analyzing both verbal and written language (Bach & Harnish, 1979; Lakeoff & Johnson, 1980).

Organizational Learning

Like the model of individual learning, the model of organizational learning has also undergone elaboration. In the beginning, Cyert and March (1963) defined the organization as an adaptively rational, information-processing, and decision-rendering system. The cycle of organizational learning, they wrote, consisted of managers' (a) consideration of alternatives and selection of means toward a goal (constrained by bounded rationality and use of standard operating procedures); (b) observation of the effect of action on the environment; and, if the effect were successful, (c) selection of similar means under later and similar circumstances.

Within 10 years of Cyert and March, a competing model of learning portrayed the organization as "anarchy," where decisions result from "the interpretation of relatively independent streams . . . " and "important decisions are made by oversight and flight" (Cohen, March, & Olsen, 1972, pp. 3, 11; see also Cohen & March, 1974). In this model, organizational decision-makers have inconsistent and ill-defined preferences, thus violating the rules for bounded rationality.

The outcome of this dialectic in organization theory was the synthesis of March and Olsen (1976). In their model of organizational learning, when the individual-in-organization perceives a stimulus in the environment, he or she processes those data according to his or her beliefs (or cognitive structures). Action is taken by individuals on the basis of this processing, and the resulting "organizational" behavior or response provokes environmental action. Such action is, of course, a stimulus, perceived by individuals, and so on, in endless loops. And in accord with the model of operant conditioning, a successful organizational action will be more likely to be produced again under conditions that are perceived to be similar to the first, and so on. . . .

About this time (in the late 1970s), another group of writers described organizational learning from a slightly different vantage. Learning, they said, can also occur as a result of deliberate, experimental forays between the organization and its environment (Hedberg, Nystrom, & Starbuck, 1976). So-called organizational learning can proceed from environmental stimulus to rewarded organizational response (the operant model), as well as the reverse. In the latter case, organizational decision-makers take an action *to provoke* some effect in the environment.

Let us say a computer company offers a voice recognition system—a unique, never-before-produced system. Let us say the environmental effect is that many people purchase these systems. Decision-makers in the computer company will respond in turn to this "reward" by offering succeeding generations of systems, in accord with what they learned from that initial provoking.

More recently, Hedberg (1981) added the dynamic of *unlearning* to the organizational learning cycle. Old ways of viewing the world, he said, must be unlearned before "adaptive and manipulative interactions between an organization and its environment" are possible (Hedberg, 1981, p. 20).

Provocative as these other perspectives on organizational learning are, I find it difficult to translate them into the setting of day-to-day management and strategic decision-making. The world in which organizations exist is continually evolving, and decision-makers face two opposing trends: first, "an increase in the speed and frequency of major changes in the physical, institutional, and cultural milieu; and, second, an increase in the time needed to mount adequate responses to such changes" (Vickers, 1965, p. 76). It is thus crucial that we have a better understanding of learning within organizations, if strategic response is to be successful.

In the following section on culture and cognition in organizations, I take the theories one step further and, using examples from my research, illustrate in detail the processes by which managers (a) perceive a stimulus, (b) construct an intersubjective reality around that stimulus, and (c) respond strategically. As noted earlier, my focus is on the *language* of organizational strategy.

CULTURE AND COGNITION IN ORGANIZATIONS

I am restricting the following discussion to the organizational culture shared by top managers, the decision-makers of organizational strategy, and do not assume that everyone in the organization necessarily shares that culture.

Of all the definitions of organizational culture, the one I find most illuminating is that of the Englishman, Sir Geoffrey Vickers. He wrote that organizational culture is a "shared appreciative system" or "set of readinesses" to (a) distinguish some aspects of the situation (i.e., the stimulus) rather than others, (b) classify them, and (c) value them in a certain way (1965, p. 67). If strategy involves a response of top managers to stimuli, then we need to understand *how* managers "select, organize, and transform the stimuli that impinge upon them" (Bandura, 1977, p. viii).

In line with the model of cognitive psychology, I propose that organizational culture influences the cognition of individuals-in-organization by first influencing what top managers *pay attention to* (what Vickers termed "distinguish" and Bandura termed "select"). Out of all possible aspects of the stimulus, Vickers suggests, managers will be predisposed by their culture to "open the door" to some and "close it to others" (Mead, 1934, p. 25; see also James, in Wilshire, 1968). Organizational culture spotlights a portion of the stimulus as salient.

Listen to how top managers in two hospitals—both faced with the same state legislation—described what was salient to them about this stimulus:

> The health care industry is beset with increasing encroachment by regulation. . . . Growing regulation continues to threaten our ability to provide the highest quality care for patients. [Hospital A]
> The regulations were the result of discussions among legislators, business representatives, and hospital leaders in good faith. . . . The business community is sharpening its pencils and demanding that we be as alert, and as aggressive, and as innovative as any business must be in order to remain viable. [Hospital B]

Organizational culture also influences how top managers *perceive* the stimulus to which they have paid attention (what Vickers termed "classify"). Simply speaking, perception is classification. Quine (1973, p. 1) suggested that people "sort things into kinds. . . . What are sensed [perceived] are significantly structured wholes." And Vygotsky (1896-1934) stated: "All human perception consists of categorized rather than isolated perceptions . . . [categorized in accord with] the internalization of culturally produced sign systems" or language (1978, p. 23). Again, listen to how top managers classified the stimulus legislation:

> What they've *really* done is put us in a box. All the law is designed to do is put us in a box! (CEO, Hospital A)
> Ach . . . ! It's not so bad. We all knew these restrictions on reimbursement were coming. (Executive Vice President, Hospital B)

Here we come to the essential dynamics of how organizational culture, by means of cognitive structures, mediates the *response* of individuals-in-organization to the *stimulus*. Top managers "talk together [and] come to share the same verbal categories and explanations"—that is, cognitive structures (Sproull, 1981, p. 207). In organizations, then, top managers will share certain cognitive structures, and these *collective cognitive structures* ensure that they organize and process information in a relatively similar manner.

How are these structures derived? The tasks of management provide the loci of social interaction that builds up communities of speech (e.g., Bloomfield, 1961; Quine, 1961; Bach & Harnish, 1979). Job socialization—the "long-term processes that teach people to function as effective members of groups," such as formal orientation, training, mentoring, and informal processes—also conveys to new managers the appropriate *language* (and other behaviors) of their face-to-face group or speech community (Sproull, 1981, p. 208; see also Asch, 1952; Homans, 1950; Salancik & Pfeffer, 1978). Collective cognitive structures are thus derived from managers' culturally determined (and rewarded) experiences on-the-job and stored in memory in the culturally determined language of their speech community. The manager quoted below is aware of these processes:

> There is a "GE manager". . . . We just instituted a mandatory first-time-manager course . . . [with] a message now that's culturally based that says: "This is what it means to be a GE manager; what the expectations are. And here are some tools and techniques and people to talk to as you go through this first year of learning to be a manager." [GE Executive Development Staff]

Finally, culture influences the cognition of individuals-in-organization by influencing what *significance* (what Vickers termed "value") top managers attach to their perceptions or classifications. Perceptions are not neutral. Top managers will judge some to be more valuable than others, and strategic decision-making will follow these significant or valued perceptions in the same way that iron will move toward the most highly charged portion of a magnetic field (cf. Boulding, 1956).

There should be little disagreement that top managers are trained, socialized, and rewarded for scanning the environment for data important to the organization. As implied earlier, I propose that what managers scan (pay attention to, or select) will be that portion of the environment made salient by their shared organizational culture. Once data are attended to, then processing of information by these individuals-in-organization will consist of endless loops of perception, communication, and reality construction (cf. March & Olsen, 1976).

Perception will be determined, first, by organizational culture and, second, by the individual's role (because of specific job socialization). For example, the chief financial officer will be most likely to scan the salient portions of the environment for data believed to be important for the financial survival of the organization.

Top managers' "communicable" perceptions—shaped by culture and role—are communicated within their peer group, or community of speech (e.g., Thayer, 1985). Such perceptions will be tested against socially constructed reality or consensually recognized "facts." If there is agreement that these perceptions are important, then they will become part of internal reality themselves and modify it in some way (e.g., Boulding, 1956; Berger & Luckmann, 1966; Argyris & Schon, 1978).

Let us say that external reality changes: there is an environmental event or stimulus like the state legislation mentioned above. "Reality," for top managers, will be socially constructed out of their communication about that event, and *this* reality will be the stimulus to which they respond strategically.

The language of organizational strategy is both an outcome of the reality construction process and an input to it. It is an outcome because it is determined by the culture of the speech group in which it is used (e.g., Sapir, 1921; Claxton, 1980). Words, phrases, acronyms, and stories repeated in organizational communications reflect the values and beliefs (i.e., culture) that make that speech community unique (see also Pfeffer, 1981). Language is also an input: words and syntax are repeated in conversations and writings. Managers hear and see this language and make it their own (meanings are implied and validated by trial and error until connotations become stable). Language thus becomes part of—that is, input to—managers' collective cognitive structures.

Images are a special class of language and a pervasive example of cognitive structures. They are so pervasive, in fact, that Lakeoff and Johnson stated, with regard to metaphors: "We draw inferences, set goals, make commitments, and execute plans, all on the basis of how we in part structure our experience, consciously and unconsciously, by means of metaphor" (1980, p. 158). That the imagery and strategy of top managers will be closely related is evidenced by the following quotation:

> I think that's the challenge at GE right now—creating some new metaphors and new visions that people really understand and own and can march toward. . . .
> The former chairman used to refer to us as the "Titanic"! That's not [Jack Welch's] vision. He wants us to be lean and agile, and move quickly. . . . There are some very consistent metaphors and themes coming from him. [GE Engineering Development Manager]

Imagery is also a linguistic flag to the third way that culture influences the cognition of individuals-in-organization. Top managers can classify aspects of the stimulus syntagmatically; that is, in a straightforward manner, without figures of speech (Leach, 1976; e.g., "restrictions on reimbursement," Hospital B). Managers can also classify aspects of the stimulus as images, which are clues to what managers feel is significant (Ortony, 1979; e.g., "the law [has] put us in a box," Hospital A). *Strategic decision-making will follow these judgments of value.* Again, images are collective cognitive structures, influencing further classification and decision-making.

Let's give this flesh by using some examples.

IMAGE-MAKING AS A STRATEGIC FUNCTION

Imagery and Strategy

In 1982–83, I observed the top management groups of two closely matched teaching hospitals as they were faced with 3-year legislation to reduce hospital budgets and set them prospectively. This first illustration is taken from one hospital in which there appeared to be six steps in the development of strategic response to that stimulus. (I began observation in the second hospital at a later date, but some steps appeared identical in the two institutions.) Three of these steps were directly observable by me; three were inferred from the subsequent steps (see Figure 1).

Figure 1. Development of Strategic Response to a Stimulus

Steps Invisible to Researcher	Steps Observable to Researcher
1 Individual perceptions of strategic stimulus, based on shared culture and organizational role	
	2 Collective discussions of individual perceptions and development of shared vocabulary
3 Coalescing of perceptions within functional groups, and development of group scripts	
	4 Collective discussions of group scripts as potential strategic response
5 Emergence of dominant image and selection of group script	
	6 Articulation of strategy, based on dominant image and group script

In hospital A, the *first step* in the development of strategic response was perception, by individual top managers, of the environmental event or stimulus legislation. Although not directly observable by me, this step was implied by the observable *second step*: collective discussion of individual perceptions.

During meetings immediately following passage of the law, there were nearly as many classifications of the legislation as there were top managers—all colored, however, by their shared culture. (Remember: These managers believed the legislation to be an "encroachment" and a threat to their "ability to provide the highest quality care for our patients.") The law was described as putting them in a "box." Legislators were believed to have "tasted blood and be out for more!" Business was involved: "All corporate presidents are screaming that their [health insurance] costs are too high." And one physician noted with heavy sarcasm: "We're becoming McDonalds. Cheap! Clean! Fast!"

It became clear to me that *how* individuals perceived the legislation depended on their roles as well as their shared culture. Medical staff "saw" the law as antithetical to teaching hospitals, because of incentives to reduce the length of stay ("they're trying to make us all community hospitals"). Financial staff "saw" the law as a means of improving the financial position of the hospital, because of incentives to cut costs quickly and invest any difference between prospectively set revenues and actual expense. Administrative staff "saw" the law as requiring rigorous cost-benefit analyses of new programs and services, because of the need to live within a predetermined budget. Each of these role perceptions, of course, captured a portion of the legislation.

Within a few weeks a shared vocabulary had developed out of these diverse perceptions. Common words and phrases appeared, some of them from the actual text of the law or public commentaries, others from colorful phrases or images used by one member or another of the top management group.

The *third step* was coalescing of interpretations around a functional group script (cf. Abelson, 1978). As implied by the *fourth step*—collective discussions of group scripts—by this stage a response was being articulated along functional lines.

The medical staff's recommendation was to address length of stay, because they were the people who controlled it. (The chief of surgery suggested: "I'll go around the floors and say: 'Wouldn't you like to go home today?'!") The fiscal staff's recommendation was a "cut and compound" tactic. Budget reductions should be made as soon as possible, because of the time value of money. ("There's a tremendous incentive to maximize budget cuts and operating margin this year. I'm almost 93% convinced that whatever we do to improve our operating margin in the first year will be carried over for 2 years and compounded.") The administrative staff's recommendation was to do detailed cost-benefit analyses of all proposed programs. ("What we do will be dictated by the economics falling out of this bill. . . . In purely economic terms, we should eliminate those services whose expenses exceed costs.") For some time, each functional script was put forth as a primary institutional response.

The *fifth step* was emergence of a reigning image of one aspect of the stimulus legislation and response to that image. Although the process by which this occurred was, like the first and third steps, invisible to me, it was implied by the *final step*: collective discussion of institutional response. Within 3 months after passage of the legislation, the "cut and compound" tactic was chosen. The maximum feasible amount of expense reduction was chosen; a target percentage was then set for all departments; and implementation of this reduced budget was scheduled to begin in January 1983.

I said above that a reigning image of one aspect of the law emerged and that managers developed a strategic response to that image. Let me now go back and review more specifically the process of imagery evolution and strategic response.

During a meeting just prior to passage of the new legislation, the CEO of hospital A went up to a flipchart, drew a rectangle, and exclaimed: "What they've *really* done is put us in a box. All the law is designed to do is put us in a box!" Shortly after his comment, one of the associate directors took up this image with regard to a proposed new program: "If we approve organ transplants, we know *that* takes up 80% of the box!"

The image of the law as a rigid and confining space became the dominant or reigning image around December. By this I mean the figure of speech was used or implied by most top managers for the remainder of the time I observed them. For example:

> At a simplistic level, if we agree to implement something, we must agree to delete something else [Chief Operating Officer].
>
> We're going to have to make sure that the costs [of the proposed organ transplant program] are extremely well spelled out. And the trustees have to understand that this would have to be funded by giving up something else [Associate Director 1].
>
> It was decided that we would go back to another committee to see what we could cut out [Associate Director 2].
>
> If we're going to do organ transplants, and we find we can't fit them into the unused portion [of the clinical department's expenses], then we can go back to the chiefs and say: 'We'll have to cut back on bypass surgery in order to do transplants' [Chief Executive Officer].
>
> We're asking everybody to look for 3% savings [in department budgets]. And we think if we can get it—and we intend to get it—we can keep it and use it for other things [Chief Executive Officer].

At hospital A, two of the major strategic decisions in response to the legislation were: an across-the-board, 3% cut in department expenses; and a reduction in the average salary increase from 9% to 5%. By the end of that fiscal year (September 1983), three organ transplants had been performed; the average salary increase was 5%; a board of trustee goal of a 1% surplus from operations was not achieved, in order to "fit in" transplants; and the hospital posted a small loss from operations.

The process of imagery evolution and strategic response was the same at hospital B. In mid-December, the executive vice president of hospital B explained to the management group: "We're going to be looking for a reduced budget by about $2M. . . . Now, the *last* thing we want to do is cause any suffering for our employees—and to lose your job is suffering. We'll do our darnedest not to get into position reductions to meet the budget." From this point on, the image of one aspect of the law as potential pain and suffering for employees was dominant. For example:

> Whatever we do [in the way of budget cuts] will hurt. . . . Nor have I put down hurting employees any more by asking them to pay more for parking, insurance, etc. [Chief Financial Officer].
> There's no way to come up with cuts without real pain [Budget Analyst].
> Grown men have come in in *tears* to see if they'll still have a job! [Associate Director].
> We need to remain *so* cognizant of the anxieties and pain that are out there [Director of Nursing].

At hospital B, two of the major strategic decisions in response to the legislation were: design of an in vitro fertilization (IVF) program expected to bring in several hundred thousand dollars in surplus revenues the first year (thus preventing layoffs to meet a reduced budget); and giving employees as large a raise as possible. By the end of that fiscal year, 12 patients had been enrolled in the IVF program; employees were given an 8% average salary increase; and the hospital posted a small gain from operations.

Comparison of Responses

To understand why these images became reigning images, we must go back to managers' shared appreciative system or culture. At each institution, managers shared a unique *core ideology*. This is my term for what Sproull described as beliefs about the "identity, purpose, and character of an organization. . . . [They are] vivid and evocative, as well as stable and enduring" (1981, p. 214; see also Nisbett & Ross, 1980). And

Hedberg (1981, p. 12) noted: "[Such beliefs] are told and carried by groups of believers, often from generation to generation."

At hospital A, managers' core ideology centered on (among other things) putting "the needs of the individual patient above all other concerns." Another quotation captures this ideology succinctly: "Throughout its history this hospital has been dedicated to the saving or prolonging of lives . . . *almost irrespective of cost*" [emphasis added]. Is it any wonder that managers perceived the state cost-control legislation to be "encroachment" and a threat to "highest quality care"? It is not surprising that managers classified the law as putting them in a box. Because of the perceived restrictions of the legislation, they felt beleaguered on all sides, that is, placed within a rigid and confining "space." For this reason, it appears, managers could only respond *by taking things out* of the box (deleting, giving up, cutting out, cutting back, etc.).

At hospital B, managers' core ideology centered on (among other things) caring for employees. Said one manager: "We've tried to make this place—not just an organization. We call ourselves a family, and we really try to live that image from the bottom up." When an employee training program was instituted, another manager explained: "Training establishes an atmosphere where the employees feel the organization *cares* for their growth." No wonder, then, that budget cuts that might affect employees were described as pain and suffering—and that managers responded by avoiding such cuts. ("If you have to make tough decisions, how can you do that to family members?")

Summary of Findings

Let me summarize the above findings:

1. The organizational culture shared by top managers will determine the collective cognitive structures that mediate managers' response to stimuli.
2. One such cognitive structure—the core ideology—will become operative as a collective cognitive structure when cued by certain characteristics of the stimulus (e.g., when threatened by such aspects, as in the earlier illustrations). When operative in this way, the strong affect with which managers hold these beliefs will result in a heightened or "magnified" perception of certain aspects of the stimulus.
3. This heightened perception will be revealed by the imagery with which managers classify that stimulus characteristic. Managers' larger-than-life perception will be depicted in larger-than-life language (imagery).

4. Because the response of top managers is to the *perceived* character-istics of the stimulus (to the intersubjective reality created by com-munication among them), that response will be in part determined by the imagery with which they classify that stimulus.

Intentionally or not, image-making is a strategic function.

IMPLICATIONS

Let me close by giving a few of my answers to the legitimate question all authors face at the conclusion of their discussion: "So what? What are the implications of all this, especially for managers of organizations?"

The *first implication* is that *top managers are the shapers of organizational imagery* as well as strategy. The impression of GE employees was that top management initiated "some very consistent metaphors and themes." Certainly, personal discussions I have had with chief executives reveal that many view themselves as shapers of imagery through myths, stories, and organizational symbols. Consider the following:

I think senior management tells the stories—starts them. I think it's a shorthand form of communication; I can't think of a major company or organization that doesn't have that kind of story that symbolizes what they stand for, how they get things done [CEO 1].

I've always got to have a "flag." I may change the colors; I may change what it says, but there's always got to be a flag out there and high enough for all the employees to see! And to see *which way we're going* [CEO 2].

I think myths are very important. I don't think top management can *plan* these stories, but they emerge. For example, when I came to this or-ganization in 1966 I closed the executive dining room. I said that was elitist. We're all working together in this organization and I won't counte-nance that. See, these are definitive actions of top management, and then they get talked about—a myth is created around the image of what this organization is about [CEO 3].

If this is the case, and if language and imagery are such powerful shapers of action, then the *second implication* is that *it behooves top managers to reflect on their language of decision-making and consider the connotations of the imagery they are using.* Jack Welch of GE uses images of speed, lean-ness, and agility in his face-to-face and videotaped discussions with his employees for a reason:

[Jack] makes speeches at every management meeting. He's very consis-tent in his themes. . . . He's also on videotapes all over the place. . . . I think having the chairman push for new technology and excellence and leaner organization, people *feel* the need for change.

Imagery is the "tip of a submerged model" (Black, 1979, p. 31). Like the iceberg, it is weighty with connotations, for better or worse. Consider the implicative elaboration of the image of the hospital cost-control law as a box. Once that became the reigning image, managers at hospital A continually spoke of cutting out, making room, taking something out to fit something else in, etc. Like the iceberg, only the tip shows, and the image is an efficient communicator of the whole. Managers at hospital A understood the new law to be "worse than a zero-sum game" by means of one word, and they understood from this image what they must do.

Unfortunately, the image of a rigid and confining space did more than efficiently communicate the impact of the law. Like military images, this image acted to "restrict flexibility [and to] narrow solutions" (Weick, 1979, p. 51). In addition to the incentive in the law to cut costs and save ("compound") any difference between prospectively set revenues and actual expenses, there was also an incentive to implement programs that brought in surplus revenues and compound these dollars. But I only heard this option mentioned twice at hospital A. It appeared that managers were "so committed to a problem frame" of the law as a box that they missed a sizable opportunity (Schon, 1979, p. 269; see also Janis, 1972). In this case, at least, the image constrained rather than enabled learning.

The *third implication* concerns the issue of change. It appears that *the process of image-making is relatively plastic—up to a point.* Remember that development of an institutional response at hospital A involved a marked "funneling down" of cognitions about the stimulus. First, there existed varied perceptions (classifications) according to the number of individuals in the top management group. Then, there was a coalescing of language around functional group scripts. Finally, there was a reigning image and the articulation of strategy in response to that image.

Cognitive consolidation and commitment to a problem frame precede the articulation of strategy. At a certain point in this process it becomes very difficult to turn back. Thus, if images should be changed, they could be altered during the stage of stimulus classification. This is a key time—when cognitive commitment is forming but has not yet "solidified." Beyond this stage, change will become progressively harder to effect, because the image has become part of reality. And we find it exceedingly difficult to admit to mistakes in our reality!

REFERENCES

Abelson, R.P. (1976). Scripts. In J.S. Carroll & J.W. Payne (Eds.), *Cognition and social behavior* (pp. 33-88). Hillsdale, NJ: Erlbaum.

Argyris, C., & Schon, D.A. (1978). *Organizational learning*. Reading, MA: Addison-Wesley.
Asch, S.E. (1952). *Social psychology*. Englewood Cliffs, NJ: Prentice-Hall.
Bach, K., & Harnish, R.M. (1979). *Linguistic communication and speech acts*. Cambridge, MA: MIT Press.
Bandura, A. (1977). *Social learning theory*. Englewood Cliffs, NJ: Prentice-Hall.
Beer, S. (1981). *Brain of the firm*. New York: John Wiley & Sons Inc.
Berger, P.L., & Luckmann, T. (1966). *The social construction of reality*. New York: Anchor Books.
Black, M. (1979). More about metaphors. In A. Ortony (Ed.), *Metaphor and thought*, (pp. 22-40). Cambridge, England: Cambridge University Press.
Bloomfield, L. (1961). Meaning. In S. Saporta & J.R. Bastian (Eds.), *Psycholinguistics* (pp. 237-263). New York: Holt, Rinehart & Winston.
Boulding, K. (1956). *The image*. Ann Arbor, MI: Ann Arbor Press.
Claxton, G. (Ed.). (1980). *Cognitive psychology*. London: Routledge & Kegan Paul.
Cohen, M.D., & March, J.G. (1974). *Leadership and ambiguity*. New York: McGraw Hill.
Cohen, M.D., March, J.G., & Olsen, J.P. (1972). A garbage can model of organizational choice. *Administrative Science Quarterly, 17,* 1-25.
Cyert, R.M., & March, J.G. (1963). *A behavioral theory of the firm*. Englewood Cliffs, NJ: Prentice-Hall.
Darwin, C. (1854). *On the origin of species by means of natural selection*.
Harsanyi, J.C. (1977). *Rational behavior and bargaining equilibrium in games and social situations*. Cambridge, England: Cambridge University Press.
Hedberg, B. (1981). How organizations learn and unlearn. In P.C. Nystrom & W.H. Starbuck (Eds.), *Handbook of organizational design* (pp. 3-27). Oxford, England: Oxford University Press.
Hedberg, B., Nystrom, P.C., & Starbuck, W.H. (1976). Camping on seesaws. *Administrative Science Quarterly, 21,* 41-65.
Homans, G.C. (1950). *The human group*. New York: Harcourt Brace Jovanovich.
Janis, I.L. (1972). *Victims of groupthink*. Boston, MA: Houghton Mifflin Co.
Kosslyn, S.M. (1978). Imagery and internal representation. In E. Rosch & B.B. Lloyd (Eds.), *Cognition and categorization* (pp. 217-235). Hillsdale, NJ: Erlbaum.
Lakeoff, G., & Johnson, M. (1980). *Metaphors we live by*. Chicago, IL: University of Chicago Press.
Leach, E. (1976). *Culture and communication*. Cambridge, England: Cambridge University Press.
March, J.G. (1978). Bounded rationality, ambiguity, and the engineering of choice. *Bell Journal of Economics, 9,* 587-608.
March, J.G., & Olsen, J.P. (1976). *Ambiguity and choice in organizations*. Bergen, Norway: Universitetsforlaget.
Mead, G.H. (1934). *Mind, self, and society*. Chicago, IL: University of Chicago Press.
Mintzberg, H. (1978). Patterns in strategy formation. *Management Science, 24,* 934-948.
Newell, A., & Simon, H.A. (1972). *Human problem solving*. Englewood Cliffs, NJ: Prentice-Hall.
Nisbett, R., & Ross, L. (1980). *Human inference*. Englewood Cliffs, NJ: Prentice-Hall.
Ortony, A. (Ed.). (1979). *Metaphor and thought*. Cambridge, England: Cambridge University Press.
Pennings, J.M. & Assoc's. (Eds.). (1985). *Organizational strategy and change*. San Francisco, CA: Jossey-Bass.
Pfeffer, J. (1981). *Organization and organization theory*. Stanford University Working Paper No. 597.
Quine, W.V. (1961). The problem of meaning in linguistics. In S. Saporta & J.R. Bastian (Eds.), *Psycholinguistics* (pp. 303-327). New York: Holt, Rinehart & Winston.
Quine, W.V. (1973). *The roots of reference*. Peru, IL: Open Court.

Rachlin, H. (1976). *Introduction to modern behaviorism.* San Francisco, CA: W.H. Freeman & Co.

Salancik, G.R., & Pfeffer, J. (1978). A social information processing approach to job attitudes and task design. *Administrative Science Quarterly, 23,* 224-253.

Sapir, E. (1921). *Language.* New York: Harcourt, Brace, & World.

Schon, D.A. (1979). Generative metaphor. In A. Ortony (Ed.), *Metaphor and thought* (pp. 253-278). Cambridge, England: Cambridge University Press.

Schroeder, H.M., Driver, M., & Streufert, S. (1967). *Human information processing.* New York: Holt, Rinehart & Winston.

Smircich, L., & Stubbart, C. (1985). Strategic management in an enacted world. *Academy of Management Review, 10,* 724-736.

Sproull, L.S. (1981). Beliefs in organizations. In P.C. Nystrom & W.H. Starbuck (Eds.), *Handbook of organizational design* (pp. 203-224). Oxford, England: Oxford University Press.

Thayer, L. (1985). *A poetic for communication.* Prepared for 35th Annual Conference of the International Communication Association, Hawaii.

Thompson, J.D. (1967). *Organizations in action.* New York: McGraw-Hill Book Co.

Vickers, Sir G. (1965). *The art of judgment.* London, England: Chapman and Hall.

Vygotsky, L.S. (1978). *Mind in society* (trans. and ed. by M. Cole). Cambridge, MA: Harvard University Press.

Weick, K.E. (1979). *The social psychology of organizing.* Reading, MA: Addison-Wesley.

Wilshire, B. (1968). *William James and phenomenology.* Bloomington, IN: Indiana University Press.

2

In Search of the Organizational Persona: A Rationale for Studying Organizations Rhetorically

Jill J. McMillan

From time to time, human beings need help in thinking about the phenomena which constitute our lives. Fortunately, when a new way of looking at our collective existence becomes necessary or desirable, we have a rich symbolic repertoire upon which to draw. For example, organizational communication has been called "the life blood of the organization," "the glue that binds the organization," "the binding agent that cements all relationships," and even "the organizational embalming fluid" (Goldhaber, 1983, p. 5). When not overtaxed or overextended, such metaphors work well to provide new frames of reference and to enhance understanding. It is only when we reify a construct that it ceases to serve us well, and rather operates to confuse or mislead us.

Such a metaphor currently taunts those who would study organizational culture—the perception of the organization-as-person. Since social scientists first suggested that organizations might have something in common with biological systems (Katz & Kahn, 1978, pp. 24-25), organizational researchers have been both compelled and constrained by the notion. While attracted to the rich and useful insights of systems theory, we were restrained by the obvious dangers of anthropomorphism, or assigning human properties to the organization.[1] Thus, the organizational culturist trips about gingerly, reluctant to admit that what he or she really seeks in each organization is the discovery of some sort of corporate personality.

---

[1] Several organizational scholars have cautioned about the problems of reification of the organization, particularly with respect to organizational goals. See Perrow (1961, pp. 854-866), Cyert and March (1963); Simon (1964, p. 1-22), and Thompson (1967).

It is possible to satisfy the nonanthropomorphic imperative of the organizational sages and, at the same time, capture the most complete cultural picture of the group when we substitute for organization-as-person the notion of "organizational persona."[2] While we are certain that the corporate body of the organization does not possess a flesh-and-bones reality, nor the human qualities of thinking, abstracting, and feeling, we do sense that there is a social presence about an organization to which it is possible to assign definite traits and qualities which are readily verifiable, i.e. "the Tandem Corporation is a warm, friendly place to work"; "Hewlett-Packard is good to its employees"; "the Unitarian Church is socially liberal-minded." These cultural impressions have emerged, not because they represent a physical presence, but because they have been created by the unique configuration of symbols with which the organization identifies. Taken collectively, these symbols reveal, not some corporate Super Person, but an image of the organization which its constituents have come to know and recognize. The researcher too must come to know this persona if he or she is to make an astute cultural assessment about the group which it represents.

There are obviously many different ways to study organizational culture, and a number of these approaches are currently being utilized effectively in studies of organizational stories, metaphors, and performances, in which data have been obtained primarily through the interpersonal medium.[3] If we take seriously, however, the warning of Deal and Kennedy that organizational culture includes "almost everything" (Deal & Kennedy, 1982, p. 4), then the researcher is faced with a critical and infinitely practical decision: where in the organization can we find (and receive access to) the richest, most potent, symbol pools and those which promise the most complete and concentrated rendering of an organization's culture? I hope to demonstrate in this essay that at least one good place to look is out front, in the organization's public words, where it both implicitly and explicitly seeks to establish its own unique persona and to spread its own particular brand of influence. The data for this particular study were obtained from a content analysis of the public or-

---

[2] *Webster's New World Dictionary*, 1978 ed., defines persona as that "outer personality presented to others."

[3] Stories in organizations have been studied by Wilkins and Martin (1979), and Brown (1982). Organizational metaphors have been analyzed by several scholars. See, for example, Manning (1979, pp. 660-671), and Koch and Deetz (1981). Pacanowsky and O'Donnell-Trujillo (1983, pp. 126-148) introduced process into the study of organizational culture.

gans of four sociologically diverse organizations for a 15-year period.[4] Organizations studied were the Tennessee Education Association (TEA), Reynolds Metals Company (RMC), Presbyterian Church in the United States (PCUS), and Kansas Democratic Party (KDP).

Realizing the impossibility of overturning every rock and stone within the organization, we hope instead for a cultural picture which might resemble an old jigsaw puzzle that we drag out of the attic on a rainy day. Several pieces are missing, but at least we know at the end of our labors whether we have a ship or a puppy. Studying organizations rhetorically does not promise a brand new, 1,000-piece look at organizational culture, but it does offer one of the better ways of constructing the organizational persona. In this essay, I will establish some general definitional parameters for the rhetorical study of organizations; examine the advantages of organizational rhetoric, both to the researcher and to the organization; and, finally, suggest how a rhetorical analysis ultimately yields that characteristic organizational persona.

STUDYING ORGANIZATIONS RHETORICALLY: SOME PARAMETERS

To study organizations rhetorically basically means to look at them in two ways: as *public* and as *persuasive* entities.

Publicity

The public symbols of the organization can include everything from newsletters to bulletin boards to pamphlets to speeches to memos to annual reports—in short, any message which the organization releases, whether deliberately or unwittingly, to the world at large.[5] To have faith in public messages, one must believe in the inherent sociability of organi-

---

[4] Utilizing critical probes which have been generated from organizational, rhetorical, and sociological literature, I analyzed the public organs of four organizations from 1965–80. The organizations represented the four major secondary socializing institutions that sociologists have identified: Education—Tennessee Education Association (TEA); Business—Reynolds Metals Company (RMC); Religion—The Presbyterian Church in the United States (PCUS); Politics—Kansas Democratic Party (KDP). This essay is derived from a rhetorical profile of organizations which emerged from my analysis of the data alluded to above.

[5] Johnson (1981, pp. 251-288) calls these official public messages "organizational documents" which are addressed "To whom it may concern' and are signed "The Organization." In other words, documents "speak for" the organization.

zations. Open systems theorists have reminded us that an organization, in order to survive, must interact with both its internal and external environments.[6] It must share, explain, even justify itself to others (Berger & Luckmann, 1966, p. 61). Therefore, when Reynolds Metals faces a crucial price hike, or the teachers in Tennessee threaten a controversial strike, or the Kansas Democrats receive an embarrassing defeat at the polls, these organizations must speak. To remain silent is to ignore the vital relationship between organization and environment, and could set in motion the organization's eventual demise (Katz & Kahn, 1978, p. 37).

Confidence in public symbols is also enhanced by the assumption that even those decisions made behind closed corporate doors are destined to face the glaring light of public scrutiny. For example, the board may decide in executive session one day to construct a well-lighted, convenient parking lot for management, and to gravel a nearby empty lot for the hourly employees. Not only is the board transaction an interesting bit of organizational news, it also tells what the organization values, how it makes and implements decisions, what it might be like to live and work in that particular organizational environment. More importantly, this cultural insight faithfully shows up 6 months later in a list of employee grievances printed in the company organ. Although the process of revelation may take a while and the whole story may never be told, most significant organizational decisions do ultimately find their way into the public record.

Persuasion

Rhetorical analysis also makes sense only if one believes that cultural transmission in the organization is largely an exercise in persuasion.[7] Sociologist Peter Berger (1969, pp. 126-153) reminds us that human beings live in a world of competing cultural cues, and that each organization must literally vie for the membership, time, and allegiance of its constituency. Karl Weick (1980) supports and extends Berger's notion when he identifies the most formidable task of the organization as fusion of all the multiple realities which reside within its constituency into "an organizational reality" around which all can rally. In other words, the

---

[6] For a comprehensive discussion of the organization's environmental dependence, see Terreberry (1973, pp. 81-100).

[7] See Johnson, p. 258, for an explanation of the persuasive dimensions of the organization's public messages.

culture which the organization continually creates and transmits is not just any culture; rather, it is a *particular* set of beliefs, values, attitudes, and behaviors, which ultimately must be endorsed by the organization's vital constituencies.

The notion of organizational persuasion appears to be an appropriate one when we consider a group's external interactions, like courting prospective customers, creating a favorable image, soliciting needed resources, and selling a product (Simons, 1972). Internally, however, organizations have often been thought of as pockets of coercion within society, where jobs get done by virtue of strict, inflexible procedures handed down by those who occupy higher positions on the hierarchical ladder. Recent organizational literature suggests that power may be more widely dispersed than the traditionalists believed. Workers do possess power over many things—resources, expertise, information, and, most significantly, over their own commitment (see, e.g., Argyris, 1974, pp. 3-17; Porter & Steers, 1973, pp. 151-176; Lawler & Hackman, 1969, pp. 467-471; Mellinger, 1956, pp. 304-309).

The day is no longer, or perhaps never was, when an organization can expect automatic adherence to its goals and procedures; workers must be viewed as viable power brokers in and of themselves—human beings who must be coaxed, cajoled, and convinced to yield to organizational commitment. And, lest we mistakenly assume that culture is only created and handed down by some arbitrary corporate mentality, we need to remind ourselves that there is no directionality to the culture flow. Though the degree of access to the organization's public media may vary among the membership, management holds no lock and key on the symbolic repertoire of the organization. At the same time organizational members are receiving culture, they are also creating it with their own reactions and counteractions.[8]

Therefore, whether culture is streaming from the inside or outside of the organization, from the bottom or the top, whether in task-related situations or socio-emotional settings, formally or informally, there is a real sense in which organizational members, both individually and collectively, are seeking to place their own distinctive stamp on the social world which they inhabit. In such a formulation, the study of rhetoric takes on interesting, even crucial, dimensions.

---

[8] See Johnson, pp. 255-56, for an interesting example of bottom-up culture creation in the organization, related by Barrett (1943, pp. 25-29).

WHY STUDY ORGANIZATIONS RHETORICALLY?

From the Researcher's Standpoint, Organizational Rhetoric Offers an Accessible and Functional Cultural Data Pool

The public messages of the organization are usually recorded, written down, *preserved*; it is difficult for them to get into the public arena otherwise. Whether the words carry the formal trappings of a speech, annual report, or company news article, or whether they display themselves casually across the bulletin board, on the bumper of an employee's car, or in a notice on the restroom door, the very translation of the symbols into written form renders them fair game for public consumption and for public scrutiny.

Organizational rhetoric is also *stationary*. Unlike the multitude of interpersonal messages which are exchanged daily within the organization, the public symbols stand still (Johnson, 1981, p. 256). Many organizational researchers, especially those who study socialization, would say that a great deal more culture is transmitted through the interpersonal medium than through organizational rhetoric.[9] While this may be true, interpersonal talk is transient. We may be lucky enough to capture it on tape, or in interview notes, or as a number in a survey questionnaire, but, for the scholar seeking to construct a cultural profile, it is advantageous to freeze the organization's total transcript for a protracted, thoughtful appraisal.

Organizational rhetoric offers a medium by which to study organizations *longitudinally*. The word "organization" itself implies process, "to bring into being" (Webster's New World Dictionary, 1978). There literally is no ad hoc corporate identity; "what an organization is" is what it has become through a series of complex and evolving interactions. It is possible, of course, to enter an organization at any given time and to describe what one sees there. Those data only make sense, or assume any predictive value, when they are compared to where the organization has been and where it is going. In the same way that culture at large is processual (Pettigrew, 1979, p. 570), a flash of culture on the organizational horizon is of little use until it takes place in some evolving pattern of beliefs, attitudes, values, and behaviors.

Cultural perceptions based on long-term organizational rhetoric are *verifiable*. Because of our ability to record, preserve, and hold still the organization's public message, we are afforded a continual, unbroken

---

[9] For discussions of organizational socialization via interpersonal mediums, see Graen (1976) and Newcomb (1958, 1961).

account of the organization which serves to validate our cultural hunches. In the ongoing stream of public data, the atypical event, the unrepresentative metaphor, the idiosyncratic account, stands out, exposes itself as a cultural imposter. Therefore, the researcher is facilitated in the assignment of status to a multitude of symbols, and only counts as representative culture those messages which stubbornly and repeatedly float to the top over time.

The study of organizational rhetoric also enables the researcher to describe the *functions* of organizational symbols; often these symbols are both "being" and "doing."[10] Not only does rhetorical analysis locate and assess significant organizational symbols, it also equips the researcher to describe how these symbols are behaving in their organizational contexts. For example, it may be helpful to identify major patterns of argument, to assess stylistic features, to categorize prominent and recurring strategies—in short, not only to describe the presence of the rhetoric, but to unravel the cultural implications which might be inherent in its behavior as well. The *Presbyterian Survey* (November, 1967, pp. 6, 10) carries a letter to the editor decrying the new liberalism invading the church. Before relegating this message to just one more letter from a disgruntled conservative, it is important for us to ask how this rhetoric is "acting." In this particular case, the rhetoric *supplies a forum* for an unhappy member, *listens* to feedback which might correct or adjust the organizational course, *presents* an open and sympathetic image to all its constituencies, *informs* about the philosophy of at least some Presbyterian members, and perhaps *recruits* those individuals of like sentiment. While it might be tempting to view thousands of organizational messages like this letter as self-evident, to do so is to ignore the versatile behavioral repertoire of organizational symbols, and perhaps to inadvertently miss the organizational story which they tell.

Finally, organizational rhetoric is *accessible*; we can get our hands on it. In fact, once an organization commits a particular statement or position to the public sector, there is no retrieving it. Unlike the executive session or the official minutes of the board or the appraisal interview, the public words of the organization are available to all. Although a manager may express surprise at an individual's interest in examining only those public messages which the organization has issued, it is unlikely that the request will be denied. At a time when researchers recognize the difficulty of "getting into an organization," the availability of so rich and thorough a data source is no small consideration.

---

[10] For a discussion and examples of the behavioral quality of rhetoric, see Austin (1971), Benjamin (1976, pp. 84-95), and Cushman and Thompkins (1980, p. 55).

From the Organization's Standpoint, Organizational Rhetoric Is an Active Cultural Medium

Some organizational theorists would insist that public words are wasted words, that they cannot be very effective at peddling culture because no one reads or listens to them anyway. If this indictment of public words is true, one wonders why organizations resolutely persist in influencing their members through that medium, each year expending vast resources in pursuit of the goal. And this dogged determination to be heard is not confined to the high and mighty organizations like IBM and Exxon (which have multi-million dollar budgets to support it). Public discourse may be held in even more esteem in the small, under-staffed, under-financed offices of the Kansas Democratic Party. In short, culture enthusiasts should value public messages because organizations do. The following propositions demonstrate why organizations across the board appreciate and utilize their public talk to pass on their particular way of looking at the world.

Organizational Rhetoric Offers Breadth and Efficiency in the Dissemination of Culture

If organizations are, in fact, continually about the business of peddling a particular cultural bias, it is understandable that they seek a medium which reaches the largest number of people in the least amount of time. For example, decision-makers of Reynolds Metals Company determine that it is important for both their internal and external constituencies to be acculturated with the message: "Reynolds will only produce a quality product."[11] (Such a message has obvious motivational implications inside the organization, and market potential on the outside.) It is staggering to ponder, however, the number of person/hours which would be required to interpersonally disperse that message throughout the organization, not to mention throughout the company's external environment. Also, when this message is transferred by word of mouth, it only has impact for the moment it is spoken, and within the sound of the voice that utters it (Johnson, 1981, p. 256). Public talk, on the other hand, can transcend time and space and address many different hearers at once. Therefore, with a few well-chosen public phrases, Reynolds Metals can take the company's case to its 37,000 employees and hope that an external constituency is listening as well.

The efficiency of public talk is further enhanced by its multi-layered, multi-functional quality of making a few words count for many. A good

---

[11] "Quality" is a recurring theme in RMC discourse. For a typical example of such rhetoric, see *Reynolds Review*, November 1975, pp. 8, 9.

example of rhetorical efficiency emerges from an account of a reading incentive program in one Tennessee classroom. Selected excerpts from the short article explain how the rhetoric is doing many things for many people at once (*Tennessee Teacher*, February, 1971, pp. 11-13):

> *Recognition and praise for an individual organizational member*: Jane Poole, a reading teacher employed in the Murfreesboro City School's Title 1 program, is currently in the midst of teaching a unit about automobiles. It is proving to be an unusual and highly successful way of teaching remedial reading to elementary students.
>
> *Norming; Standard-setting for expected performance among individual members*: Finding information suitable for a child whose reading level might be several grade levels below his age was particularly tedious; and, to individualize her program, she searched through many books and references to find automobile stories and information that remedial students would be able to read.
>
> *Appreciation of and cohesion with fellow organizational members*: The end result was incorporation of all subject areas in the unit taught in the remedial reading class. A multi-media method was used to teach reading, spelling, and phonetics and to expose students to creative writing, poetry, music, and art.
>
> *Credibility-building and positive image-making for the teaching profession*: To teach a unit of this type successfully is especially demanding and Mrs. Poole devoted much time to finding appropriate material that would interest her students and be appropriate to their particular reading level . . . It is difficult to do justice to the rewarding nature of Mrs. Poole's program at Bellwood. A visitor to the center sees many wonderful things at a glance, and—most wonderful of all—that the children are really learning.

Organizational Rhetoric Also Displays Versatility and Creativity in its Form and Substance. A criticism often leveled at official organizational discourse is that it is notoriously bland and boring, rendering it questionable as an effective cultural carrier. However, close scrutiny of such messages reveals interesting variations in both the form and the substance of the organization's public message. Of course, there are the expected media—feature articles, speeches, editorials, public pronouncements—but the "company line" is also spread through such unexpected methods as fiction, poems, posters, cartoons, recipes, crossword puzzles, and even prayers. The Kansas Democrats are especially inventive in their use of rhetorical forms; in 1971, they published their own annual awards ceremony which they entitled Kandid's Year-End Dubious Distinction Awards. (The following are among the more illustrious examples):

"The Most Tasteless Acronym of the Year Award"
Award to GOP Senator Bob Dole who said, "GOP means
generation of peace."

"The Christopher Columbus Award"
Award to GOP Senator James Pearson, who upon hearing
next year is an election year, discovered Kansas.

"The Best Imitation of Spiro T. Agnew Award"
Award to GOP Senator Bob Dole who said, in one breath,
"Media merchants of defeatism" and later,
"Left-leaning marshmallow." (*Kandid*, November, 1971, p. 2)

While each of us can recall personal experiences with sterile, calcified institutional rhetoric, the forms of organizational messages are not necessarily so uninteresting. Apparently, wise organizational rhetors reason that, if their particular message is to survive the multitude of competing cultural stimuli, that message must be outfitted in its most attractive and compelling attire.[12]

Perhaps more important than this flexibility of form is an efficiency and a creativity in the substance of organizational talk. I have alluded to the multi-functional quality of organizational discourse, in which a single message performs multiple tasks. Organizational rhetors also employ a multi-layering process,[13] stacking meanings on top of one another in a neat, concise verbal package. To watch this phenomenon at work, it is necessary to strip away the layers of meaning hidden beneath the organization's public symbols much as one would peel an onion. On the surface, Reynolds' litter campaign identifies the organization as environmentally concerned, quite a remarkable position at that time. At a deeper level, the observer might discern a strange irony at work. As well as creating a favorable image, RMC desperately needs to insure its own survival by convincing America that disposable cans can be a workable and viable option, that litter and aluminum production need not be, must not be perceived as, synonymous.

Examples of multi-layering consistently emerge from rhetoric of various organizational types. Even as the Tennessee teachers attempt to explain why Johnny can't read, they are pleading at a deeper level for public appreciation and professional credibility (*Tennessee Teacher*, Feb-

---

[12] In the psychological perspective of communication theory, the individual is surrounded by an informational environment containing an infinite array of competing stimuli from which he or she will ultimately choose. See Fisher (1978).

[13] Numerous scholars have addressed the phenomenon of multilayered meaning. See, for example, Tyler (1978) and Hopper (1981, pp. 195-211).

ruary, 1974, pp. 18-22). When the Kansas Democrats enthusiastically announce a 25-dollar per-plate Washington Day gala, the message they hope to hide is that party survival may depend on your 25 dollars (*Kandid*, April, 1971, p. 1). And, finally, when the Presbyterians celebrate diversity throughout their ranks, they are really saying to unhappy members, "Don't leave us. We care for you. There's room for everyone" (*Presbyterian Survey*, November, 1971, p. 23).

Besides being multi-functional and multi-layered, organizational talk is also often designed to be multi-interpretive. Confounding the rhetorical task of the organization as it transmits its particular culture is the fact that its listening audience consists of various and sometimes competing groups both inside and outside its boundaries, and some individuals who are "partially included" (Allport, 1933) in both groups. While the needs and aspirations of these groups may be quite different, the organization is expected to speak a message which is somehow compelling and pleasing to all. So the organization sets up its message to facilitate multiple interpretations.

For example, when the *Presbyterian Survey* (November, 1971, p. 23) reports on a ministry for minorities, it can do so with certain hopes and expectations—perhaps the message will be heard by PCUS liberals as a move toward social consciousness; perhaps the *same* message will be heard by church conservatives as, "We're giving them soup so that we don't have to go to church with them." When the KDP touts itself as the party of the "little man" (*Kandid*, May, 1969, p. 1), it, too, counts on multiple interpretations. If the rhetoric hits its mark, all sorts of diverse types may rally beneath the Democratic banner—from the economically deprived to the small farm owner to short people.

Also contributing to the versatility and thus to the usefulness of organizational talk is the fact that it is highly malleable, taking any shape or form which the organization might desire. When the KDP reports on the 1971 legislative session, the party seeks to also score some points with the listening public. To do so, it verbally constructs the account to suit Democratic interests at the expense of the Republican majority:

A potentially people-conscious 90 days was fraught with political partisanship, self-interest, and one self-inflicted pay raise. . . . The 1971 Kansas Legislature had an opportunity to enact people-oriented measures to eliminate gaping tax loop-holes, upgrade higher education, strengthen law enforcement. . . . Who lost? Because special interest had the reins of Republican leaders, and an incorrigible majority party's obsession to "get the Governor," the people of Kansas suffered a crippling blow (*Kandid*, April, 1971, p. 1).

The KDP kneads and shapes this message like bread for baking: it defines the issues of Republican failure (tax, education, law enforcement, etc.); assigns its own descriptive terms ("political partisanship," "self-interest," "incorrigible obsession"); asks the important question—"Who lost?"; and even answers it: "The people of Kansas."

Finally, organizational discourse is ostensibly infallible. From its perspective it is seldom wrong—a highly useful trait in a world of competing cultural cues. One liability to doing organizational business through face-to-face interaction is that receivers have a tendency to talk back. Public discourse precludes such an unfortunate occurrence. Because of its monologic form, it rests on the printed page, virtually insulated from attack. Therefore, when RMC defines the major problems confronting industry in 1975 as "the high cost of environmental controls; the increasing cost of energy; and the increasing cost of raw materials on which we have been mainly dependent on other countries" (*Reynolds Review*, January, 1975, p. 20), who will argue? And who will debate the Tennessee teachers when they say that the legislature *must* provide them financing for guidance, instructional supplies, building maintenance and operation, etc. (*Tennessee Teacher*, January, 1970, p. 5)? There will be no argument because the medium of public discourse does not allow it. If the organization wants the last word, it says the first word in public.

Organizational Rhetoric is Capable of Both Preserving and Propelling the Organization. The phrase "But we've always done it that way" sparks instant recognition with anyone who has ever belonged to an organized group. This universal epithet, while sometimes functioning to protract, even impede progress, does reflect the fact that organizations sense their longitudinal nature. Although they may not know exactly how to capitalize upon their past or how to effectively program the future, they do appreciate the need to operate in multiple time frames, and they have learned to utilize a medium which can reconstitute organizational roots and simultaneously provide a compelling vision and rationale for the future.

Rhetorical Preservation —In its role as preserver (Cherwitz & Hikins, 1982, pp. 135-162) rhetoric functions to tell the organization's story, whether that tale be fact or myth. For years, organization watchers have been tripping over the compulsion to separate reality and illusion in organizations. However, we have come to admit of late that there may be as much reality in an organizational myth or in an apocryphal story or in an office ritual as there is in an office building or a typewriter or a managerial grid.[14] In fact, Pettigrew argues that it is precisely the study

---

[14] For examples of recent studies in organizational symbolism, see Martin and Powers (in press), Brown, McMillan, and Blackman (1981), and Boje, Fedor, and Rowland (1982, pp. 17-28).

of humankind as a "creator and manager of symbolic meaning" (Petti-grew, 1979, p. 572) that yields to us the essence of an organization.

Therefore, the wise organization never misses an opportunity to call forth the past, usually through celebration or company ritual. At Reynolds, anything is cause for a party—from the top salesman award to a 25th birthday party for Reynolds Wrap. The celebratory discourse usually repeats the company legends: Old Mr. Reynolds' trip to Germany to view aluminum production; his return home and subsequent warning to the U.S. government; RMC/USA alliance to produce aluminum and to "protect America"; U. S. government leasing of Reynolds' first plants (*Reynolds Review*, May, 1967, pp. 4, 18; May, 1966) . . . and the story goes on.

Public discourse also puts the organization "on record"—declares to the world where it stands. Organizational talk which occurs in the board room or at coffee break or during the company picnic is often irresponsible. Especially when we really need to count on it (e.g., a promised raise, allusion to an overdue promotion, an anticipated company policy), private organizational talk is invariably elusive. No one remembers exactly what words were said, and, certainly, no one wants to be responsible for them.

Public talk, on the other hand, cannot retreat to anonymity; it is there on the table for all to see and hear. So it faithfully claims its calling as guardian of the organizational record—what the organization endorses, what it supports, what it stands for. When the PCUS goes on record in favor of amnesty, the *Presbyterian Survey* captures the message (*Presbyterian Survey*, June, 1976, p. 24). When Reynolds speaks for nuclear power, not a single phrase is omitted (*Reynolds Review*, September, 1976, p. 2). When the TEA endorses teacher negotiations (*Tennessee Teacher*, November, 1979, p. 21), every word is faithfully recorded and preserved for posterity.

Finally, when the organization's public record proves to be a liability rather than an asset, the organization invariably taps its vast symbolic store for messages with which to defend itself. Therefore, if the PCUS is called by feminists a "sexist organization," it is important to be able to pull out messages of women's ordinations, minority quotas, and language adaptation; if the KDP is linked with the rich and powerful, it can parade "little man" talk; and if RMC is accused of excessive energy use, it may deftly switch the verbal arena to the economy of recycling. Through public discourse, the organization is able to marshall an impressive assemblage of messages aimed at any impinging philosophy which may threaten it, and frequently the mere presence of this preventive rhetoric, carefully preserved in its public record, is sufficient to ward off attack.

Rhetorical Activation. —While rhetoric's preservative function is continually pulling the past to the fore and giving the organization a continuing social presence, public messages are existentially active in the workplace as they mobilize, socialize, and energize the membership for participation in the future. This blue collar, hard hat characteristic of organizational rhetoric may be surprising to those who believe it to be reserved for ceremonial occasions only, like the company anniversary, the annual fund-raiser, and the supervisor's pep talk. Such formal talk is predictable fluff, the critic might say, devoid of substance or surprise; the real workhorse of the organization is that interpersonal variety of talk that transpires in the actual workplace.

However, a long, hard look at rhetoric in organizations of all types reveals the active presence of organizational rhetoric in the trenches. For example, in the ongoing life of the organization, norms must be continually established and transferred. The favored rhetorical device for organizational norming is the member feature (e.g., spotlighting the valued maintenance supervisor at the Reynolds Building in Richmond, *Reynolds Review*, May, 1975, p. 4; the innovative little congregation in Florida *Presbyterian Survey*, April, 1972, p. 21; the dedicated reading teacher from Murfreesboro *Tennessee Teacher*, February, 1971, pp. 11-13). Repeatedly, organizations locate those people who are essentially "doing their jobs well," adorn them with the finest of rhetorical trappings, and parade them out as examples for all the world to see. In some of its best multi-purpose work, this message implies to the external audience that the featured paragon is a typical TEA member, while quietly and unobtrusively holding up a model for the internal membership to see and to emulate. And, in the often costly process of member training and mobilization, no one has to lose. One member receives recognition; norms and values are established; other members get a painless, uncostly nudge; and the onlookers envision dedicated, hard-working public servants when they think of the TEA.

Organizational discourse also acculturates the member to appropriate organizational values and, at the same time, presents a value package which it hopes will sell in Peoria as well. Values march forth proudly and unashamedly in such visible places as speeches, editorials, technological and philosophical pronouncements. They are a little less bold in company-wide memos, articles, member features, and question/answer series. And they are almost hidden from view in contests, charts, announcements, poems, calendars, etc. The following list of accumulated "do's" and "don'ts" was extracted from the pages of the *Kandid*, and clearly demonstrates what the organization values:

· It is "good" to be:

1. Holding the line on taxes
2. Helping the blind, aged, handicapped
3. The esteemed editor of the *Kandid*
4. A recipient of the Wheat award
5. Connected to everything "good"—Navy, school, family, and apple pie.

· It is "good" *not* to be:

1. Republican
2. Right wing
3. Ultra anything
4. A faction
5. Powerful
6. Partisan
7. Wealthy
8. Ambitious
9. A puppet
10. A sacrificial lamb
11. A name caller.

· It is "good" to say:

1. "Help the blind, aged, and handicapped"
2. Attach metaphors of death to refer to the GOP, e.g., "GOP Legislature kills spending lid"
3. Attach metaphors of life to refer to the Democratic party, e.g., "the Democrats have caused the birth of new legislation"
4. Republicans are "plotting takeover"
5. "Celebration" instead of "fund-raiser"
6. "Red neck" instead of "reactionary arch-conservative"
7. "Two-party system"
8. "JFK"

Organizational literature tells us that simply getting people to work is not enough; workers must experience some degree of satisfaction and commitment if the work of the organization is to proceed smoothly. Job satisfaction is enhanced when people feel some sense of power, some notion that they "count" in the organization.[15] Rhetoric proves to be an active medium for spreading power around in the organization, employing some fancy footwork in the process. Often, organizational discourse disperses power frontally, as in public accountability for organizational resources; disambiguation of political processes; and member testimonials or admonitions. More subtle and perhaps more interesting is a covert tactic which might be labelled "the illusion of participation." While organizational rhetoric is by definition monologic, astute organizational rhetors compensate for that fact. Sensing that members may resent a one-way communication flow, organizations seek to simulate the form and spirit of dialogue through such devices as solicited question/answer series, suggestion boxes, contrived question/answer series, and, in some organizations, "Letters to the Editor."

It seems to matter little that these rhetorical forms are highly controlled by the organization, or that most of the actual member messages may wind up in File 13; what does matter is that members perceive that they, or those of their ranks, are being heard. And, in this symbolic power exchange, it appears that both the Indians and the Chiefs of the organization win.

Another prominent weapon in the rhetorical arsenal for power dispersion is metatalk, or talk about talk. In the organizational setting, this strategy takes the form of the organization's publicly contemplating or evaluating its previous messages or those options which lie ahead. For example, when the Driver's Education Program in Tennessee was facing resistance, the discourse about it did not preach; it did not prescribe; it did not pontificate. Rather, it analyzed and strategized about the exigence in public. We can almost picture two old friends sitting over a cup of coffee as we hear these words about the issue:

> The "sell" will continue to be the biggest problem. There are a lot of people who are against driver education. . . . They say: 1) Driver education does not reduce accidents. . . . 2) As the engineering aspects of driving improve there will be less need for driver education; and 3) Certified school driver educators do little more than commercial driving instructors. We shall be able to answer these critics only when high school instructors can prove that driver education does indeed reduce accidents (*Tennessee Teacher*, May, 1968, p. 17).

The significant switch in this organizational metatalk is from discourse that "dictates" to discourse that "conspires with" the member. Because of this subtle yet significant transformation, the member gains

---

[15] Traditionally, power within the organization was thought to be residing in and around the hierarchy. For an alternative view, see McMillan (1980).

perceived status in the symbolic exchange, and the organization has effectively presented its cause to the listening public as well. Once again, rhetoric has proven its worth in the workplace, as well as on the ceremonial stage.

So, in the dual role of both preserving and propelling the organization, rhetoric reveals some of its greatest strengths as a cultural carrier. Astute organizations have apparently learned that, while their interpersonal exchanges operate efficiently to do organizational business in the here and now, organizational rhetoric can also operate well in the present, and offers the additional bonus of easy movement in and out of the organization's other significant time frames. In summary, this section has attempted to demonstrate that we should look for culture in a group's public statements, because we will find it there—busily disseminating information, norms, and values; creatively packaging its own particular cultural bias; and calling forth a significant past, as it also provides the symbolic impetus to propel the organization into the future.

THE ORGANIZATIONAL PERSONA

At the beginning of this essay, I suggested that, residing within every organization—whether business, social, profit, nonprofit, giant corporation or small family company—is a persona, not a flesh-and-blood entity, but an organizational image which has been *created* from the accumulated symbols by which the organization represents itself. Taken together, these symbols fall into a unique configuration which reveals the attitudes, values, hopes, dreams, and fears of a group of people, and thereby constitutes, as well as reflects, their corporate existence—or their persona. I have also argued that at least one good place to look for this persona is in the public talk of the organization, where "who we are" is both deliberately, and sometimes quite accidentally, unfolding before our eyes. In this final section, I will discuss the characteristics of the persona which emerge across organizations.

The Organizational Persona has a Voice. While some of its other manifestations may be less distinct, there is no doubt about its ability to transmit messages in behalf of the organization. For the many reasons which have been submitted throughout this essay, the organizational persona usually speaks *in public*.[16] This inherent publicity should not sug-

---

[16] Geertz (1973, p. 12). In this essay, Geertz discusses the inherent publicity of culture: "Culture is public because meaning is . . . you can't wink (or burlesque one) without knowing what counts as winking."

gest that the substance of the message is not repeated, reinforced, perhaps even instigated, in the organization's private domain; it simply attests to the organization's implicit understanding that it must ultimately share itself with the social world which it inhabits.

The organizational persona also speaks *in chorus*; in other words, the voice of the persona is louder, more commanding, and more definitive than that of any one individual organizational member. Critics may argue that what we hear when the organization "speaks" is a strong executive or a particular editor or an especially active board, and it is true that a particular segment of the public record may carry such imprints. However, when one assumes the macro, longitudinal perspective, such temporary trends are mediated and corrected by the totality of the organizational record.

Therefore, when an organization speaks, we not only hear words which come from David Reynolds, or the General Assembly of the Presbyterian Church, or the State Democratic Chairman, or the Legislative council of the TEA, but we also hear how a school teacher in Murfreesboro prepares her lesson plans (*Tennessee Teacher*, February, 1971, pp. 11-13), how a Reynolds' employee plays Santa Claus for his community each year (*Reynolds Review*, November, 1974, p. 16), and why a concerned church member feels that Presbyterian ladies should not wear pantsuits (*Presbyterian Survey*, June, 1974, p. 60). In short, it is these collective voices, in chorus, which help to construct the persona of the organization.

The Organizational Persona Suggests a Visual Image. As the organization talks about itself, we receive distinct visual impressions of a physical nature. Whether those visual cues construct a sterling white, immaculately groomed high-rise in Richmond, or a quiet, stately, stained-glass sanctuary somewhere in the South, or a disheveled two-room office building in the Midwest, one thing is certain: the organization will most consistently appear in its finest technological trappings. In other words, when we envision the organization, it hopes that we will see it working—making aluminum or conducting a class or carrying a Bible.

Consistent with the findings of numerous other organizational studies, I found the chief determinant of identity in organizations to be technology;[17] in short, we *are* what we *do*. And if we are unable to envision

------

[17] Examples of organizational research which have emphasized the importance of technology may be found in the work of Woodward (1965) and Lawrence and Lorsch, (1967). In fact, so pervasive has been the power of technology in organizational research that many scholars have embraced the notion of "technological determinism" which Katz and Kahn define as "the major causal factor affecting other organizational attributes, interorganizational activities, and interorganizational behavior" (Katz & Kahn, 1978, p. 137).

ourselves at work, and to sell that same vision to our social world, then we just may not have the right to be there. So invariably, RMC will show up adorned in Reynolds Wrap, the Tennessee Teachers will be wearing specs and holding the hand of a child, and the Democrats will be sporting a campaign button and waving a flag. No other attire is so flattering or so useful to the organizational persona.

The Organizational Persona has a Character. "Life is hectic at Xerox." "IBM is a stuffy company." "GE treats you fairly." The world of organizations is filled with such perceptions.[18] While the bearer of organizational folk wisdom might be hard-pressed to produce concrete data in support of such claims, skeptic or challenger beware. Organizations do possess a sort of character on which their constituents would stake a life.

The researcher might identify those organizational *character traits* by dominant symbolic clusters within the organizational record, which examined longitudinally, began to spell out discernible attitudes, values, habits, etc. Less significant symbols fall by the wayside and allow us to extract the figure from the organizational ground which surrounds it.[19]

Gleaned from 15 years of public talk about themselves, the following characteristics describe a "Reynolds person." Not only are these traits clear and distinct in the discourse, they are abundant.
A Reynolds person is:

safety conscious

community active—a good citizen

enterprising

energetic and hard-working

a product of the American dream

educated, or values education

concerned for troubled people

dependable

quality-oriented

versatile

political

a "company man"

persistent

integrated, with personal and professional skills

professional

a team player

patriotic

heroic

loyal

Rounding out the organizational character is a behavioral dimension; as we come to know the organizational persona, we recognize that it

---

[18] Deal and Kennedy (p. 23), offer an extended list of organizational character traits which have come to typify some national organizations.

[19] See Cherwitz and Hikins for an explanation of how rhetoric assists in the cognitive differentiation process which helps us to ultimately confirm dominant organizational traits.

"acts" in distinctive and somewhat predictable ways. *Behavioral clues* usually can be found residing in the ritualistic repertoire[20] of the organization, or in "the way we do things around here" (Marvin Bower, quoted in Deal & Kennedy, 1982, p. 53). Whether the ritual be *work-related*—as in hiring and firing, reward systems, meeting formats, writing style, or *ceremonial*—as in company anniversaries, employee rites of passage, change of corporate command—the wise organization literally orchestrates its activities.

Just as certain corporate traits fall into neat and discernible clusters, so do organizational behaviors. For example, if we notice in the public record that the Kansas Democrats only announce a celebration (alias fund-raiser) when they are "in the red," or that the Presbyterians tend to call forth basic theological warrants in times of turbulence, then, after sufficient sampling, we are able to confidently assign to these organizations those distinctive behavioral traits, and to predict the likelihood that they will act the same way again under similar circumstances. Linguistic choices, argumentative shortcuts, stylistic preferences, and degree of emotional appeal are just a few of the strategies which enable us to identify and describe the actor which is the organizational persona.

The Organizational Persona Has a Story. One of the questions typically asked of a new acquaintance is "Where are you from?" The question suggests not only a place or an origin, but a *story*. Just as a person's story is helpful in coming to know him or her, so too is the story of the organization, and the organizational saga is usually passed along via its fables, myths, and legends. Therefore, when an organization admits publicly that "the Civil War split us from our Northern brethren"; "In the early 1900's, we made tin foil for tobacco packs"; "we were once known as 'bleeding Kansas,'" these organizations are not just making a statement of historical fact, but are passing on a piece of themselves, telling you who they are, even who they aspire to be. And it is only in this evolving story, in this unbroken line, that the murky image of the organizational persona begins to clear and to take on recognizable features. Just as in human interaction, however, first impressions can be deceiving, so it is vital that we return again and again to verify longitudinally the organizational persona which we have discovered.

The Organizational Persona Is a Rhetorical Actor as Well as a Rhetorical Creation. I have attempted to demonstrate that the viabil-

---

[20] The subject of ritual in the corporate lives of individuals has been a favored one. Selected references include Eliade (1958), Goffman (1967), Geertz (1972, pp. 1-37), and Campbell (1973).

ity of the concept of the persona lies in the fact that it does not reflect an actual physical being, but rather the *image* of the organization which it attempts to create. Thus, as Edwin Black reminds us, there may be some distance between "reality" and illusion in the organizational record (Black, 1970, p. 111). This distance may bother those critics who believe that focus upon the persona precludes the discovery of organizational warts which can only be exposed in private, interpersonal interaction.

While the rhetorically sophisticated organization does put on quite an impressive show,[21] I submit that the organizational persona is not only a rhetorical creation but also a rhetorical actor, and thus susceptible to all the dangers of opening one's mouth in public. While larger and mightier than any one individual rhetor, the persona of the organization is not exempt from all the mistakes, miscalculations, and failures of rhetorical strategy. In fact, the very size and clumsiness of the organization often function to impede the clean and efficient handling of its rhetorical task. As with any rhetor, the organization is prone to verbal outbursts, susceptible to fads, and sometimes seduced by the sweet sounds of its own words. The organizational persona seems alternatingly brilliant and bumbling; sometimes it talks big and bossy, sometimes offends or bores us, and frequently preaches and pontificates, but, in the next breath, finds the words to instruct, to comfort, to support, and even to inspire us.

The organizational persona will never leave us alone. If we are on the inside of the organization, it will beg for our continued participation and commitment; if we are on the outside, it must have our resources and renewal. Its survival demands it. Whether consciously strategizing or stumbling headlong into a public posture, the organizational persona offers a formidable, but infinitely worthwhile, challenge for those culturists who would construct the ship or the puppy which is the modern organization.[22]

CONCLUSION

The rationale for this study began with a fear—the fear of turning a concrete edifice or a managerial grid or a corporate board room into a per-

---

[21] McMillan (1982, pp. 212-236). The data from this particular study revealed an ideal type, or specific rhetorical postures which an organization might assume if it were at its best. The rhetorically sophisticated organization displayed proficiency in rhetorical complexity, economy, empowerment, utility, longevity, responsiveness, forecasting, and image-making.

[22] See Krippendorff and Eleey (1986) for a practical approach to assessing and utilizing the organization's symbolic environment.

son. My study of organizational rhetoric and the commentaries concerning it has completely reversed that fear. I now suspect that the real danger lies in transforming the persons of organizations into mindless, voiceless, inanimate objects—"the company," "the government," "the institution"—totally divorced from human responsibility and attribution (Lakoff & Johnson, 1980, p. 38). Literature and research strongly reflect the tendency, not only to embue organizations with extra-human characteristics, but to view them as separate from, even antithetical to, the individuals who constitute them. Thus, organizational members are often portrayed as helpless victims of arbitrary, usually reprehensible, organizational messages descending upon them from some inverted Black Hole somewhere (e.g., Bowers, 1974, p. 132). Perhaps it is because of this organizational disassociation that so much of our organizational literature is "steeped in criticism" (Lumsden, quoted in Weick, 1979, p. 12); by viewing the Organization as Other, we can regard it in both thought and practice as we would never dare to regard ourselves.

I submit that one reason we engage in this convoluted attribution process is that, historically, we have failed to understand the rhetoric of collectivities. This study has given us some new insights in that regard: organizations as persuasive arenas; organizational rhetoric as dispersed and reciprocal; organizations as collective symbolic constructions. The good news of this study is that there is a human being behind each organizational message, and, because the creation of organizational rhetoric is widely dispersed, oftentimes *I* am that organizational messagemaker. The potentially bad news is that, as a member, I am held accountable for the symbols of my organization, just as fellow members must share in the consequences of the organizational messages which I create. Participation in and association with collective rhetoric does not allow me to pick and choose only those symbols which please me. I *shall* be represented by, identified with, the group's entire symbolic repertoire, for such is the nature of the persona.

Karl Weick has declared that the time has come for organizational research which "appreciates" organizations (Weick, 1979, p. 12); a rhetorical approach does that. It sees organizations as human beings symbolically constructing and reconstructing the organizational worlds which they inhabit. Those symbols may not always be aesthetically pleasing, or rhetorically appropriate, or even morally justifiable, but they are *our* symbols and they stubbornly stand to represent the imperfect human collectivity that created them.

REFERENCES

Allport, F.H. (1933). *Institutional behavior*. Chapel Hill, NC: University of North Carolina Press.

Argyris, C. (1974). Personality vs. organization. *Organization Dynamics, 3*, 3-17.

Austin, J.L. (1971). *How to do things with words* (J.O. Urmson, ed.). New York: Oxford University Press.

Barrett, W. (1943). Senor Payroll. *Southwest Review, 29*, pp. 25-29. Reprinted in W.R. Nord (Ed.), *Concepts and controversy in organizational behavior.* Pacific Palisades, CA: Goodyear, 1972. 319-322.

Benjamin, J. (1976). Performatives as a rhetorical construct. *Philosophy and Rhetoric, 9* (2), 84-95.

Berger, P. (1969). *The sacred canopy.* Garden City, NY: Doubleday.

Berger, P. (1970). *A rumor of angels.* Garden City, NY: Doubleday.

Berger, P. (1979). *The heretical imperative.* Garden City, NY: Doubleday.

Berger, P., & Luckmann, T. (1966). *The social construction of reality.* Garden City, NY: Doubleday.

Black, E. (1970). The second persona. *Quarterly Journal of Speech, 56*, 109-119.

Boje, D.M., Fedor, D.E., & Rowland, K.M. (1982). Myth-making: A qualitative step in OD interventions. *Journal of Applied Behavioral Science, 18*, (1), 17-28.

Bowers, J.W. (1974). Communication strategies in conflicts between institutions and their clients. In G.R. Miller & H.W. Simons (Eds.), *Perspectives on communication and social conflict.* Englewood Cliffs, NJ: Prentice-Hall.

Brown, M.H., McMillan, J.J., & Blackman, B. (1981). *Investigation into the implications of organizational myth-making in a nursing care facility.* Paper presented at the SCA/ICA Conference on Interpretive Approaches to Organizational Communication, Alta, Utah, May.

Brown, M.H. (1982). That reminds me of a story: Speech action in organizational socialization. Unpublished dissertation, University of Texas.

Campbell, J. (1973). *Myths to live by.* New York: Bantam Books.

Cherwitz, R., & Hikins, J. (1982). Toward a rhetorical epistemology. *Southern Speech Communication Journal, 47* (2), 135-62.

Cushman, D.P., & Thompkins, P.K. (1980). A theory of rhetoric for contemporary society. *Philosophy and Rhetoric, 13*, 43-67.

Cyert, R.M., & March, J.G. (1963). *A behavioral theory of the firm.* Englewood Cliffs, NJ: Prentice-Hall.

Deal, T.E., & Kennedy, A.A. (1982). *Corporate cultures: The rites and rituals of corporate life.* Reading, MA: Addison-Wesley.

Eliade, M. (1958). *Rites and symbols of initiation.* (trans. by W.R. Trask). New York: Harper.

Fisher, B.A. (1978). *Perspectives on human communication.* New York: Macmillan.

Geertz, C. (1972, Winter). Deep play: Notes on the Balinese cockfight. *Daedalus*, 1-37.

Geertz, C. (1973). *The interpretation of cultures.* New York: Basic Books.

Goffman, E. (1967). *Interaction ritual.* New York: Doubleday.

Goldhaber, G.M. (1983). *Organizational communication* (3rd ed.). Dubuque, IA: William C. Brown.

Graen, G. (1976). Role-making processes within complex organizations. In M.D. Dunnette (Ed.), *Handbook of industrial and organizational psychology.* Chicago, IL: Rand McNally.

Hopper, R. (1981). The taken-for-granted. *Human Communication Research, 7*, 195-211.

Johnson, B.M. (1981). *Communication: The process of organizing.* Boston, MA: The American Press.

Kandid: Kansas Democratic Information Digest, 1965-80, Topeka, Kansas: Kansas State Democratic Party.

Katz, D., & Kahn, R.L. (1978). *The social psychology of organizations*, (2nd ed.). New York: John Wiley and Sons.

Krippendorff, K., & Eleey, M.F. (1986). Monitoring a group's symbolic environment. *Public Relations Review*, Spring, 13-36.

Koch, S., & Deetz, S. (July, 1981). Metaphor analysis of social reality in organizations. *Pro-*

ceedings of the Conference on Interpretive Approaches to the Study of Organizational Communication. Purdue University, West Lafayette, IN.

Lakoff, G., & Johnson, M. (1980). *Metaphors we live by*. Chicago and London: The University of Chicago Press.

Lawler, E.E., & Hackman, J.R. (1969). Impact of employee participation in the development of pay incentive plans: A field experiment. *Journal of Applied Psychology, 53*, 467-471.

Lawrence, P.R., & Lorsch, J.W. (1967). *Organization and environment: Managing differentiation and integration*. Boston, MA: Division of Research, Harvard Graduate School of Business Administration.

Manning, P.K. (1979). Metaphors of the field: Varieties of organizational discourse. *Administrative Science Quarterly, 24*, 660-671.

Martin, J., & Powers, M.E. (in press). Truth or corporate propaganda: The value of a good war story. In L. Pondy, P. Frost, G. Morgan, & T. Dandridge (Eds.) *Organizational Symbolism*.

McMillan, J.J. (1980). *Power reciprocity and upward distortion within the organization*. Paper presented at the annual meeting of the Speech Communication Association, New York.

McMillan, J.J. (1982). *The rhetoric of the modern organization*. Unpublished dissertation, University of Texas.

Mellinger, G. (1956). Interpersonal trust as a factor in communication. *Journal of Abnormal and Social Psychology, 52*, 304-309.

Newcomb, T.M. (1958). Attitude development as a function of reference groups: The Bennington study. In E.E. Maccoby, T.M. Newcomb, & E.L. Hartley (Eds.), *Readings in social psychology*, (3rd ed.). New York: Holt, Rinehart and Winston.

Newcomb, T.M. *The acquaintance process*. (1961). New York: Holt, Rinehart and Winston.

Pacanowsky, M., & O'Donnell-Trujillo, N. (1983). Organizational communication as cultural performance. *Communication Monographs, 50*, 126-148.

Perrow, C. (1961). The analysis of goals in complex organizations. *American Sociological Review, 26*, 854-866.

Pettigrew, A. (1979). On studying organizational cultures. *Administrative Science Quarterly, 24*, 570-581.

Porter, L.W., & Steers, R.M. (1973). Organizational, work and personnel factors in employee turnover and absenteeism. *Psychological Bulletin, 80*, 151-176.

Presbyterian Survey, 1965-80. Atlanta, Georgia: Presbyterian Church in the United States.

Reynolds Review, 1965-80. Richmond, Virginia: Reynolds Metals Company.

Simon, H.A. (1964). On the concept of organizational goal. *Administrative Science Quarterly, 9*, 1-22.

Simons, H.W. (1972). Requirements, problems, and strategies: A theory of persuasion for social movements. In Ehninger (Ed.), *Contemporary rhetoric*. Glenview, IL: Scott Foresman.

Tennessee Teacher, 1965-80. Nashville, Tennessee: Tennessee Education Association.

Terreberry, S. (1973). The evolution of organizational environments. *Contingency views of organization and management*. Chicago: IL: Science Research Associates.

Thompson, J. (1967). *Organizations in action*. New York: McGraw-Hill.

Tyler, S.A. (1978). *The said and the unsaid: Mind, meaning, and culture*. New York: Academic Press.

Weick, K. (1979). *The social psychology of organizing* (2nd ed.). Reading, MA: Addison-Wesley.

Weick, K. (1980). *Loosely coupled systems*. Paper presented at the AERA Convention, Boston.

Wilkins, A., & Martin J. (1979). *Organizational legends.* (Research paper No. 521), Graduate School of Business, Stanford University.

Woodward, J. (1965). *Industrial organization: Theory and practice.* London: Oxford University Press.

3

Implications of Interpretive Approaches for Organizational Communication Research and Practice

Nick Trujillo

In recent years, "interpretive" approaches to the study of human behavior have attracted widespread attention from organizational researchers (see, e.g., Burrell & Morgan, 1979; Louis, 1980; Mitroff & Kilmann, 1975; Morgan & Smircich, 1980; Pacanowsky & O'Donnell-Trujillo, 1982, 1983; Peters, 1978; Pettigrew, 1979, Pfeffer, 1981; Pondy, Frost, Morgan, & Dandridge, 1983; Putnam & Pacanowsky, 1983; Sanday, 1979). Generally speaking, interpretive approaches focus on the *symbolic* aspects of human nature, examining how people use various symbols to make sense of their everyday experiences. Organizational researchers of late have been interested in interpretive approaches to examine how organizational members use symbols to make sense of their organizational experiences, and to examine how such symbol use and sense making impacts the nature of management. Pfeffer (1981), for example, suggests that management is "symbolic action" and that the critical administrative task is the construction and maintenance of systems of shared meanings. Pondy (1978) similarly argues that effective leaders not only change the behaviors of others but also "give others a sense of understanding what they are doing" (p. 94). As Weick (1979) more colloquially puts it, the manager is now coming to be understood as an "evangelist" as well as an "accountant." In short, the call is clear to consider closely the impact that organizational members, especially managers, have in defining organizational reality for themselves and for others.

Despite this heightened interest in interpretive approaches, the implications of such approaches for management research and practice remain somewhat unclear. This essay develops in more detail some of the implications of interpretive approaches for the research and practice of management. Specifically, this essay first introduces interpretive research as relevant to organizational inquiry. Second, the essay outlines key characteristics of interpretive approaches, and develops implications for management research and practice which follow from these characteristics. These implications are presented in terms of five interpretive challenges of management. Finally, the essay develops two types of interpretive skills that contribute to managerial effectiveness.

INTERPRETIVE APPROACHES AND ORGANIZATIONAL INQUIRY

As developed by Burrell and Morgan (1979), the "interpretive" paradigm is one overarching perspective that, unlike the "functionalist" paradigm, adopts a more *subjective* than objective view of organizational reality and focuses more attention on the *symbolic* than instrumental aspects of organizations. While functionalist research examines how instrumentally real entities—like hierarchies and technologies—impact organizational members, interpretive research examines how organizational members interpret such entities as real. In other words, the functionalist paradigm emphasizes how organizational reality "determines" organizational behavior, whereas the interpretive paradigm emphasizes how organizational behavior "creates" organizational reality.

Of course, the interpretive and functionalist paradigms are actually umbrella labels that cover a variety of academic traditions, including behaviorism (e.g., Skinner, 1957), systems theory (e.g., Emery & Trist, 1965), cybernetics (e.g., Wilden, 1972), social action theory (e.g., Silverman, 1970), symbolic interactionism (e.g., Louis, 1980), ethnomethodology (e.g., Gephart, (1978), and phenomenology (e.g., Jehenson, 1973). Each of these traditions adopts orientations toward organizational reality that vary in different ways and different degrees and, as Morgan and Smircich (1980) suggest, each can be viewed as different positions on an objective-subjective continuum. At the objectivist extreme are behaviorism and social learning theories, which view organizational reality as an externally real "concrete structure" and which treat organizational members as "responding mechanisms" who are conditioned by stimuli in the environment "to behave and respond to events in predictable and determinate ways" (Morgan & Smircich, 1980, p. 495). At the subjectivist extreme are phenomenological traditions which view organizational reality as a "product of human imagination" and which treat organizational members as "transcendental beings" who direct their psychic energies to "shape the world within the realm of their own immediate experience" (Morgan & Smircich, 1980, p. 494). Morgan and Smircich note that most organizational researchers fall between these polar perspectives and usually incorporate assumptions from adjacent positions in the actual practice of their research. As they conclude:

> The transition from one perspective to another must be seen as a gradual one, and it is often the case that the advocates of any given position may attempt to incorporate insights from others. Consequently, the success of efforts to determine who advocates what may be limited to determining the relative emphasis an advocate gives to one or more adjacent positions. (Morgan & Smircich, 1980, pp. 492-493).

As noted earlier, this essay focuses on interpretive approaches, those approaches which share, to a greater or lesser degree, more subjectivist orientations toward organizational reality.[1] In particular, this essay develops implications of these approaches for management practice and research. In the next section, the essay reviews five characteristics that interpretive approaches generally emphasize. As will be seen, these interpretive emphases suggest particular implications for management research and practice.

CHARACTERISTICS OF INTERPRETIVE APPROACHES

Subjectivity

Interpretive Approaches Tend to Emphasize the Subjectivity of Organizational Realities and to Deemphasize Their Objectivity. As noted earlier, interpretive approaches do not focus on how organizational phenomena like hierarchies and technologies impact organizational behavior, but rather focus on how members *interpret* these organizational phenomena. In other words, interpretive approaches emphasize the *meanings* of organizational phenomena to organizational members. Those who adopt extremely subjectivist positions (e.g., phenomenologists), for example, argue that organizational phenomena exist only as they are interpreted by individuals—that organizational realities are "social constructions" (Berger & Luckmann, 1967). Moderately subjectivist proponents (e.g., social action theorists) argue that organizational members assign subjective meanings to al-

---

[1] Approaches which incorporate subjectivist orientations toward organizational reality include, among others, social action theory, symbolic interactionism, dramatism, grounded theory, rhetorical theory, ethnomethodology, hermeneutics, critical theory, and phenomenology. As noted, phenomenological traditions adopt the most subjectivist positions, whereas social action theorists are closer to the "border" between interpretive and functionalist paradigms. For a review of various interpretive and functionalist approaches, see Burrell and Morgan (1979), Morgan and Smircich (1980), and Putnam (1982).

ready existing structures and thus "mediate" or "reflect" organizational realities. Whatever the particular emphasis on subjectivity, "interpretive approaches aim to explicate and, in some cases, to critique the subjective and consensual meanings that constitute social reality" (Putnam, 1983, p. 32).

Implications of Subjectivity—Managing Meanings. Interpretive approaches discourage management researchers and practitioners from assuming too quickly the instrumental status of organizational entities, like hierarchies and technologies, and encourage them to consider how organizational members ongoingly interpret these hierarchies and technologies. Interpretive approaches do not deny the existence of such phenomena, but, rather, focus on the meanings these phenomena have for particular organizational members. Thus, the hierarchy "exists" not only in its objective formalization in the organizational design but also in its subjectivity *use* in everyday actions. And managers manage the hierarchy not only by objectively redesigning organizational structures but also by subjectively encouraging members to "go straight to the top" or to "go through the chain of command."

As suggested earlier, organizational researchers have recently argued that a fundamental managerial task is to help create and maintain shared meanings in the organization (Pfeffer, 1981; Pondy, 1978; Smircich & Morgan, 1982). Indeed, as Smircich (1983) notes, strategic management "is devoted to bringing about a shared vision and shared interpretation of experience" (p. 235). The first interpretive challenge of management, thus, is to *manage meanings*—to help create and maintain particular interpretations of organizational reality with organizational others.

Dynamism

Interpretive Approaches Tend to Emphasize the Dynamism of Organizational Realities and to Deemphasize Their Stability. Interpretive approaches typically endorse more dynamic views of organizations. As Morgan (1980) asserts: "the interpretive paradigm directly challenges the preoccupation with certainty that characterizes the functionalist perspective, showing that order in the social world, however real in surface appearance, rests in precarious, socially constructed webs of symbolic relationships that are continuously negotiated, renegotiated, affirmed, or changed" (p. 9). Interpretive approaches, for example, describe the hierarchy less as a stable configuration and more as an interaction pattern that both persists and evolves. In short, those who adopt more dynamic positions focus on how organizational members create or mediate reality in their actions and interactions.

Implications of Dynamism—Managing Processes. Interpretive approaches discourage management researchers and practitioners from taking too static a view of organizations. Indeed, interpretive approaches ask us to take seriously the idea that organizations are constantly (if subtly) in flux, since organizational members ongoingly engage in actions which shape and reshape their view of the organization. Indeed, those who endorse positions of extreme dynamism describe the organization as "a continuous process, created afresh in each encounter of everyday life" (Morgan & Smircich, 1980, p. 494) though moderates qualify this description by recognizing a continuity of organizational life. Even so, these moderates are quick to assert that this continuity "is always open to reaffirmation or change through the interpretations and actions of individual members" (Morgan & Smircich, 1980, p. 494).

The process orientation of interpretive approaches invites managers to (re)examine how they reify various structures, products, and decisions in their organizations. In so doing, interpretive approaches may assist managers in cultivating what Peters and Waterman (1982) call a "bias for action"—an organizational "fluidity" characterized by chunking, experimenting, and most importantly, communicating with others (pp. 119-155). Perhaps as important, interpretive approaches encourage managers to recognize the symbolic importance of organizational processes independent of their instrumental importance. As Bolman and Deal (1984) recently assert: "Even if processes do not produce results, they are still important. They serve as rituals and ceremonies that provide settings for drama, opportunities for self-expression, forums for airing grievances, and arenas for negotiating new understandings and meanings" (p. 175). In sum, the second interpretive challenge of management is to *manage processes*—to help create active and fluid orientations in the organization.

Relativity

Interpretive Approaches Tend to Emphasize the Contextual Relativity of Organizational Realities and to Deemphasize Their Causality. Although most organizational researchers have taken the lead of Lawrence and Lorsch (1967) and acknowledge the contingencies of organizational behavior, many (including Lawrence and Lorsch) pursue generalizable explanations that cover a wide range of organizational contexts. Thus, most organizational research seeks to discover more deductive patterns of cause–effect relationships that predict patterns of behavior across organizational situations. Interpretive approaches more intensely consider the contingencies of organizational life, inasmuch as they directly focus on how members uniquely behave in particular organizational contexts. As Putnam (1983) summarizes, interpretive approaches "aim to understand social phenomena by extracting the unique dimensions of situations rather than by deducing generalizable laws that govern social behaviors" (pp. 40-41).

Implications of Relativity—Managing Contexts. Interpretive approaches invite organizational researchers and practitioners to develop more detailed understandings of particular organizational contexts. And interpretive approaches suggest that those who manage contexts also manage meanings, insofar as wider relational, situational, and historical frameworks influence the meanings of all organizational actions. Thus, interpretive approaches alert organizational researchers and practitioners to consider particular events and to ask questions like, Who are the participants? Where did these events take place? And when did these events take place? Those who adopt positions of moderate relativity assert that these contextual features shape organizational actions, whereas those who adopt positions of greater relativity argue that actions and contexts mutually elaborate each other, a characteristic known as "reflexivity." As one ethnomethodologist (Leiter, 1980) summarizes, "the setting gives meaning to the talk and behavior within it, while at the same time, it exists in and through that very talk and behavior" (p. 139).

The emphasis on contextual relativity suggests that managerial work is richly textured and that it cannot be easily "programmed" if it can be programmed at all. Managerial work involves a multiplicity of elements, all of which infuse ongoing significances into organizational realities. The research challenge ahead for those who study managing, then, is to avoid ignoring and simplifying the contextual features of managerial performances. "Context free arguments," Weick (1981) explains, "are irrelevant when applied to actors who are never free of contexts." And the practical challenge ahead of managers is to *manage contexts*. As Smircich (1983) summarizes, "wisdom among strategic managers lies in their recognition that they cannot control events, but they can influence the context against which events take on meaning" (p. 235).

Voluntarism

Interpretive Approaches Tend to Emphasize the Voluntarism of Organizational Realities and to Deemphasize Their Determinism. Organizational researchers who adopt more deterministic positions assert that the external environment determines human behavior in organizations. Indeed, extremely deterministic approaches (e.g., behaviorism) consider humans to be reactive individuals who respond to externally controlled events rather than to their own self-interests. Interpretive approaches, in contrast, adopt more voluntaristic views of organizational behaviors and assume that organizational members are active choice-making individuals who do not conform to behavioral laws. Moderately voluntaristic positions argue that organizational members act in ways which reflect social conventions of other members, whereas extremely voluntaristic positions suggest that organizational reality exists only as intended in each individual's consciousness. Whatever the case, interpretive approaches argue that organizational members' personal choices are very important indicators of organizational realities.

Implications of Voluntarism—Managing Choices. Interpretive approaches encourage management researchers and practitioners to recognize the choices that organizational members, including themselves, make. Interpretive approaches, for example, focus on the *improvisational* nature of management and try to identify the wide range of alternative actions available to organizational members. Thus, although the idea of organizational goal(s) may imply some managerial patterns or routines, interpretive approaches are quick to remind us that managers (should) ongoingly adjust and adapt these routines as they deal with the contingencies of everyday organizational phenomena.

Interpretive approaches also challenge management researchers and practitioners to actively confront the choices that they and other members make. As Smircich (1983) suggests: "Managers must look to their actions and inactions, not to the environment, for explanations of their situation. The environment often serves as a convenient scapegoat for placing blame and denying responsibility" (p. 230). Those who adopt voluntaristic positions, thus, are less inclined to deny their responsibility (as in "I had no choice but to let you go") and more inclined to actively assume responsibility for their choices. They are also more committed to understanding the reasons and strategies underlying such choices. In short, interpretive approaches challenge organizational researchers and practitioners to *manage choices* more actively in their organizational lives.

Pluralism

Interpretive Approaches Tend to Emphasize the Pluralism of Organizational Realities and to Deemphasize Their Unity. Organizational researchers and practitioners who talk about what goes on inside "*the* organization" often reveal their implicit assumption that organizations are single, coordinated entities. And those who endorse extremely unitary views often treat organizational members solely as singular components of these coordinated entities or as "instruments of purposeful-rational action aimed at technological effectiveness and organizational efficiency" (Putnam, 1983, pp. 36-37). Interpretive approaches, in contrast, adopt more pluralistic views of organizations. Although extremists argue that organizations have as many realities as individuals, most would qualify that organizations are collections of different individuals, groups, and coalitions with differing interests and priorities. Those more critically inclined additionally examine issues of power among these various individuals, groups, and coalitions. In sum, interpretive approaches invite organizational researchers and practitioners to look for multiple meanings of organizational behaviors and, thus, multiple interpretations of organizational realities.

Implications of Pluralism—Managing Coalitions. Those who adopt more pluralistic approaches to organizations believe that "the" organization is comprised of different individuals and groups that have their own unique interests. As Pfeffer (1981) suggests: "since organizations are coalitions, and the different participants have varying interests and preferences, the critical question becomes not how organizations should be designed to maximize effectiveness, but rather, whose preferences and interests are to be served by the organization. . . . The assessment of organizations is dependent upon one's preferences and one's perspective" (p. 223). Interpretive approaches, thus, see politics as an inevitable and even healthy element of organizations.

Along these lines, interpretive approaches invite organizational researchers and practitioners to consider the "same" organizational event from different perspectives. Indeed, those who adopt pluralistic views tend to assume misunderstandings rather than understandings among organizational communicators and, thus, often take greater care in articulating their intended meanings as they interact with others. Those who adopt pluralistic perspectives, too, spend more time cultivating bargaining and negotiation skills so as to help them ongoingly deal with multiple perspectives in their organizations. In short, the fifth interpretive challenge of management is to *manage coalitions.*

Summary

This section has discussed five key emphases of interpretive approaches and the corresponding implications (or challenges) for management research and practice. Not surprisingly, these interpretive emphases suggest somewhat different implications for organizational research and practice than do functionalist emphases. As Smircich (1983) summarizes:

> There is a major shift in emphasis from managing and controlling to interpreting and knowing. The major concerns for an interpretive practitioner is the examination and critique of organizational realities. The adoption of the interpretive perspective leads managers to clarify the various realities in a setting and to remove distortion in their understanding of what is going on, in order to contribute to the more informed practice of organization (p. 225).

In this way, then, interpretive and functionalist approaches can both critique and complement each other in organizational research and practice. Functionalist approaches stress the objectivity, stability, causality, determinism, and unity of organizational behavior, whereas interpretive approaches stress the subjectivity, dynamism, relativity, voluntarism, and pluralism of organizational behavior. Functionalist approaches challenge practitioners to manage facts, products, causes, reactions, and coordinated systems, whereas interpretive approaches challenge them to manage meanings, processes, contexts, choices, and coalitions. And while those who adopt positions near one paradigmatic extreme might ignore the challenges from the other paradigm, it seems most constructive to promote theoretical and practical discussions which further our understandings of the many functionalist *and* interpretive challenges and of the managerial skills required to meet these challenges.

This essay attempts to further our understanding of the managerial skills needed to confront the *interpretive* challenges of management, skills which can promote the symbolic effectiveness of a manager. I focus here on interpretive challenges and symbolic effectiveness, because these issues have generally been overlooked or understated in the organizational literature. A manager's "symbolic" effectiveness, after all, is a somewhat ephemeral concept when compared with instrumental measures of "profit," "productivity," "absenteeism," and the like (though I would note that measuring these instrumental indicators of effectiveness has been—and still is—fraught with difficulties). In short, a manager's symbolic effectiveness has been difficult to adequately assess, and in fact may be evidenced over the *long run* in an organization and thus escape short run effectiveness measures. Additionally, organizational researchers have only recently legitimized the importance of interpretive management skills in the organizational literature. As Pfeffer (1981) points out, the admission that symbolic skills are important to managerial effectiveness is not consistent with the dominant ideology of management as a rational enterprise. In sum, organizational researchers have generally overlooked interpretive management skills and the importance of symbolic effectiveness. This next section, thus, addresses the symbolic effectiveness of managerial action, and is organized around two general management skills that follow from interpretive approaches.

INTERPRETIVE MANAGEMENT SKILLS

> Dramaturgical skill has become increasingly essential to the hierarchical role, and technical competence increasingly irrelevant. (Thompson, 1963, p. 133)
>
>   If management involves the taking of symbolic action, then the skills required are political, dramaturgical, and language skills more than analytical or strictly quantitative skills. (Pfeffer, 1981, p. 44)

In order to perform the interpretive challenges of management, managers require skills that are sensitive to the symbolic aspects of organizations. This section discusses two such skills—"subtlety" and "eloquence." These two skills complement each other, in the sense that subtlety is a *perceptual* skill, whereas eloquence is a *behavioral* skill. I will argue that effective managers are both subtle and eloquent. This discussion does not endorse an amoral view of management which encourages managers to manipulate organizational realities solely for their own needs, but rather seeks to promote a more informed and more self-conscious research and practice of management.

Subtlety

In *Theory Z*, Ouchi (1981) notes that one important characteristic of an effective "theory Z" organization is "subtlety." Ouchi argues:

> Relationships between people are always complex and changing. A foreman who knows his workers well can pinpoint personalities, decide who works well with whom, and thus put together work teams of maximal effectiveness. These subtleties can never be captured explicitly, and any bureaucratic rule will do violence to them. (p. 6)

Ouchi's point is well taken. Relationships among workers do indeed have nuances which are often overlooked. As used here, though, "subtlety" involves more than a keen understanding of particular work relationships. As developed here, subtlety refers to one's sensitivity to the variety of ways that organizational members interpret their organizational realities. Stated differently, subtlety refers to one's nuanced understanding of the complexities of organizational life.

There are several reasons why organizational researchers and practitioners should be concerned with the variety of ways that other members interpret their organizational realities. First, as Weick (1979) has suggested, "a person can never do *one* thing" because "any action ramifies and has far reaching consequences" (p. 240). Some of these consequences will be viewed as immediate, direct, and desired, whereas other consequences will be viewed as delayed, indirect, and undesired. Organizational members who are sensitive to organizational complexities may be better able to read these interpreted consequences and, thus, accomplish more in any given activity. Second, every organizational action has retrospective and prospective aspects (Mehan & Wood, 1975). That is, past actions are often used to better understand present actions (and vice versa), and, similarly, present actions sometimes frame future ones. Finally, some events which may seem unimportant or trivial to some are often considered by others to be very important. Weick (1979), for example, suggests that, in long agenda-less meetings where nothing much seems to get accomplished, members exchange a great deal of talk and may learn to accommodate to one another's idiosyncratic styles, which enhances meeting productivity over the long run. Kanter (1977), too, illustrates how even casual remarks made by a manager can be translated into action by members who overhear such remarks. In short, those who are sensitive to the complexities of organizational life may be more aware of the potential interpretations of their own and others organizational actions.

Developing Managerial Subtlety. In order to develop a more subtle appreciation of organizational actions, researchers and practitioners need to *complicate* and *integrate* their interpretations of those actions. They, first, need to complicate, not simplify, their understanding of organizational actions. To simplify one's understanding is to interpret an event from a limited number of perspectives and to ignore additional possibilities; to complicate one's understanding is to interpret an event from multiple perspectives and to consider additional (alternative and simultaneous) possibilities. Subtle managers and researchers, thus, assume that every activity they engage in and that others engage in can be interpreted in multiple ways and from different points of view.

Organizational researchers and practitioners can develop more complicated understandings of organizational actions in many ways. First, they can usefully employ "critical incident" (Flanagan, 1954) and "diary" (Stewart, 1967) techniques to get more detailed and more self-conscious descriptions of their own and others' behaviors. Critical incident and diary methods require individuals to describe particular episodes of organizational behavior (including such things as what was said to whom in what location and on what occasion), and thus, sensitize these individuals to some of the interpersonal, historical, situational, and political details through which they and others interpret these episodes.

Researchers and practitioners, then, can use these descriptive details to help them multiply the potential meanings of their actions. Weick (1981) uses a textual metaphor to make this point when he argues that individuals can complicate and enrich their understandings of organizational action by "glossing" that action. "To 'gloss,' " Weick writes, "is to 'annotate' or append comment in the interest of helping a reader interpret an obscure passage or text" (p. 112), and he invites us to think of such glossings as a glorified version of the everyday marginalia we add to more traditional texts we read (books, manuscripts, etc.). These marginalia, Weick suggests, "variously interpret, personalize, embed, direct attention, provide links with other writings or other commentators, point to multiple meanings" (p. 114), and thus help a reader understand an event in more of its potential fullness. (Weick (1981) concludes that, when applied to texts of organizational behavior, such annotations add to the list of overdetermined factors of any given event and recapture requisite variety by enriching the event. In glossing, then, the manager or researcher multiplies the possible meanings of an organizational action so as to develop a richer understanding.

To complicate one's understanding of organizations is necessary but insufficient for developing subtlety. *Integration*, defined here as the development of broader coherent interpretations of organizational actions, is also needed. Managers in particular should cultivate broader interpretations of organizations, since they are inclined to be generalists more than specialists (Mintzberg, 1973). As managers move up the hierarchy, their duties and responsibilities increase in breadth and depth, as should their understanding of the organization.

Managers can cultivate broader pictures of organizations by considering various ways that organizational actions fit together. In other words, managers can analyze how organizational actions are connected to multiple other actions, and how all of these actions are connected together to accomplish broader strategic sets of actions and goals. In short, subtle managers and researchers develop a puzzle-solving curiosity and talent for fitting pieces of organizational action together in order to understand the broader organizational pictures of their everyday working worlds.

Subtle managers, thus, are better equipped to perform the five interpretive challenges of management developed earlier in the essay. First,
they can manage *meaning* better, because they are more aware of the different ways their own and others' actions can be interpreted. Thus, they
don't assume that their intentions are completely understood, and are
ready to handle "misunderstandings." Second, subtle managers manage
processes better because they are more aware of the temporality of organizations. Thus, they use past actions to frame present ones, and present
ones to frame future ones. And they ultimately learn to weave sequences
of actions together to accomplish long term goals. Third, subtle managers manage *contexts* more effectively, by using the situational and historical details which frame the meanings of events. They are predisposed to
use more flexible and adaptable styles of management to maximize their
effectiveness in different contexts. Fourth, subtle managers manage
choices more effectively, by taking a more active role in their organizations. They are likely to treat their appointment books, telephone calls,
and walking tours more seriously, since these phenomena represent potentially important choices that frame the manager time at work. Finally,
subtle managers manage *coalitions* better, because they are more aware
of the interpersonal and political details which influence meanings. Subtle managers, thus, are more likely to treat everyday events as bargaining
episodes and consider the self-interests of particular groups in more detail.

Subtlety is important for any organizational member, but for managers it is critical. As many have observed, managers experience their lives
in brief, varied, and fragmented episodes. Although some may find this
character of work distracting for accomplishing their tasks, subtle managers can interpret fragmentation more positively. As Deal and
Kennedy (1982) explain, "to the symbolic manager, this fragmentation
of a typical working day is a goldmine—the manager gets literally hundreds of different events to use in influencing the culture around him or
her" (p. 142). The challenge is to realize the potential significances of
these fragmented acts and to develop meaningful interconnections
among them. The challenge, then, is to use these subtle understandings
of organizations to perform management more effectively.

Eloquence

Managerial effectiveness not only depends on a subtle awareness of organizations but depends on how managerial *actions* are performed. And
organizational researchers have recently argued that the *communicative
actions* of management may be the most critical. Weick (1983), for example, describes managerial work as a "talk job" and says that we need to

spend more time developing job descriptions of such managerial talk. Pondy (1978), too, following Wittgenstein, characterizes leadership as a "language game," and he invites us to explore how leaders use language to influence others. These and other researchers argue that one's managerial effectiveness is intimately related with one's interaction with organizational others. Following Weick (1980), the term "eloquence" is used to describe effective language use in organizations.

For some, the term "eloquence" may sound archaic and, at first blush, may seem inappropriate for describing effective communication in everyday organizational contexts. The term has a tradition in public oratory and is associated with the so-called "grand style" of rhetoric—a style which doesn't seem to fit the often mundane performances of most managers. Moreover, contemporary critics often use the term pejoratively as "mere rhetoric" or "all talk and no action." And, as Weick (1980) points out, managers especially "like to characterize themselves as people of action who distrust words" and who avoid being "branded a 'wordsmith,' one who is wordy and passive rather than taciturn and active" (p. 18).

Weick (1980), however, is quick to counter that language use and eloquence are indeed essential for managerial effectiveness. As he argues:

> The management of eloquence in language is a key tool for effective leadership. Eloquence, defined as fluent, forceful, moving expression, is crucial, not so much because it stirs followers as because it affects what followers tell themselves when they try to discover what they are thinking. (p. 18)

Indeed, if organizations are filled with "talk jobs" and "language games," then language effectiveness is particularly critical. Moreover, as Baskerville (1979) notes, "words can provide the impulse to action—can explain and justify, can focus and canalize determination, and thus make action possible" (p. 240). To the extent that the social construction of reality is considered organizational "action," then language *is* action in a foundational sense. And so at second (or perhaps third) blush, the term "eloquence" may be a useful way of describing managerial effectiveness.

Developing Managerial Eloquence.   As used here, eloquence refers to one's use of *appropriate* and *dramatic* language with organizational others. Eloquence, first, refers to the use of language which is *appropriate* to the context in which it is used. Eloquent managers, thus, make language adaptations which best correspond with the particular contexts they encounter. For example, managers are "situationally" eloquent when they adapt to the exigencies of their immediate surroundings. Certain "front stage" settings require particular protocols, whereas other situations may suggest similar, though less formalized, rituals. Managers are "historically" eloquent when they adapt to the temporal contingencies of their organizations. When managers fail to address the precedents of organizational actions, for example, they ignore potentially important considerations which can impact the effectiveness of a current performance. Managers, finally, are "interactionally" eloquent when they adapt their communicative behaviors to the communicative behaviors of specific others. Eloquent managers, thus, "listen" to others, not only to acquire informational content, but also to understand and adapt their interaction as it unfolds and to play a more conscious part in their relationships with others.

Eloquence, second, refers to language which *dramatically* presents images of organizational reality. Such a quality is characteristic of what Hymes (1975) calls "true performance" and describes as "something creative, realized, achieved, even transcendent of the ordinary course of events" (p. 13). Bauman's (1975) comments about cultural performance best capture this dramatic sense of eloquence:

> There is . . . a distinctive potential in performance by its very nature which has implications for the creation of social structure in performance. It is part of the essence of performance that it offers to the participants *a special enhancement of experience*, bringing with it a heightened intensity of communicative interaction which binds the audience to the performer. . . . Through his performance, the performer elicits the participative attention . and energy of his audience (p. 301, emphasis added).

Bauman's assertion that performance offers participants a "special enhancement of experience" is the key to managerial eloquence. Whereas all communicative performances may help mediate organizational realities, eloquent performances enhance those organizational realities for others. Eloquent managers, thus, may indeed be more like "evangelists" than "accountants," to use Weick's (1979) labels, insofar as they socially enrich organizational realities for others.

In order to develop eloquence, managers must develop a flexibility in their communicative actions. In other words, managers should examine and then broaden their current repertoires of communicative strategies. Most importantly, managers should consider communicative forms like myths, stories, and metaphors, since these are more powerful vehicles for presenting organizational realities to others. Fortunately, organizational researchers have renewed their interest in these and other dramatic forms (see Dandridge, Mitroff, & Joyce, 1980; Daft & Wiginton, 1979; Koch & Deetz, 1981; Pondy et al., 1983; Wilkins, 1983). These communicative forms hold much promise as the dramatic vehicles through which managers can more actively enrich organizational reality for others.

Eloquent managers, thus, are better equipped to perform the five interpretive challenges of management. First, eloquent managers manage *meanings* more effectively by using flexible repertoires for communicating intended meanings. They additionally disclose other possible readings of their own and others' actions that could be important to the interactants. Second, eloquent managers manage *processes* better by creating a timeliness in their interactions with others. They are more likely to use and encourage verbs rather than nouns (Weick, 1979) and active voice rather than passive voice, and to make explicit connections among past, present, and anticipated events. Third, eloquent managers manage *contexts* more effectively by adapting to (and by adapting) the situational, historical, interpersonal, and political exigencies they experience. Thus, they change their own behaviors to fit various audiences as well as help these various audiences to likewise adapt. Fourth, eloquent managers manage *choices* better by actively acknowledging their own and others' choices. They are less likely to dichotomize options and more likely to suggest a variety of possibilities and opportunities. Finally, eloquent managers manage *coalitions* more effectively by developing bargaining and negotiation skills. They are more likely to understand different positions and better able to advocate certain positions.

Summary

To conclude, subtlety and eloquence are two managerial skills that follow from interpretive approaches. And the most effective managers are both subtle and eloquent. Effective managers need to understand the complexities of their organizations so they can appropriately adapt their actions to the situation at hand. So, too, effective managers use language which more dramatically presents their own images as well as organizational images. As Pondy (1978) summarizes, "this dual capacity . . . to make sense of things *and* to put them into language meaningful to large numbers of people gives the person who has it enormous leverage" (p. 95). Effective managers use this "leverage" to enhance organizational life for themselves and for others.

REFERENCES

Baskerville, B. (1979). *The people's voice.* Lexington, KY: University of Kentucky Press.

Bauman, R. (1975). Verbal act as performance. *American Anthropologist, 77,* 291-310.

Berger, P.L., & Luckmann, T. (1967). *The social construction of reality.* New York: Anchor.

Bolman, L.G., & Deal, T.E. (1984). *Modern approaches to understanding and managing organizations.* San Francisco, CA: Jossey-Bass.

Burrell, G., & Morgan, G. (1979). *Sociological paradigms and organizational analysis*. London: Heinmann.

Dandridge, T.C., Mitroff, I., & Joyce, W.F. (1980). Organizational symbolism: A topic to expand organizational analysis. *Academy of Management Review, 5*, 77-82.

Daft, R.L., & Wiginton, J.C. (1979). Language and organizations. *Academy of Management Journal, 2*, 179-191.

Deal, T.E., & Kennedy, A.A. (1982). *Corporate cultures: The rites and rituals of corporate life*. Reading, MA: Addison-Wesley.

Emery, F.E., & Trist, E.J. (1965). The causal texture of organizational environments. *Human Relations, 18*, 21-32.

Flanagan, J.C. (1954). The critical incident technique. *Psychological Bulletin, 51*, 327-358.

Gephart, R.P., Jr. (1978). Status degradation and organizational succession: An ethnomethodological approach. *Administrative Science Quarterly, 23*, 553-581.

Hymes, D. (1975). Breakthrough into performance. In D. Hymes (Ed.), *Folklore: Performance and communication* (pp. 4-23). The Hague, Netherlands: Mouton.

Jehenson, R. (1973). A phenomenological approach to the study of formal organizations. In G. Psathas (Ed.), *Phenomenological sociology: Issues and applications* (pp. 219-249). New York: Wiley & Sons.

Kanter, R.M. (1977). *Men and women of the corporation*. New York: Basic.

Koch, S., & Deetz, S. (1981). Metaphor analysis of social reality in organizations. *Journal of Applied Communication Research, 9*, 1-15.

Lawrence, P.R., & Lorsch, J.W. (1967). *Organization and Environment*. Boston: Graduate School of Business Administration, Harvard University.

Leiter, K. (1980). *A primer on ethnomethodology*. New York: Oxford University Press.

Louis, M.R. (1980). Surprise and sense making: What newcomers experience in entering unfamiliar organizational settings. *Administrative Science Quarterly, 25*, 226-251.

Mehan, H., & Wood, H. (1975). *The reality of ethnomethodology*. New York: John Wiley & Sons.

Mintzberg, H. (1973). *The nature of managerial work*. New York: Harper & Row.

Mitroff, I.I., & Kilmann, R.H. (1975). Stories managers tell: A new tool for organizational problem solving. *Management Review, 64*, 11-20.

Morgan, G. (1980). Paradigms, metaphors, and puzzle solving in organizational theory. *Administrative Science Quarterly, 25*, 600-615.

Morgan, G., & Smircich, L. (1980). The case for qualitative research. *Academy of Management Review, 5*, 491-500.

Ouchi, W.G. (1981). *Theory z*. New York: Avon.

Pacanowsky, M.E., & O'Donnell-Trujillo, N. (1982). Communication and organizational cultures. *Western Journal of Speech Communication, 46*, 115-130.

Pacanowsky, M.E., & O'Donnell-Trujillo, N. (1983). Organizational communication as cultural performance. *Communication Monographs, 50*, 126-147.

Peters, T.J. (1978). Symbols, patterns, and settings: An optimistic case for getting things done. *Organizational Dynamics, 7*, 3-23.

Peters, T.J., & Waterman, R.H. (1982). *In search of excellence*. New York: Harper & Row.

Pettigrew, A.M. (1979). On studying organizational cultures. *Administrative Science Quarterly, 24*, 570-581.

Pfeffer, J. (1981). Management as symbolic action: The creation and maintenance of organizational paradigms. *Research in Organizational Behavior, 3*, 1-52.

Pondy, L.R. (1978). Leadership is a language game. In M.W. McCall & M.M. Lombardo (Eds.), *Leadership: Where else can we go?* Durham, NC: Duke University Press.

Pondy, L.R., Frost, P.J., Morgan, G., & Dandridge, T.C. (Eds.). (1983). *Organizational symbolism*. Greenwich, CT: JAI.

Putnam, L.L. (1983). The interpretive perspective: An alternative to functionalism. In L.L. Putnam & M.E. Pacanowsky (Eds.), *Communication and organizations: An interpretive approach*. Beverly Hills, CA: Sage.

Putnam, L.L. (1982). Paradigms for organizational communication research: Overview and synthesis. *Western Journal of Speech Communication, 46*, 192-206.

Putnam, L.L., & Pacanowsky, M.E. (1983). *Communication and organizations: An interpretive approach*. Beverly Hills, CA: Sage.

Sanday, P.R. (1979). The ethnographic paradigm(s). *Administrative Science Quarterly, 24*,

Silverman, D. (1970). *The theory of organizations*. London: Heinemann.

Skinner, B.F. (1957). *Verbal behavior*. New York: Macmillan.

Smircich, L. (1983). Implications for management theory. In L.L. Putnam & M.E. Pacanowsky (Eds.), *Communication and organizations: An interpretive approach*. Beverly Hills, CA: Sage.

Smircich, L., & Morgan, G. (1982). Leadership: The management of meaning. *Journal of Applied Behavioral Science, 18*, 257-273.

Stewart, R. (1967). *Managers and their jobs*. London: Macmillan.

Thompson, V. (1963). *Modern organizations*. New York: Alfred A. Knopf.

Weick, K.E. (1983). Organizational communication: Toward a research agenda. In L.L. Putnam & M.E. Pacanowsky (Eds.), *Communication and organizations: An interpretive approach*. Beverly Hills, CA: Sage.

Weick, K.E. (1981). Psychology as gloss. In R.A. Kassachau & C.N. Cofer (Eds.), *Psychology's second century*. New York: Praeger.

Weick, K.E. (1980). The management of eloquence. *Executive, 6*, 18-21.

Weick, K.E. (1979). *The social psychology of organizing* (2nd ed.). Reading, MA: Addison-Wesley.

Wilden, A. (1972). *System and structure*. London: Tavistock.

Wilkens, A.L. (1983). The culture audit: A tool for understanding organizations. *Organizational Dynamics, 12*, 24-38.

PART II

Historical Perspectives on Organizational Dynamics

4

How We Got To This Point: A Brief History of Organizational Communications Technologies

Jib Fowles

INTRODUCTION

Stationed in these times, towards the close of the twentieth century, we are susceptible to taking for granted the widespread existence of organizations. Modern day organizations are so commonplace, ordering so many spheres of life from the economic to the recreational, that we never pause to consider the historical novelty of this phenomenon. We can be enthralled with the potentialities of the organization, but ignorant of how the present organizational landscape came into being.

It was not so long ago that organizations were rare, and that those few that did exist were characterized by a rigidity which, from a present perspective, would seem to make them candidates for extinction. Before the nineteenth century, the most common organizations were governmental; the organizational embodiment of their power were armies and navies. Some religions were organized—the Roman Catholic Church was one—but most were not. None of these organizations generated wealth; they survived by appropriating it one way or another.

Economics then only partially resembled the market economy of modern times. Most goods and services produced before the nineteenth century were consumed by the producer, or were entered into local barter. The kind of business organizations we live with were historically the least frequent type of organization, although not totally absent—a few European banking houses, the British East India Company, the French Tobacco Trust, and the like.

But as the nineteenth century moved along, strong and supple organizations began to appear everywhere. Most dramatically, they came to dominate economic life by the close of the century. The twentieth century has seen the continued growth of organizations in number and size. To what do we owe this quantitative, if not to say qualitative, change? It is the contention of this chapter that the phenomenal expansion of organizations can in some good measure be credited to advances in the technologies of organizational communication. A description of the sequence of these technologies will help in understanding what Kenneth Boulding has described as the organizational revolution: "It consists in a great rise in the number, size, and power of organizations of many diverse kinds, and especially of economic organizations" (1953, p. xi).

There are several reasons, in a collection of emerging perspectives on organizational communication, to briefly glance backwards. The first is that, within the annals of scholarship, the tale of organizational communications has scarcely been told. While the individual histories of the various communication technologies have been ably researched and described, virtually nowhere has the entire sequence been set down.[1] I suggest that history here in the interest of stimulating further scholarly effort into the relationship of communications technologies and the rise of the organization. As a subject area, the history of organizational communication is emergent in its own right, and deserves to be cultivated.

Second, if the past is prologue, then it is good to know what that prologue is. What is the nature of the historical momentum in communications technologies? What imperatives are at work here? Is there anything to constrain possibilities for the future? A sense of the past may convey a sense of what is more likely, and less likely, to emerge in the future of organizational communication.

The modern era in organizational communications began as quills were giving way to steel pen nibs. In the all-male offices, clerks perched on tall chairs set behind high desks and laboriously scratched out one entry or one message at a time. Whatever was sent outside the office was often dispatched several times over, so unpredictable were the mails. The owner of the typical small firm may well have wished to expand his enterprise, as most businessmen do, but the means of controlling and coordinating great numbers of dispersed employees was lacking. It was not until several communications advances had transpired that the modern business organization—which Alfred Chandler defines as having a large mid-management tier and multiple units (1977, p. 3)—could come into being. The history continues to the present, where the organization's internal and external communication is increasingly handled electronically.

---

[1] Two attempts, each only partially successful, are Delgado (1979) and Giuliano (1982). In addition, a brief sketch is found in Rice (1984, pp. 159-161).

The history to be outlined here cannot account for all the technologies that have influenced organizational communication, but will consider the major ones. It does no great disservice to the uneven flow of historical events to think of four stages in the development of organizational communication technologies, each about 40 years long and each initiated by one or two inventions:

1. (1840–1880) *The telegraph* led to the appearance of large prototypical organizations.
2. (1880–1920) *The telephone and the typewriter* permitted the proliferation of organizations.
3. (1920–1960) *The vertical file* created organizational memories.
4. (1960–   ) *The photocopier and the computer* vastly increased the communications capabilities of organizations.

One step at a time, the sequence of technologies overcame hindrances in external and internal communication processes. They also overcame problems with the storage of communication—although, as we will see, at a surprisingly late date. It is interesting to note that many advances created an imbalance, from a communication perspective, which led to the need for the next advance. Perhaps an awareness of present imbalances can result in statements about the future.

TELEGRAPH

"What hath God wrought?" was the question Samuel F. B. Morse flashed between Baltimore and Washington on May 24, 1844, and the answer was, something beyond compare—the miracle of distant and instantaneous communication. From our perspective, saturated as we are with electronic communication, it is nearly impossible to appreciate the spectacular nature of the first telegraphed messages. But in its time, the significance of the invention was recognized by all, as suggested by the word commonly used for it, a word which captures its force and impact: the "lightning."

Morse had been ready to demonstrate his astonishing device for several years. He had a working model at least by 1836, and had filed for a patent in 1837. What he lacked was the financial backing to string out a lengthy line and prove the entire system. For funds, he turned to the federal government, to which in his desperation he offered to assign all rights. But, at this historic juncture, the government declined the offer, and, henceforth, electronic communication has remained in private hands.

What Congress eventually did do, in August 1843, was to allot Morse $30,000 for his experiment. The project began inauspiciously, for the copper wire which Morse had ordered laid underground shorted itself repeatedly. Nearly out of money, halfway to Baltimore, in mid-winter, Morse had to back up and start again using poles.

Once proven, the telegraph diffused rapidly through the young nation. Robert Thompson, the historian of the telegraph, terms the period from 1845 to 1852 that of "methodless enthusiasm," during which many small companies sprang up to exploit the new invention (1947, p. 441). As the numerous competing firms raced to stake out new territories, the network spread south and west. By 1851, lines reached New Orleans.

From the beginning, the telegraph was primarily an instrument in service to businesses. "Increasingly, the telegraph allowed businessmen to obtain immediate and extremely accurate information on market prices and quantities and to reduce intermarket uncertainties of all kinds. Such price data are essential when producers have several potential markets, or suppliers, at their disposal, and the superiority of the telegraph for executing these transactions seems to have been recognized almost at once," writes business historian Richard DuBoff (1980, p. 477). This utility to business stands in contrast to the European experience, where the telegraph first found its chief employment in interpersonal correspondence. DuBoff, estimating that such noncommercial messages comprised less than 10% of the United States volume, quotes a nineteenth-century observer, " 'Thus the great difference between the telegraph systems of Europe and America is, that abroad the telegraph is used principally by the people for social correspondence, here by business men for business purposes' " (1980, p. 466).

Some businesses soon learned that the telegraph was not just a device for external communication. It could be used for internal administrative purposes too. According to DuBoff, "As business units grew in size, the telegraph proved to be compatible with hierarchical and multi-functional enterprise" (1980, p. 477). The first firms to recognize the managerial benefits of the "lightning" were the telegraph companies themselves. Having so many of their employees out of sight, scattered in telegraph offices across the countryside, a company would use the wires to implement policies, issue work orders, monitor performance, call in sales records, and so forth. The greater the success was at managing a far-flung enterprise, the larger the firms and its central staff could grow. In effect, broadness led to largeness; a helpful image of this process is that of a tent, where greater expanse demands a higher tentpole in the center. Electronic communication permitted organizational "tents," so to speak, to increase in geographical breadth and hierarchical height.

For telegraph company employees, the telegrams from headquarters were both timely and influential—the two qualities necessary in organizational communication when employees are not within close range. Speed means that messages from headquarters can be appropriate to changing conditions; influence means that the messages will have effect. The influential aspect is in part accomplished when messages are committed to writing—an advantage of the telegram.

The telegraph industry began to consolidate following the period of "methodless enthusiasm," and the tens of small companies were amalgamated into six major firms. So sizable were these corporations that, when they entered into an agreement in 1857 to ensure each other's territory and provide for interconnections, the pact was popularly known as the "Treaty of the Six Nations."[2] Due to their internal communications systems, these six companies (which included Western Union and American Telegraph) had appeared in the 1850s as the first modern multi-unit, professionally managed organizations.

Right on the heels of the telegraph companies came the railroads, who also exploited the technology of telegraphy to manage their dispersed operations. A railroad would either develop its own private telegraph system, or work jointly with a telegraph company. There were advantages to a mutual effort; "Each industry had something to offer the other," Thompson notes (1947, p. 443). The railroads, for their part, had the rights-of-way that the telegraph companies ached for. Each station could shelter a telegraph apparatus, and each stationmaster could be a part-time telegrapher. In return, the telegraph provided the communication links which greatly improved the safety record of the railroads, since management could keep track of each train. Once the telegraph system was in place, railroad executives learned they could also keep track of each employee, and administer the whole with an unimagined efficiency. By the Civil War, the railroads had shot past their comrade companies, and become the premier large-scale organizations.

The use of the telegraph to effectively manage railroads had a secondary effect upon communications. The transportation and delivery of mail became routinized and much less expensive. While only 10% of the long distance mail was carried by railroads in 1857, 10 years later nearly a third of it was. Before 1851, the Post Office charged $.05 an ounce for each 300 miles; after 1851, the tariff was $.03 for each 500 miles; and, in 1855, the cost dropped to $.03 for 3,000 miles (Pred, 1980, p. 147). Businesses came to rely on cheap, predictable delivery of their letters.

The ability of the telegraph to facilitate the management of large organizations was not lost on the government. According to Thompson, "Both the States and the Federal Government were quick to recognize

---

[2] A reference to the six major Iroquois tribes, or "nations."

the value of the telegraph in carrying out their functions, and they made extensive use of it" (1947, p. 444). The Civil War especially was a stimulus to the administrative use of the telegraph. The need to direct the Union armies resulted in telegraph lines being laid up to the very edge of battle (Thompson, 1947, p. 385).

After the Civil War, the lessons in organizational communication which had been learned in the telegraph and railroad industries, as well as in government, began to diffuse elsewhere, especially to new industries which could make profitable use of large, complex multi-unit organizations. One carrier of these lessons was Andrew Carnegie, who began his career as a telegraph operator at the Pittsburgh office of the Atlantic and Ohio Telegraph Company (one of the "Six Nations"), then went to work for the Pennsylvania Railroad where he rose to be superintendent of the Pittsburgh Division before leaving for the steel industry and his own company (Chandler, 1977, p. 267).

But, for all the revolutionary advantages of the telegraph in managing organizations, there were shortcomings. While telegraphed communication was instantaneous in concept, it was not instantaneous in practice. A two-way exchange of messages entailed having the original message encoded, waiting for a reply to be formulated, and having the return message transcribed. This process necessitated skilled operators, which severely restricted the access of most employees to the system. Such obstacles were not crippling for a geographically dispersed firm, but for a company at one location, such as one of the new manufacturing plants, the telegraph was less than satisfactory. How could a manager telegraph the bookkeeper down the hall, the foreman in the yard? A less restrictive, more immediate communication device was called for.

TELEPHONE AND TYPEWRITER

The years from 1880 to 1920 were the time when the form of the modern organization, with its particular internal and external message systems, diffused throughout American life. Not only were governmental organizations strengthened, and business organizations endlessly replicated, but other organizations began to appear in unlikely areas— organized baseball, for instance. In order for the organizational form to diffuse so far from its place of origin in a few large, dispersed businesses which had exploited the telegraph, several advances in communications technologies were necessary.

The telephone held the answer to many of the liabilities of the telegraph. In particular, the problem of accessibility was solved. The access pains which had been discounted for long-range transmissions by telegraph could not easily be discounted for short-range ones. Since anyone could operate a telephone, the new device lent itself to communication over short distances within a centralized firm. The very first telephoned words—"Mr. Watson, come here, I want you," said Alexander Graham Bell to his assistant on March 10, 1876—were typical of what was to come. Even for that two-person organization, timely local messages were the essence of communication by telephone.

Just as with the telegraph, in the United States the telephone too was an instrument of business rather than social transactions (Aronson, 1977, p. 28). This had not been clear to Bell when he had tried to anticipate its uses; he had imagined several purposes, including using it as a broadcasting device for musical performances. Being unsure of its role-to-be, Bell offered to sell his patent to Western Union for $100,000 in late 1876, but was rebuffed by the firm's president, who said, "What use could this company make of an electrical toy?" (Aronson, 1977, p. 15).

Other businesses proved more receptive (Aronson, 1977). Largely to replace inter-company telegraph lines, 230 telephones had been installed in the United States by June 30, 1877, 750 by July 30, and 1,300 by August 30. The first telephone exchange began operation in Boston on May 17, 1877, to connect three businesses. The Pittsburgh directory of 1879 lists 300 telephones, all but six being businesses. Even the railroads switched to the newer system: the first to install lines was the Pennsylvania Railroad in 1879, and, by 1910, its system had 175 exchanges, 400 operators, 13,000 telephones, and 20,000 miles of wire.

By means of this new nervous system, management could effectively monitor and administer multi-unit enterprises with numerous employees. Down through a firm's wires flowed orders which were timely and appropriate. The speed and volume of instructions were vastly superior to what the telegraph had achieved. Sidney Aronson asks rhetorically what the effects of the telephone upon business life were, and answers, "Perhaps the most conspicuous of these effects has been the dramatic contraction in the time needed to establish communication, transmit orders, and consummate business transactions, what for the sake of brevity, may be called 'transaction time' " (1971, p. 154). And since the telephone was much more accessible to all, ample monitoring information could also flow back up through the hierarchy. The more phones a company had, the greater were the lateral flows also, so that out-of-sight employees could synchronize themselves to each other.

Despite solving the matter of accessibility and allowing for the high volume of short-range transmissions that can hold an organization together, the telephone still did not respond to all the communication imperatives of the organization. On a formality-to-informality scale, telephoned communication is located too far towards the informality end, while organizations depend on the formal. The chief reason that telephone calls are less than official is that the telephone leaves no written record, as the telegraph did. Something in writing has more chance of eliciting compliance than something merely spoken, which cannot be precisely duplicated or successfully stored. The telephone was limited in authority.

When Alexander Graham Bell had exhibited his invention for the very first time at the 1876 Centennial Exposition in Philadelphia, another inventor had stood in the shadows, begrudging Bell all the attention and honors that resulted from the display of the prototypic telephone. The envious figure was Christopher Lathom Sholes of Milwaukee; he felt the accolades were due him, since his own invention was already in production and on the market (Bliven, 1954, p. 63). Sholes was the person holding the patent on the first efficient typewriter.

The telegraph was succeeded, not just by the telephone, but by the telephone plus the typewriter. The eighteenth century had seen several European attempts to devise a mechanical writing instrument, and in 1829 a U.S. patent was issued for a device which is clearly a predecessor of the typewriter. In spite of analogous machinery in the telegraph and printing industries, a fully developed personal typewriter was not finally patented until 1868. The patent was transferred to the Remington Arms Company, which in 1874 produced the first of these instruments for sale (Bliven, 1954, p. 56).

Among the earliest purchasers of the Remington typewriter was Mark Twain. In a letter to his brother Orion Clemens, typed on December 9, 1874, Twain commented, "The machine has several virtues. I believe it will print faster than I can write. It piles an awful stack of words on one page. It doesn't muss things or scatter ink blots around. Of course it saves paper" (Bliven, 1954, p. 61). Speed, orderliness, and economy are values of organizations, especially of competitive businesses, so it is not surprising that, from this time forward, when companies put something into writing, increasingly it was typewriting rather than handwriting.

The typewriter also upheld another organizational value, that of impersonality. A typewritten message does not have the familiar, human touch of a handwritten one. On this count, the machine was resisted by some. When Sears Roebuck began sending "machine-made" letters to its customers, the outcry was great enough for the company to return for a time to handwritten correspondence (Boorstin, 1973, p. 399). But, in the end, there was no stopping its diffusion. The typewriter was invaluable to organizations because, by being impersonal, or supra-personal, it lent needed authority to communication. By 1900, more than 100,000 typewriters had been sold, and more than 20,000 new ones were being manufactured each year (Giuliano, 1982, p. 149).

The typewriter did more than reassert the formality and influence of organizational communication. Both the telegraph and the telephone feature point-to-point communication; for any one message, there were rarely more than two parties involved. But as organizations expanded in size and became more complex, often the same message had to be widely circulated internally so that the various offices and units could be coordinated with each other, and the whole could operate more or less harmoniously. This meant that documents had to be copied.

The typewriter played a key role in the increasingly important act of duplication. Carbon paper had been around for some time, but it was not until the 1880s, as the typewriter was becoming common in organizations, that this copying paper did too. Ralph Delgado writes, "When the hard-hitting typewriter showed that not only one carbon copy could be obtained very satisfactorily, but numerous additional copies of outstanding quality, it was an important stage in copying and added to the paperwork which was gradually gaining ascendancy" (1979, p. 81). The ripple of office paper became a stream when the rotary duplicator appeared shortly thereafter—a machine that used stencils cut on typewriters.

The telephone and the typewriter were the communication technologies that brought organizations well into the twentieth century. The forte of the telephone was fast if informal communication, and the forte of the typewriter was official and thus influential communication. But the added dimension, beyond speed, range, and influence, was volume. Some of the enormous volume came from cross-boundary communication, but much of it resulted from internal efforts to integrate the organization through duplicated messages. So great was the demand for voluminous communication that a vastly expanded office force was hired after 1880. Enter into the once all-male terrain the legion of secretaries—to intercept the cascade of calls, to operate the typewriter more efficiently than the opposite sex. In the Census of 1880, office clerical numbers were almost totally male, but, by 1910, they were 83% female (Scott, 1982, p. 172).

Thanks to the new technologies, the internal and external messages which were the life-blood of the expanding organizations were mounding up. But, odd as it may seem to us, there was no effective way to store them.

VERTICAL FILES

Records are the very keel of an organization. Containing what has transpired before in time, they are the basis of the organization's continuance and responsiveness. Yet, before World War I, only a minority of American firms possessed what could be judged from a present day vantage point to be a satisfactory system for storing and retrieving documents.

Throughout the nineteenth century, most businesses had kept copies of outgoing letters in a press book. This bound volume had several hundred tissue pages; a letter to be reproduced would be placed between dampened sheets and pressed, making a copy. The only index was that of chronology; an office worker would have to know roughly when a letter had been mailed in order to track down the duplicate. Incoming correspondence was kept even less systematically, in pigeonholes, on spindles, or in boxes. "In any case," reports JoAnne Yates, "incoming and outgoing correspondence on the same topic was always separated, since the outgoing correspondence was in the press book" (1982, p. 8).

The next step in the evolution of filing systems, one the railroads embraced in their need, was the use of flat files stored in shallow boxes. The chief advantage was release from the chronological bondage of the press book. Also, the outgoing and incoming correspondence on a subject could be filed together, and the whole indexed alphabetically (or numerically, as the railroads largely did). The remaining disadvantage was accessibility; the boxes were stacked, and for any but the topmost, access involved unpiling and repiling.

This was clearly an inadequate system. In her investigation of the communications evolution of a large Connecticut brass manufacturer, Professor Yates uncovered a telling piece of inter-firm correspondence, written just before the company switched to vertical filing in 1914: " 'Replying to yours of the 24th regarding terms to Jos. L. Porter and Co., we are sorry that our record for 1908 is quite as inaccessible as yours seems to be, and unless you consider the matter of enough importance, you will let the matter pass' " (1982, p. 9).

The solution was the vertical file. It makes sense that the system would arise in institutions which had most directly confronted the problem of storing and accessing vast amounts of written material—libraries. The vertical file was the direct descendant of the card catalog, the earliest system to store unbound paper on edge. Card catalogs had been first offered for sale in 1876. The firm that manufactured them subsequently developed the vertical file for business correspondence, and exhibited it at the 1893 Chicago World's Fair. Acceptance of the new device was slow; it was not until 1920 that this simple technology had become commonplace in American businesses.

With a system in place for the easy storage and retrieval of written material, American business experienced a river of paper. Not only was more mail sent and received, but the internal single-subject memo came into its own at this point. On the basis of her study of Scovill Manufacturing, JoAnne Yates is ready to venture, "A dramatic increase in the number of internal memoranda resulted and reports circulated routinely within companies during this historical process" (Markus & Yates, 1982, p. 118).

This increased note and letter-writing, encouraged by the new filing system, occurred as managers took responsibility for yet larger corporations. Top management now had the information on tap which served as the basis of thoughtful planning. Middle management saw the productivity of each white-collar worker increase when records came easier to handle. Every filed document added luster to the others, so that, when a file was considered in its entirety, it formed a complete picture; the file-user could then respond appropriately to new situations. And new employees found access to the corporation's memory to be near effortless. Because of this feature, the organizational form grew sturdier still, since it was no longer dependent upon the recollections of individuals.

Yates takes note of the fact that the vertical file is not a very glamorous technology, and that people are likely to undervalue it: "Yet the development of vertical filing was as important in the communications system of that time as the shift to computer storage, transmission, and access is to our time" (1982, p. 6).

COMPUTER AND PHOTOCOPIER

Following World War II, the communications requirements of organizations were stepped up as a period of economic growth led to increased competition among the rising number of businesses, and increased pressure within each for more extensive and efficient message systems. This demand was addressed in time primarily by two new technologies—one usually thought of as prosaic, and the other unquestionably revolutionary.

In increasing the communication capacities of businesses, the photocopier has played a significant if sometimes unappreciated role. The first electrophotographic image was produced in 1938 by an American inventor, Chester F. Carlson. The millions of dollars necessary to develop the instrument were not available until after World War II, and it was not until 1960 that the first production-line photocopiers, the Xerox 914, were delivered to customers (Boorstin, 1973, pp. 401-402). In very little time, photocopiers became universal in offices.

The photocopier solved one enduring problem in business communications, that of making copies of incoming correspondence. Additionally, it created a great savings of employee time in the copying of both outgoing and internal messages. The abundance of copies served two broad purposes central to the maintenance of an organization. They brought about synchronous control and coordination of the numerous individuals and units of a company, and they created the extensive files which a modern business operates from.

The paper that the photocopier generates will not soon be eliminated from offices because paper and the writing on it have an authoritative cachet not yet found in other modes of communication. In part the continuing power of words-on-paper stems from the fact that they are near indelible, not easily subject to revision. But while the photocopier has been fulfilling the communications potential of paper-based systems, another technology coming in at the same time, the computer, has had an unparalleled effect upon the organization.

Since the late 1950s, when computers first gained entry to businesses, there have been several changes in the use of this technology. Its content, from the employee's viewpoint, has shifted from a small amount of data processing to a large mix of data and word processing. At the outset, computers were often housed in accounting departments to carry out such humble tasks as payroll processing; from that starting point, computer capacity has been distributed throughout the organization, up and down, to control production lines or to supply top management with highly processed information for decision-making. The key to this technological diffusion was the microprocessor (the semiconductor chip that contains the essential logic circuitry of a computer), which made possible smaller and less costly units. According to Ronald Rice, "The microprocessor was invented by Dr. Ted Hoff at Intel Corporation in Santa Clara, California, in 1971, thus opening the way for the continued miniaturization of computers. Hoff's invention was a key event setting off the Information Revolution; it made possible the microcomputer" (1984, p. 36).

It is as a word processing device that the computer is having its widest effect upon organization communications. The notion of "word processing" was initially promoted by IBM in the 1960s as a way to stimulate sales of their machines. When microcomputers grew common, more and more employees were able to participate in the electronic writing, editing, sending, receiving, storage, and printing of text. As time goes by, the requisite hardware and software are becoming ever more accessible to personnel; Benjamin Compaine of Harvard University's Center for Information Policy Research reports, "The trend in computer and communications use has been to lower the labor involved as well as the skill required" (1984, p. 3). Not only are word processing and electronic mail increasingly accessible, and not only do they meet many other communications dicta, but they accomplish this through a single integrated system, which lends to the whole an unheard-of efficiency.

A review of over thirty different field studies of the impact of computer-mediated communication upon organizations resulted in the following list of common effects (Rice, 1984, p. 211):

1. Electronic mail capabilities increased asynchronous communication activities within function groups and in superior-subordinate relations.
2. Remote communications enabled executives to work outside the office during nontraditional work hours.
3. Word processing reduced document preparation turnaround time.
4. Office automation systems produced a daily time savings by reducing the number of clerical tasks per activity . . .
5. Users perceived a qualitative improvement of their work frequently in the form of greater control, improved communications, and greater access to information.

No wonder organizations are rushing to embrace this technology. As testimony to this diffusion, Compaine and his colleagues have annually analyzed the employment advertisements in the *New York Times* on a particular day (the fourth Thursday in June) since 1977; of all ads for secretaries, those specifying word processing skills rose from 0% in 1977 to 26% in 1984 (1984, pp. 39-40).

Since 1960, the photocopier and the computer have vastly increased the volume of communication within organizations—to the point that the abundance can threaten to overwhelm employees and paralyze organizations. "Information overload" is the new communication obstacle to be removed. How ironic this condition would seem to the businessman of 1840, could he be transported to the present.

CONCLUSION

With hindsight, we can see what the communications imperatives were which had to be technologically addressed if the organizational form was to grow and spread. Message systems had to provide for these things:

1. Speed
2. Variable range
3. Accessibility
4. Influence
5. Duplication
6. Storage

As each of these factors was obliged by a technology, sometimes an imbalance was created which set the stage for the next advance.

As a summary narrative: the hardest and most remarkable task was probably the first one—breaking free of age-old constraints through the discovery of a means for instantaneous distant communication. For all its glories, though, the telegraph was biased away from short-range transmissions, and away from convenience of access. Balance was struck with the arrival of the telephone, which created its own imbalance due to its lack of authoritativeness and influence. Influential messages were instituted by the typewriter, which also contributed, in the context of expanding organizations, to the important business of duplicating messages. This led to yet another imbalance by straining existing storage systems, a problem solved by the vertical file.

Available communications technologies could not satisfy the growing need for the internally circulated messages which integrate an organization, so the photocopier found a ready market. The facile creation of copies helped to meet the duplication and storage requirements of organizational communication, but also added to the increasingly burdensome volume of messages.

Almost all the imperatives are obliged by the introduction of computer-mediated communication. Speed, range, access, influence, distribution, and storage are all handled in these increasingly efficient unified systems. Beyond these, the systems extend backwards into the enterprise of fabricating messages (by contributing material from their information bases, applying spelling programs, and so forth) and forwards into the enterprise of responding to them (automatically forwarding messages, for instance, or regulating office lighting). Their chief liability, from a human perspective, is their contribution to the overabundance of communication.

All this leads to a seventh imperative. Imperatives 1 through 6 have to do with augmenting communication; number 7 points to the need to curtail information flows and discriminate among items. Let's call it:

7. Filtration

Secretaries used to be the main communication filters as they intercepted telephone calls, opened and sorted letters, and misplaced files. Now that computer-mediated communication may be diminishing the secretarial role, something else is warranted.

It may come to be that a paramount function of the computer is to filter and dampen communication. One of the main advantages of electronic mail is that it is not intrusive like the telephone, but holds messages patiently until the user logs on. The computer can be programmed to reject messages on certain topics or from certain sources. In a similar vein, computers cull from their information bases using key word searches. The use of key words and other filtering protocols hold great promise as ways to manage the torrent of communication descending on today's employee.

While in a predictive frame of mind, let's go ahead and forecast the technologies which will be in place by the year 2000, to get organizations off on their next 40-year stint. I foresee the voice-activated, conversing computer (the limit in accessibility) and its cousin, the printing telephone (increasing the formality and influence of this device).

REFERENCES

Aronson, S. (1971). The sociology of the telephone. *International Journal of Comparative Sociology, 12,* 153-167.

Aronson, S. (1977). Bell's electric toy: What's the use? In I. de Sola Pool (Ed.), *The social impact of the telephone* (pp. 15-39). Cambridge, MA: MIT Press.

Bliven, B., Jr. (1954). *The wonderful writing machine.* New York: Random House.

Boorstin, D. (1973). *The Americans: the democratic experience.* New York: Random House.

Boulding, K. (1953). *The organizational revolution.* New York: Harper.

Chandler, A.D., Jr. (1977). *The visible hand: The managerial revolution in American business.* Cambridge, MA: Belknap.

Compaine, B. (1984). *Information technology and cultural change: toward a new literacy.* Cambridge, MA: Harvard University Program on Information Resources Policy.

Delgado, A. (1979). *The enormous file: A social history of the office.* London: Murray.

DuBoff, R. (1980). Business demand and the development of the telegraph in the United States 1844-1860. *Business History Review, 54,* 459-479.

Giuliano, V. (1982). The mechanization of office work. *Scientific American, 247*(3), 148-165.

Markus, M. L., & Yates, J. (1982, June). Historical lessons for the automated office. *Computer Decisions,* 116-119.

Pred, A. (1980). *Urban growth and city-systems in the United States, 1840-1860.* Cambridge, MA: Harvard University Press.

Rice, R., et al., (1984). *The new media: Communication, research, and technology.* Beverly Hills, CA: Sage.

Scott, J. W. (1982). The mechanization of women's work. *Scientific American, 247*(3), 166-189.

Thompson, R. L. (1947). *Wiring a continent: The history of the telegraph industry in the United States 1832-1866.* Princeton: Princeton University Press.

Yates, J. (1982). From press book and pigeonhole to vertical file: A revolution in storage and access systems for correspondence. *Journal of Business Communications, 19*(3), 5-26.

5

From Hand Copy to Xerox Copy: The Effects of Duplicating Technology on Organizational Communication in American Firms in the 19th and 20th Centuries

JoAnne Yates

The appearance of the Xerox 914 on the American market in 1960 marked the end of one era and the beginning of another in office technology. It has become almost a commonplace to remark on the role of Xerox and other plain-paper photocopying machines in promoting the bureaucratization of the office by allowing the reproduction of endless numbers of copies of any document at any time. The word "promote" is probably too strong. As David Noble (1977, p. 258n) has stated, "In actuality, technical imperatives define only what is *possible*, not what is *necessary*; what *can* be done, not what *must* be done. The latter decisions are social in nature." Nevertheless, this innovation in the technology of duplicating, like a series of innovations that preceded it, created new possibilities for communication and information flows within firms. Organizational needs led to the exploitation of these possibilities.

Plain paper photocopying was certainly not the first copying technology to affect communication and information flows within firms. Beginning in the early nineteenth century, a series of innovations have transformed duplicating in the workplace, making possible the copying of few or many copies. The innovations in copying technology fall into four general categories, in roughly chronological order:

- Copying of single, bound copies
  - letter press
- Copying of one to ten unbound copies
  - rolling press copying of single copies
  - carbon copying of up to ten copies with typewriter
- Mass duplicating of large numbers of copies
  - stencil duplicating of hundreds of copies
  - gelatin/spirit duplicating of up to 100 copies
- Photographic copying of any number of copies
  - photocopying on treated paper
  - plain paper photocopying

Hand copying gave way to letter press copying of single copies into bound volumes in the early- and mid-nineteenth century. In the late 1870s and 1880s, two technologies allowed the creation of unbound copies. The rolling copier was an adaptation of press copying that produced loose copies. Carbon paper, which only became widely used with the spread of the typewriter, allowed the creation of one to ten unbound copies. In the same period, various means of producing many copies from a single, specially prepared master were also being developed. Mimeograph, hectograph, and other related processes opened up new possibilities for producing multiple copies. All of these processes allowed people to make planned copies at or right after the point of origin of the document. By the turn of the century, the first technology for making unplanned copies *after* the point of origin appeared: expensive and slow photographic processes using treated paper. Finally, 60 years later, and almost as an afterthought to this sequence of innovations, came the spectacularly successful plain paper copiers.

This paper explores the impact of these nineteenth and twentieth century innovations in duplicating technology on communication and information flows within American firms, concentrating primarily on the pre-Xerox period.[1] These innovations in duplicating technology, I contend here, opened the way for new uses of communication and information, while concurrent changes in the size and organizational needs of firms led to the exploitation of these possibilities. Successive innovations in copying had the following effects on the types and uses of organizational communication:

---

[1] Much of the material in this paper is covered in a broader context in my book-in-progress, currently titled "Control through Communication: The Emergence of Internal Communication in American Firms, 1850-1920."

- facilitated the growth of correspondence,
- allowed filing systems to serve as organizational memories,
- permitted the decentralization and proliferation of files,
- allowed and encouraged the growth of hierarchical and some lateral internal communication, and
- allowed increased nonhierarchical flows of information.

Without these technological innovations, certain other organizational developments might have been stiffled. Thus, the role of these innovations in the evolution of intra-firm communication is significant and well worth exploring. Moreover, the impact of recent innovations in communication technology may be better understood in light of less recent developments.

Methodology and Mode of Presentation

My research methods in this study have been primarily historical and nonquantitative. I have studied published and unpublished materials from the nineteenth and early-twentieth centuries, as well as more recent analyses of earlier events. Published period sources such as text books, office manuals, advertising literature, and government studies provided general information on why and how the technologies were used in organizations. Unpublished, archival materials from three specific companies—the Illinois Central Railroad, Scovill Manufacturing Company, and E.I. du Pont de Nemours and Company[2]—illuminated the adoption and effects of duplicating technology in individual firms.

The results of this study, in keeping with the historical research methodology, are presented here in a roughly chronological, narrative mode. The first section below explores the effects of mechanical copying of single, bound copies in the mid-nineteenth century. The next section treats the impact of late-nineteenth and early-twentieth century copying methods that produced small numbers of unbound copies. The third section analyzes the effects, during approximately the same period, of mass duplicating technologies that produced large numbers of copies. The final section looks at the impact of photocopying methods that allowed the production of unplanned copies.

---

[2] The Illinois Central Railroad archives are housed at the Newberry Library, Chicago, Illinois; the Scovill Manufacturing Company records are housed in the Archives Department, Baker Library, Harvard Business School, Boston, Massachusetts; and the records of E.I. du Pont de Nemours and Company are housed at the Hagley Museum and Library, Wilmington, Delaware. Access to the archives is provided courtesy of these institutions.

MECHANICAL COPYING OF SINGLE, BOUND COPIES

In the first half of the nineteenth century, the demand for inexpensive and fast methods of duplicating was not very strong in manufacturing firms, and thus the few technological advances made in duplicating were not widely adopted. Firms were generally small, often family-run businesses (Chandler, 1979). Their written communication consisted almost exclusively of external correspondence, since internal management was all handled orally. The total volume of correspondence was generally small enough to be handled by the owner, frequently with the help of one or two salaried clerks.

At this time, the standard copying technology was primitive, but adequate to the needs of most firms. The pen—initially the quill pen but by the second third of the century the steel pen (Daniels, 1980)—was the principle tool for both production and reproduction of written documents in firms. Letters were written by hand, then recopied, also by hand, usually into a bound book of blank pages called a copy book. Although most manufacturing companies were not large enough to employ someone solely to copy correspondence, copying was a normal part of every firm's routine. The copy books, if used consistently, provided a complete, centralized, and chronological record of all outgoing correspondence. They were often indexed by correspondent.

The letter press, the first mechanical method of copying to gain widespread use in American firms (other methods, such as the double pen device used by Thomas Jefferson, were never adopted by more than a few individuals), was invented three-quarters of a century before it became generally used (Proudfoot, 1972). The letter press process of copying outgoing correspondence was patented by James Watt in 1780. Although press copying devices were available from that time on, they did not become widely used in business until the second half of the nineteenth century. The form of the device to become popular then was a screw press used in conjunction with a press book, a specialized form of bound copy book with tissue paper pages. A letter freshly written in a special copying ink was placed under a dampened tissue page of the press book, with other pages protected by oil cloths. The book was closed and the letter press was screwed down tightly on it. Pressure on the damp letter transferred an impression of it onto the underside of the tissue sheet. After the original was removed and the pages dried, the impression, if dark enough, could be read through the top of the thin paper. (For a more detailed description of the process, see, for example, Wigent, Housel, & Gilman, 1916.) The process made only a single copy of a given letter (though several different letters could be copied simultaneously), and this copy had to be made before the letter was more than

one day old. Thus this method, like all of the nineteenth century duplicating methods, copied documents at point of origin, not point of
receipt. Indexing, when used, was still by correspondent only.

In spite of the obvious time savings of press copying (especially with
several letters at once) over hand copying, use of the apparatus was
confined to a relatively small number of individuals and firms until the
second half of the century. The Scovill Manufacturing Company, for example, switched from hand copying to press copying sometime between
1830 and 1854 (Scovill I, v. 254, 1830 and v. 456, 1854), while E.I. du
Pont de Nemours and Company, quite conservative in its business practices at this time, did not adopt press copying at its main office until 1857
or later. Its main series of letterbooks from 1857 to the early twentieth
century has not survived, but the letterbooks up to the cut-off point in
1857 were still hand copied (Du Pont 500/I/I/A). An inventory taken at
the end of 1857 (Du Pont 500/I/2/M/486) indicated that they had acquired a press by this point, though they may not yet have begun using it
regularly. Many other companies adopted press copying even later than
1857.

The reasons for the belated but widespread adoption of press copying
in the second half of the century were both social and technological, with
the social reasons taking precedence. Technologically, the quality of
copying inks was improved significantly by the development of aniline
dyes, beginning in 1856 (Proudfoot, 1972, p. 29). Previous copying inks
produced relatively dim copies that faded rapidly. The aniline dyes produced clearer and more permanent copies, and even allowed a second,
paler copy to be made from the original if all conditions were optimal.
This development made letter press technology more satisfactory, and
may have been one factor in the increased business use of the letter press
in the second half of the century. The probable date of Du Pont's switch
to press copying would support this influence. On the other hand,
Scovill adopted the letter press before aniline dyes were developed, indicating that the technological breakthrough was not necessary for wider
adoption of the press copier.

Despite this technological factor, the major reason for increased use
of the letter press in the mid-century period was social: the increase of
business activity that began in the 1840s with the spread of railroad and
telegraph. As a company grew, so did its correspondence. At Scovill, for
example, correspondence between the New York agent and the main
office averaged seven letters a month in the 1830s (Scovill II, Case 13,
January-April, 1829), when letters were copied by hand. By 1854, the
company had established a store in New York, and correspondence between it and the main office had doubled to 15 letters a month (Scovill I,
Vol. 456, February-June, 1854). We can probably safely assume at least a

comparable increase in correspondence with external individuals and companies. Under the pressure of this growth in correspondence, hand copying necessarily became an increasing burden and expense. Scovill adopted press copying sometime between these two periods. Thus the *need* for a rapid and inexpensive copying method spurred the adoption of the letter press.

In a period of expansion and speeding up of business, the letter press enabled companies to increase their correspondence while reducing the time and cost of duplication. Thus the innovation that had gained very limited acceptance in the preceding 70 years became increasingly popular as the need for it grew. In this case, because the technology appeared before businesses really needed it, its diffusion was delayed. Once the need became apparent, however, the technology spread rapidly.

New Organizational Needs in the Late Nineteenth Century

The increased speed and decreased expense of press copying eased the pressures of expanding external correspondence during the mid-century period. During the final quarter of the century, however, radical changes were occurring in firms. Growth and the development of a new philosophy of management brought both increased correspondence with external parties and other company sites, and the development of internal flows of communication. Press copying was not adequate to the new organizational needs that were manifesting themselves. Pressures toward change began to build.

Growth of many companies from small, family businesses to large, often dispersed corporations, along with a consequent growth of external correspondence, was the first and most obvious change in firms (Chandler, 1979). The railroads and telegraph companies, in their push to span the country, were the first large corporations. Moreover, they were by definition dispersed. Then, spurred by the expanding railroad and telegraph networks and by the new technologies of mass production, manufacturing firms expanded to serve national markets beginning in the 1880s and continuing into the early twentieth century. Many of these companies established sales forces around the country, as well as expanding their production facilities. This growth and dispersion required increased correspondence with external parties and other company sites.

Changes in managerial philosophy, and consequent changes in organizational communication patterns, followed growth. First the railroads in the 1850s and 1860s, then the manufacturing firms in the decades surrounding the turn of the century discovered that the ad hoc management techniques used in small firms were not adequate for the expanded firms (Chandler, 1979). The new philosophy, later designated systematic management, sought efficiency by replacing individual, oral, idiosyncratic methods with "systems" for carrying out and evaluating various functions (Litterer, 1961a,b, 1963; Jelinek, 1980; Nelson, 1974, 1975).

These systems required the establishment, for the first time, of regular upward and downward flows of written communication, and indirectly encouraged lateral flows (Yates, 1985). Regular reports documenting activities at lower levels flowed upwards to enable managers to monitor and evaluate those activities. Downward communications to large numbers of employees established rules, procedures, and systems. Lateral communication, though for the most part ignored by those who wrote about the theory and techniques of systematic management, evolved to coordinate activities and document relations between various departments and units in the firm. Primarily documentary lateral communication, which had probably appeared partially by analogy to documentary vertical communication, gained particular importance as loyalties to departments and units grew stronger and rivalries among such units were exacerbated by changes in traditional divisions of responsibility. All of these internal flows of written communication, whether horizontal or vertical, contributed to establishing a corporate memory independent of specific individuals.

These changes in communication needs exacerbated some old problems and created some new ones with press copying. The sheer increase in volume of external correspondence (including correspondence with dispersed sales offices and sites) compounded the problem of locating copies. Correspondence from Scovill's main office, for example, increased from filling an average of five press books (of 1,000 pages each) a year from 1880 to 1885, to filling nine press books a year from 1885 to 1890, and the company continued to grow, quadrupling its labor force between the 1890s and the beginning of World War I (Bishop, 1952, pp. 205-6). Thus by 1890, the main office was already going through a press book every month and a third. This made locating copies, always somewhat difficult, even more difficult. Even when the indexes were well maintained, they only indexed by correspondent, not by date or subject. Thus it was time-consuming to locate a specific letter. This problem was made even worse when the correspondent was, for example, the company's New York store. The company often wrote several times a day to the store, and to locate one of those copies the searcher would have had to check each page number listed in the index under the New York store as correspondent.

A more basic set of copying, storage, and access problems, also made worse by firm growth, centered around the fact that press copying was done with bound volumes. The bound letter press books were essentially a *centralized* copying and storage system. This centralized system became less convenient as the facilities expanded. All outgoing correspondence had to go to a central location to be copied before being sent out. Even more inconvenient was the fact that individuals from all over the facilities had to go to that same central location to see copies of their letters at a later time. Moreover, while the bound volumes guaranteed a complete set of copies of outgoing correspondence, they prevented these copies from being stored with related incoming letters, kept in pigeonholes or letter boxes (Yates, 1982b). Thus, locating a set of correspondence on an issue required going to two different storage systems. The two systems were organized differently, as well. While loose incoming letters were generally organized according to how they were likely to be used, such as by recipient or by subject, the press copies were frozen into a less useful chronological order. Thus, a copying technology depending on bound volumes posed increasing problems as firms grew larger.

The development of internal communication as a tool of systematic management posed even more serious problems for press copying as the primary duplicating technology. Internal correspondence could serve as an organizational memory, to be consulted when needed, only if access was easy and functional. It did not make much sense for copies of all internal correspondence to be stored only in the single centralized set of press books. Then the sending party could only refer to the copy by going to that central location. Finding such a copy later was difficult as well as inconvenient, since press books were indexed only by correspondent. And locating all of the internal correspondence on a single issue was even more time-consuming. Loose copies, which could be stored with originals and copies of related correspondence, would be much more functional than bound press books.

The developing need for downward communication to large numbers of employees also caused problems. Press copying produced one, or at the very most two, copies. Yet an executive might want to send the same instructions, procedures, or information to half a dozen department heads or to 1,000 employees. The large railroads encountered this problem first, as early as the 1850s and 1860s, because safety demanded that uniform instructions be issued to all employees. They were forced to use the only technology then capable of producing large numbers of copies: printing. The Illinois Central Railroad, for example, had its "Bulletins" and "Notices" to large groups of employees printed (ICRR 2.8). This technology, however, was expensive and time-consuming. A cheaper and quicker method was needed.

Finally, a need for copies at the receiver's end was now becoming evident. In the larger companies, several individuals or departments might need to see or use a letter or document that had been received. Even if the letter had not been press copied at its point of origin, it could not very successfully be copied at its point of receipt, since press copying worked best when the letter to be copied was less than 24 hours old. The letter had to be passed around or recopied by hand or, later, by type-writer.

All of these new or exacerbated needs created pressures on the old system of press copying. As these pressures built, new innovations or new applications of old ones appeared to relieve some of them. New methods of copying facilitated the organizational changes then under-way. They made feasible further growth of external correspondence and the development of the internal written communication required by techniques of systematic management. Let us look first at the new meth-ods of copying that emerged to fill the need for small numbers (one to ten) of unbound copies to be stored where and how they were needed.

UNBOUND COPIES

The press book method of copying outgoing correspondence required, as its necessary consequence, centralized and chronological storage sepa-rate from storage of incoming correspondence. In the 1880s and 1890s, two methods of creating unbound copies appeared: the rolling copier and carbon paper. Both remained in use through the 1920s, when car-bon paper gained clear ascendancy for reasons of economy, efficiency, and flexibility. Unbound copies opened the way for more functional and often decentralized storage, which made internal written communica-tion more accessible and usable. Decentralized storage, in turn, further encouraged the growth of internal written communication by allowing it to document internal differences and points of view.

The rolling copier was a simple adaptation of press copying, using a pair of rollers rather than a screw press to produce press copies on a continuous roll of tissue paper (Wigent et al., 1916, pp. 55-57). The con-tinuous sheet was then cut apart to produce loose copies that were exact, if often faint, copies of the original. Ironically, the portable version of Watt's original press copying machine, introduced around 1780, em-ployed a pair of rollers to produce loose copies (Proudfoot, 1972, p. 21). At that time, however, loose copies were not considered an advantage, and consequently that mechanism died out in favor of the screw press used with bound volumes. One hundred years later, when loose copies were desirable, the principle of a rolling press was rediscovered.

The loose copies produced by the reinvented rolling press could be stored with related incoming correspondence in letter boxes or flat files (drawers or containers in which letters were stored flat) in a central filing area or in a manager's office, and could be rearranged as needed. Copies of internal correspondence could be stored as desired by the sender. For the first time, users were freed from the centralized and chronological tyranny of the press book. One Du Pont manager, for example, bought a rolling press copier in 1890 (Du Pont 504/40/24 February 1890) and immediately began interfiling copies of his outgoing letters with related incoming letters in one form of flat filing system (Du Pont 504/40/March 1890). The files were organized by correspondent, whether internal or external, so that all the correspondence to and from a given person, internal department, or external company was stored together. His correspondence with the company selling him the rolling copier, cited above, indicated that he found his new duplicating and filing system much more convenient.

Loose press copies did not solve all the problems of small scale copying, however. Press copying onto a roll of paper, like press copying into a press book, produced only a single copy. It was a messy process, sometimes resulting in smeary, hard-to-read copies, and it took extra time before letters were sent out. Since it was generally done in mail rooms, internal correspondence that would not otherwise need to go to the centralized mail room had to be diverted there for copying. Moreover, the copies were on flimsy tissue paper and of varying lengths. They produced disorderly flat files and collapsed down to the bottom of vertical files, which appeared in 1893 (Yates, 1982b). The other innovation in small-scale copying, carbon paper, solved some of these problems.

Carbon paper was not new at all when it suddenly became popular in the late nineteenth century. Carbon copying, like press copying, was invented long before it rose to popularity. In this case, however, the delayed acceptance was as much the result of a technological development as of social developments. Ralph Wedgewood invented "carbonic" or "manifold" paper in England in the first decade of the nineteenth century, and it was available in the United States by at least 1823 (Proudfoot, 1972, pp. 25, 32-33). But carbon paper could not be used with quill, steel, or gold-tipped pens without ruining the pen or tearing the paper. Moreover, the carbon paper of this period was soaked in the carbonic ink, giving it a carbon coating on both sides. It was meant to be placed between a top sheet of tissue paper and a bottom sheet of normal writing paper and written on with a stylus. In this system, the "original" was the carbon copy on the letter paper, while the "copy" was the carbon copy on the bottom of the tissue paper, which was viewed through the sheet, as a press copy was viewed. By mid century, single-sided carbon paper was available for use with a pencil. In this form it was often used for receipts, orders, and telegrams, but not for correspondence, since polite business correspondence was always written in ink. Carbon paper, then, had limited business use in the mid-century period.

Just in time to help handle the increased external and developing internal correspondence of the 1880s and 1890s, another technological advance converted carbon paper from a minor curiosity into a major copying technology. The typewriter, introduced in the 1870s (Current, 1954; Bliven, 1972), could readily be used with carbon paper, a fact discovered by its inventors and users almost immediately (Proudfoot, 1972, p. 33). This combination of technologies opened up new possibilities for carbon copying.

Like the rolling press, carbon paper produced unbound copies that could be stored with related correspondence. However, its many advantages over the rolling press led to its dominance of the small-scale copying market by the early twentieth century. While letters had to be taken to a centrally located rolling press *after* they were created, carbon copies were created at the typewriter at the same time the original was created. Thus, carbon copies took less time to make and did not require transmitting the original to a centralized location or collecting the copy from the location later. Carbon copies were also more readable than the often blurry press copies. And the paper used for carbon copies was of even lengths and had more body than the soft tissue used in press copying. It did not create messy flat files or fall down into the bottom of vertical files (after they were introduced) as rolling press copies did. Moreover, by 1912, a government study showed, carbon copying was considerably cheaper than press copying (President's Commission, 1912). Perhaps most importantly, however, the typewriter could easily produce more than one carbon copy, greatly facilitating internal communication. Four or five carbon copies could be made relatively routinely, and, under optimal conditions (a good typewriter, thin paper, and a strong typist), up to ten.

Moreover, the possibility of making multiple copies made small-scale downward communication, such as a general manager's communication to a handful of department heads or a department head's communication with half a dozen foremen, possible without extra work. Previously, such communication demanded either retyping a document multiple times, a costly process, or, more frequently, circulating a document from one department head to the next, a time-consuming process. Moreover, when downward communications were circulated from one person to the next, each recipient got to *read* it, but not to *keep* a copy. A surviving collection of downward communications saved by one foreman at Scovill shows that he had each circulating communication retyped in his department in order to maintain his own file of rules, procedures, and announcements (Scovill II, Case 34, E.G. Main's "Orders and Instructions," 1905-1914). His procedure was time-consuming and costly, and apparently few followed his example. But when enough carbon copies for a small circulation list were created, each recipient could keep a copy for local files, thus establishing a local, decentralized segment of corporate memory in an easily accessible location.

Although downward communication benefited most obviously from this innovation, upward and lateral communication benefited as well. Reports to be sent up the hierarchy could be made in as many copies as necessary to allow the sender and each intended recipient to keep a copy. Similarly, sender and recipient of lateral communications could both keep copies, in addition to any copies sent to higher levels. With carbon copies, sets of records that served as a corporate memory of some particular function could be available to several interested parties. Thus while loose copies made decentralized files possible, multiple loose copies allowed further decentralization.

The decentralization of files that generally followed rapidly on the adoption of loose copies happened in spite of expert advice. Books on establishing vertical filing systems (Griffith, 1909; Duffield, 1926) argued for maintaining central files. Experts insisted that an efficient central filing system could deliver the requested document to a clerk or manager faster than that person could get it from local files. Whether or not that was literally true, centralized filing was doomed from the time that loose and multiple copies were available. The rapid decentralization of files testifies to the fact that departments and even smaller units at least *perceived* that local files were more accessible to them and more under their control.

By allowing the decentralization of files, loose copies not only made internal communication more useful and accessible; indirectly it apparently encouraged the proliferation of that internal correspondence. A causal relationship between decentralized files and growth in internal written communication was frequently given as a reason to attempt (usually unsuccessfully) to restrict existence of local files. The chairman of a committee that investigated methods of handling correspondence in the Pennsylvania Railroad proposed to reduce internal correspondence by such a method (Hanna, 1913, p. 61):

> Probably the most effective means of reducing the number of letters written is the elimination of correspondence, as far as possible, between the head of a department and his subordinates, or staff officers. This is facilitated and made practicable by combining all of the files of the various staff officers with that of the department head. The principle of consolidating files to effect economies of time and the elimination of unnecessary letters, has been in use by many of our largest commercial enterprises, as well as on several railroad systems, for a number of years.

Some letters, Hanna argued, were only written to document something for all the sets of files. When the files were eliminated, these letters were no longer written. He went on to assert that the Pennsylvania Railroad reduced internal correspondence by 20% by consolidating files. Whether or not the consolidation of files lasted, Hanna's experiment provides evidence that decentralized files indeed led to further proliferation of internal correspondence.

While Hanna focused on the effect of dispersed files (made possible by loose copies) on vertical correspondence between superiors and subordinates, dispersed files probably encouraged internal lateral correspondence, as well. Scovill Manufacturing Company adopted carbon paper and vertical files in 1913 (Yates, 1982a). Dispersed, local files were rapidly established, although the official announcement of the change to vertical files assumed that the files would still be centralized. Almost no lateral correspondence dated before that year has survived, although some vertical correspondence has. In the single surviving set of local vertical files from the period following the changeover, however, lateral communication is plentiful, forming the largest single component of the files.

While this sudden appearance of lateral communication in the archival records almost certainly reflects in part the survival of lateral correspondence that previously existed but was not preserved, the amount and nature of that lateral correspondence was probably affected by the existence of the decentralized files. As I noted earlier, lateral correspondence was acquiring a documentary function, partially in indirect response to the systematic management movement's emphasis on corporate, rather than individual, memory, and partially in response to the frictions resulting from growth. Such correspondence documenting lateral relationships was much more accessible, controllable, and permanent when it was preserved in local files (both sender's and recipient's). Thus the decentralization of files would increase the potential value of lateral documentation, consequently encouraging its increased use. Documentary lateral correspondence would then be assumed to increase in absolute and relative terms.

Although no direct comparisons are possible in the Scovill case (since no lateral correspondence at all has survived from the days before decentralized filing), this hypothesis is indirectly supported by the fact that many of the letters surviving from the period right after the decentralization of filing were clearly written primarily to document one side of a power struggle, rather than to communicate with the other party. In one such letter, for example, the writer states, "I would like to go down on record as saying . . . ," a clear indication that his letter, which was also copied to other recipients, was written to document more than to communicate (Scovill II, Case 26, 25 March 1918). Fewer such letters might have been written if both parties had not wanted to go on record in their separate files. Thus, the shift in emphasis from communication to documentation that accounts for the rise of what we would today call CYA ("cover your ass") correspondence, I would speculate, was encouraged by the decentralized files made possible by new copying technologies.

In summary, the advent of the technology of loose copies, itself affected by the development of internal communication, affected internal communication both directly and indirectly. The technology that produced loose copies had been at least in part available earlier, but was not adopted until the systematic management movement greatly increased the amount of internal written communication in firms. This technology, in turn, helped that increased internal communication serve the desired functions more cheaply and easily. By making it possible to copy and store internal communication more functionally and accessibly, loose copies made internal correspondence more useful as a corporate memory. Indirectly, loose and multiple copies allowed the decentralization of files, which in turn encouraged more internal communication by providing local storage and access to primarily documentary communications.

MASS DUPLICATION

While the rolling copier and carbon paper solved some of the problems created by the growth of internal written communication, they did not solve all of them. Firm growth and the systematic management philosophy had created the need to communicate identical information, rules, and procedures to large numbers of employees. Carbon paper could enable one communication to reach up to ten individuals, but it could do no more. Mass duplication demanded different technologies. The growing railroads, which discovered the basic principles of systematic management very early, were forced to use printed notices and rules. Printing, however was expensive and slow, and as manufacturing companies began to grow and systematize themselves in the late nineteenth century, they were not eager to turn to that example.

In response to the newly developing need for inexpensive and convenient methods of mass duplication, a series of duplicating devices were developed in the closing decades of the century. The technology of mass duplication fell into two general types: (a) the stencil duplicating methods, which required a master with holes through which ink could be forced; and (b) the gelatin and spirit duplicating methods, which required a master produced with aniline dyes that were then transferred to other sheets of paper by means of a gelatin or spirit (alcohol-based) medium. The new duplicating devices both satisfied the growing companies' needs to communicate with their employees and facilitated further firm growth and systematization.

The history of stencil duplicating, which Proudfoot (1972) has studied extensively, began in the 1870s. The initial form of stencil duplicating to appear in America was Thomas Edison's "Autographic" or "Electrical" pen, patented in 1876. This device, powered by an electric motor, had a vibrating needle for its point. When the user "wrote" with it, it made tiny holes in the paper on the pen's path. The paper then served as a stencil master through which ink was passed to make copies of the spidery writing.

An early brochure advertised the device as an economical way to produce many copies of anything ("Edison's Electrical Pen," c. 1876), but the list of uses included more external types of communication (producing price lists and advertising circulars) than internal ones. Nevertheless, the brochure did suggest that it could be used for "notices to sub-agents from general agents." If Edison did not initially emphasize such internal uses, railroads and other big businesses certainly saw its potential. Within the first year of the electrical pen's appearance, the Illinois Central Railroad was using one for some of its widely distributed circulars (ICRR 2.8/2/1876). The fact that the railroad turned to the new technology so immediately after its appearance illustrates the pent-up demand for such a device. The railroad's reversion to printing within a couple of years says more about the state of the technology at that point than about the railroad's needs. In any case, the immediate demand for the Edison electrical pen, as imperfect as it was, was probably a factor in the innovations in stencil copying that followed.

The electrical pen was an early and unnecessarily complex application of the stencil principle, which only required the creation of holes in paper to let ink through. Several other non-electric methods of producing stencils of handwriting were devised in the late 1870s and 1880s (Proudfoot, 1972, pp. 46-52). One apparatus used a metal stylus on a sheet of waxed paper laid over a grooved surface. It was developed in England but marketed in America by the A.B. Dick Company as the Edison Mimeograph. Another method, developed by David Gestetner in England, used a wheel pen with perforating points on special, porous Japanese paper coated with wax. The stencil produced by these methods could be used to make hundreds of copies from a single original. By the late 1880s, according to Proudfoot (1972, p. 78), "the duplicating of handwriting by means of stencils became an accepted and necessary routine in the rapidly expanding office of that time."

By that time, however, the typewriter was superceding handwriting in most offices. The stencil process required adaptation to make it suitable for the typewriter (Proudfoot, 1972, pp. 82-104). A new type of wax-coated Japanese paper, even more porous than that already used for creating stencils of handwriting, could be used with the typewriter to produce a master from which large numbers of clear, legible copies could be made. Further improvements in the speed and neatness with which the copies were actually duplicated from the master, including the development of the rotary stencil copier to replace the earlier flat-bed apparatus, made the technology even more effective for making large numbers of copies. Stencil copying thus became a familiar necessity of the expanding firms.

Less is known about the early history of gelatin and spirit duplicating methods, which both used an original document written or typed in ink with aniline dyes as the basis for making up to one hundred copies (Proudfoot, 1972, pp. 34-36). The gelatin method, which became known in this country as the hectograph or, after one brand name, the Shapirograph process, apparently appeared in America in the 1870s. This duplicating method involved transferring the ink from the original master onto a gelatin bed, from which the ink was in turn transferred to the copies. It was, as it sounds, a messy process, though improvements to the original, fully manual devices made gelatin duplicating more automatic (though not electric). By 1923, a related but more convenient process, spirit duplicating, was developed in Germany. It became known in the U.S. (after one of its manufacturers) as Ditto. Spirit and gelatin copying methods produced fewer copies than stencil duplicating but were less expensive. Thus, they were popular for applications involving more than 10 but fewer than 100 copies.

Both types of duplicating devices, stencil and gelatin (later replaced by spirit), were widely adopted in the early decades of the twentieth century by growing companies attempting to systematize their operations. (They were also adopted by all sizes of companies for external, advertising purposes, but those uses are not relevant to this paper.) These large companies, unlike the railroads earlier, were enabled to issue large numbers of internal downward communications easily and cheaply.

Du Pont, for example, went through a major period of growth and systematization in the early twentieth century, beginning with a change in ownership in 1902 (Chandler & Salsbury, 1971, Chaps. 3-4). A system of mass downward communication was rapidly established to standardize rules and procedures. The company employed a variety of the duplicating devices then available to reproduce the downward communications. Headquarters of the High Explosives Operating Department (HEOD) started a numbered series of circular letters addressed to plant management in the various plants scattered around the country (Du Pont 500/II/2/HEOD/Boxes 550-551). The distinctive purple color and the survival of one of the masters indicate that these circular letters were reproduced by one of the gelatin devices. By 1912, one internal communication announces, the Sales Department had acquired a more modern Shapirograph, which made up to 40 copies (Du Pont 500/II/2/Box 1005/2/14 Oct. 1912). While Sales used it for external sales letters as well as internal communications, that department made it available to other department offices in headquarters for internal communications.

Du Pont adopted stencil duplicators when larger numbers of copies were required. Loose leaf manuals of standard rules and procedures were sometimes printed, but at other times were reproduced by stencil duplicators. The Engineering Department's *Standard Practice Book*, for example, had stencilled pages that were issued at different times to add to or replace existing printed pages (Du Pont 500/II/2/Box 111). Thus, the higher cost of printing was accepted in materials issued rarely and intended to be used for a long time, but not in periodic updates. Even forms, widely adopted for routine data gathering, were mimeographed when demand for them ran in the hundreds rather than the thousands (Du Pont 500/II/2/HEOD/Box 550/2/#417).

In Du Pont and other growing companies, then, duplicating provided quicker and less expensive modes of mass producing internal, especially downward, communication than printing could. Had the firms had, as their only option, the expensive and time-consuming process of having communications printed, they might not have depended so heavily on downward written communication in systematizing operations, and management methods might have differed radically from the form they actually took. Had the companies continued to depend on oral orders and documents circulated from person to person for most downward communication, they would never have achieved the standardization for which they strove. Moreover, the lack of an up-to-date corporate memory would have hampered their ability to learn from their past experience. They might have supplemented expensive printed communications with a more systematic form of oral communication, with heavy dependence on meetings, such as is found in Japanese firms. Such a communication system, while perhaps not as efficient for many matters, might have avoided some of the labor problems firms faced in the early years of the twentieth century.

Speculation on what might have been is, of course, highly problematic. Nevertheless, duplication technology clearly made feasible the heavy dependence of systematic management methods on written communication, a dependence that has continued to the present.

UNPLANNED COPIES

Carbon paper made it possible to make up to ten loose copies, and the duplicating methods just discussed made it possible to make hundreds of them. Both these technologies copied at the point of origin of the document, thus requiring advance planning. Extra sheets of paper and carbon paper had to be inserted in the typewriter at the point of creation for carbon copying, and stencil or gelatin/spirit copies could only be made from a specially prepared master. Neither of these types of technologies could be used to make unplanned copies. If a document from an external source needed to be seen by several people within a company, or if an internal document was created with insufficient carbon copies for internal needs, the document could only be reproduced by retyping (or writing) it, with extra copies as needed. Since retyping a document was costly, many documents were simply circulated to a list of people indicated on an attached buck slip. This process, though less costly, was slow.

Thus a technology was still needed to make copies after the point of creation. As early as 1900, the first such process was developed, but it was not until 1960, with the appearance of the Xerox 914, that the technology became economic and convenient for routine use. Photocopying opened the way for much wider informal dissemination of information within firms, as well as further promoting the proliferation of decentralized files.

The first photocopying process, patented in 1900 by a Frenchman (Nasri, 1978) and known in the United States by at least 1906 (Dessauer, 1971), was slow and expensive. The photostat, as it was called in the U.S., used a camera and light-sensitive paper to produce a negative photographic image. At a speed of only one copy per minute, it could only make about 500 copies in a day. Moreover, the average cost per copy, according to a government commission, was $98 per thousand (or approximately $.10 apiece), 175 times as costly as the $.56 per thousand for carbon copies at that time (President's Commission, 1911, n.d.).

Even at this cost, however, the photostat had a market, but not for routine copying. The government commission found the photostat cost effective for reproducing complicated documents, especially tables or diagrams, that would take a long time to retype or redraw. Du Pont clearly concluded likewise, for the company had a photostat by at least 1915, and probably earlier (Du Pont 500/II/2/Box 133/File ES-196-B/12 Feb. 1915). In fact, this machine was so popular for duplicating tables, graphs, and organization charts that the chairman of the executive committee had to send a communication to the heads of departments pointing out that printing by means of electrotypes was cheaper if many copies were to be made (Du Pont 1662/Box 29/18 June 1919).

The government or a large company like Du Pont could find cost-effective uses for the photostat, but they were specialized uses. Routine copying of normal written documents at point of receipt was still not feasible with this slow, expensive technology. The next major breakthrough in the technology did not come for half a century, when Xerox introduced the 914 copier, the first electrostatic, plain-paper copier, in 1960. Ironically, as Dessauer (1971) has shown, Xerox brought the 914 to market despite gloomy market projections. In fact, according to one executive involved in the initial production of the 914, a market research study performed by Arthur D. Little showed a total potential market of only 5,000 copiers (Horace Becker, telephone interview, Sept. 30, 1985). That study, however, was based on a major misperception of the Xerox machine's role in the copying market—that it would simply absorb some of the carbon copying market. Yet, as we have seen, carbon copying only worked at point of origin. That market did not begin to tap the demand for fast and inexpensive copying at the point of receipt. While photostats were too slow and expensive to reach that market, the Xerox copiers were not. Even the first Xerox copier, the 914, made 400 copies an hour, almost as many as photostats made a day, and later Xerox copiers were many times faster (Dessauer, 1971, p. 177). And the copies cost only $.05 per copy, roughly $.02 in 1912 terms (U.S. Bureau of the Census, 1960), or 1/5 the cost of copies made on the photostat in 1912.

Since my archival research does not extend beyond the 1920s at this time, future research will have to explore the effect of Xerox and other plain paper copiers on organizational communication in specific firms. Like its predecessor technologies, however, it clearly paved the way for further changes in organizational communication, most of them continuing earlier trends.

Like the earlier innovations in copying, Xerox copying contributed to the proliferation of decentralized files. Many have blamed the proliferation of files entirely on the Xerox machine (Dessauer, 1971, p. 224). In fact, as we have seen, it simply continued a trend begun by carbon copying and by stencil and gelatin/spirit duplicators. By breaking away from the centralized, bound letter books, the earlier technologies made it possible to establish decentralized files. These technologies, however, limited the number of recipients of a document to those planned for in advance. Plain paper copiers could make as many copies as desired, at any time after the original creation of the document. This capability allowed even further proliferation of decentralized files as more individuals had access to copies of documents.

Plain paper copying contributed to another, less established trend in dissemination of information within the organization: nonhierarchical flows of information. The planned copies created by the earlier technologies for the most part supported the hierarchical flows of information up and down the firm, as required by systematic management principles. At the originator's option, however, copies could be made for recipients outside of the main hierarchical flows. The unplanned copies made by a plain paper copier could be disseminated as widely as was desired, not just by the originator of the document, but by any recipient of the original communication. This innovation, then, made it easier to supplement the hierarchical channels of communication established by systematic management around the turn of the century. As such supplementary flows of information became desirable, they could readily be established. In this case, the demand for accessible information throughout organizations seemingly already existed, although the market research had not discovered it. The spectacular success of the early Xerox machines reflects that reality.

CONCLUSION

A series of innovations in the technology of reproduction in the nineteenth and twentieth centuries made possible enormous changes in the ways in which information and communication could be used within organizations. While the technology did not cause the changes, as we can see from the delayed initial acceptance of letter press copying, it allowed changes made necessary or desirable by firm growth, evolving managerial philosophy, and a growing need for information. Without the technological breakthroughs in duplicating, monetary and temporal constraints would have limited some developments, causing organizational communication and possibly even organizations themselves to take very different forms. However, without the changes in firms, some of the technologies might never have become commercially successful.

We may look for similar interactions between technologies and organizational needs with today's new computer-based communication technologies. Researchers studying the effect on organizational communication of the easy "copying" allowed by electronic mail, for example, might find the effects of earlier copying technologies useful in suggesting hypotheses. Since electronic copying, like plain paper photocopying, can occur at any time after the creation of the document, it is also likely to encourage nonhierarchical communication. Moreover, we might assume that further proliferation of copies is likely to encourage yet further decentralization of files (especially since electronic files take so much less space), which in turn may encourage yet further documentary internal communication.

On a more general level, an understanding of past interactions between communication technologies, organizational needs, and communication practices highlights typical patterns still in evidence. For example, we saw that some new communication technologies, such as carbon paper, initially fail to catch on because no organizational need for them yet exists or because the technology is not yet well enough developed to fulfill any organizational needs. Yet, as organizational needs change and as the technology continues to advance, they may suddenly be in demand. This pattern may be relevant to such contemporary technologies as teleconferencing. Initially, many of its proponents saw it as an answer to large corporate travel bills. When it did not fulfill this function, especially in its less expensive, freeze-frame mode, teleconferencing seemed to be a flop. As companies discover uses for it other than as a substitute for travel, however, and as the technology improves and becomes less expensive, it may gain a new market.

Learning from the past, then, may provide useful perspectives for examining the present and future—even in an area as seemingly "modern" as the effects of communication technology on communication in organizations.

REFERENCES

Published Sources

Bliven, B., Jr. (1972). *The wonderful writing machine*. New York: Random House.

Chandler, A.P., Jr. (1979). *The visible hand: The managerial revolution in American business*. Cambridge, MA: Belknap Press of Harvard University Press.

Chandler, A.P., Jr., & Salsbury, S. (1971). *Pierre S. du Pont and the making of the modern corporation*. New York: Harper & Row.

Current, R.N. (1954). *The typewriter and the men who made it*. Champaign, Illinois: University of Illinois Press.

Daniels, M. (1980). The ingenious pen: American writing implements from the eighteenth century to the twentieth. *American Archivist, 43,* 312-324.

Dessauer, J.H. (1971). *My years with Xerox: The billions nobody wanted*. Garden City, NY: Doubleday.

Duffield, D.W. (Comp.). (1926). *Progressive indexing and filing for schools*. Tonawanda, NY: Rand Kardex Bureau for Library Bureau.

Griffith, J.B. (1909). *Correspondence and filing* (Instruction Paper). Chicago, IL: American School of Correspondence.

Hanna, J.L. (1913). Efficient methods of handling correspondence. *Railway Age Gazette,* (10 January), *54,* 61-63.

Jelinek, M. (1980). Toward systematic management: Alexander Hamilton Church. *Business History Review, 54,* 63-79.

Litterer, J.A. (1961a). Alexander Hamilton Church and the development of modern management. *Business History Review, 35,* 211-225.

Litterer, J.A. (1961b). Systematic management: The search for order and integration. *Business History Review, 35,* 461-476.

Litterer, J.A. (1963). Systematic management: Design for organizational recoupling in American manufacturing firms. *Business History Review, 37,* 369-391.

Nasri, W.Z. (1978). Reprography. In A. Kent, H. Lancom, J.E. Daily, & W. Nasri (Eds.), *Encyclopedia of Library and Information Science* (Vol. 25). New York: Marcel Dekker, Inc.

Nelson, D. (1974). Scientific management, systematic management, and labor, 1880-1915. *Business History Review, 48*, 479-500.

Nelson, D. (1975). *Managers and workers: Origins of the new factory system in the United States, 1880-1920*. Madison, WI: University of Wisconsin Press.

Noble, D.F. (1977). *America by design: Science, technology, and the rise of corporate capitalism*. New York: Oxford University Press.

Proudfoot, W.B. (1972). *The origin of stencil duplicating*. London: Hutchinson & Co.

U.S. Bureau of the Census. (1960). *Historical statistics of the U.S., colonial times to 1957*. Washington, DC: U.S. Government Printing Office.

Wigent, W.D., Housel, B.D., & Gilman, E.H. (1916). *Modern filing: A textbook on office systems*. Rochester, NY: Yawman and Erbe.

Yates, J. (1982a). The development of internal correspondence in American business: A case study. In S.J. Bruno (Ed.), *Cultural crossroads in the 80's*. Proceedings of the 1982 American Business Communication Association International Convention, American Business Communication Association.

Yates, J. (1982b). From press book and pigeonhole to vertical filing: Revolution in storage and access systems for correspondence. *Journal of Business Communication, 19*, 5-26.

Unpublished Sources

Bishop, P.W. Unpublished manuscript history of the Scovill Manufacturing Company, c. 1952. In Scovill Archives, Archives Department, Baker Library, Harvard Business School, Boston, Massachusetts.

Edison's Electrical Pen and Duplicating Press. (Advertising brochure.) c. 1876. Courtesy of Edison National Historic Site, Menlo Park, New Jersey.

E.I. du Pont de Nemours and Company, courtesy of Hagley Museum and Library, Wilmington, Delaware. Text citations are indicated by "Du Pont," followed by the Hagley accession number; the numbers and symbols necessary to indicate the relevant section, part, box, and/or volume where the document is located; and the date.

Illinois Central Railroad, courtesy of the Newberry Library, Chicago, Illinois. Text citations are indicated by "ICRR," followed by the Newberry call number and date.

President's Commission on Economy and Efficiency, courtesy of National Archives and Records Service. "Report to the President on the Use of a Photographic Process for Copying Printed and Written Documents, Maps, Drawings, etc." (Dec. 1911); also undated memorandum and attached "Photostat" advertising brochure. In National Archives, Washington, D.C., Record Group 51, PCEE Box 12, File 045.2. Text citation indicated by "President's Commission 1911, n.d." Also Circular #21, "Memorandum of conclusions reached by the commission concerning the principles that should govern in the matter of handling and filing correspondence and preparing and mailing communications. . . ." Washington, D.C.: U.S. Government Printing Office, 1912. In National Archives, Washington, D.C. Text citation indicated by "President's Commission, 1912."

Scovill Manufacturing Company, courtesy of Archives, Baker Library, Harvard Business School, Harvard University, Cambridge, Massachusetts. Text citations are indicated by "Scovill," followed by collection number, volume or box number, and date.

Yates, J. (1985). "Control through communication: The emergence of internal communication in American firms, 1850-1920." Unpublished work-in-progress.

PART III

Understanding Organizational Communication Cross-Culturally

6

Spoken Japanese: Linguistic Influence on Work Group Dynamics, Leadership, and Decision-Making.*

Fredrik Ulfhielm

1. INTRODUCTION

Face-to-face verbal interaction in Japan is the focal point of this paper. The main aim, however, is neither a linguistic nor a cultural anthropological study per se, but an examination of the role of language in work group processes. Japanese was chosen for analysis to enrich the discussion of the broader issue:

> How can group cohesion and functioning be influenced linguistically, and what are the implications for leadership and decision-making?

The strong emphasis on group membership in Japan makes this culture a particularly rewarding target for analysis. Since Japanese is a rather "exotic" language, at least from a non-Japanese point of view, it readily invites comparison, making the dynamics of verbal interaction more visible. The current study is theoretical rather than empirical; I have drawn upon a number of works on various aspects of Japanese culture. Participatory observation was also carried out for a period of 6 weeks in 1983, within various types of groups in Japan.

2. LANGUAGE AND CULTURE

Language, as Berger and Luckmann (1967, p. 38) observe, "retains its rootage in the commonsense reality of everyday life." It conveys infor-

---

* This paper is an expanded version of a contribution to the First International Conference on Organization Symbolism and Corporate Culture, held at the University of Lund, Sweden, June 26–30, 1984.

mation, not only through the overt meaning of the utterance (i.e., se-
mantically and syntactically), but also through reference to—and dependence on—the specific circumstances of each particular interaction
situation (what linguists call "pragmatics"). Language is not neutral; it
mirrors the dominant values of the cultural context, subtly guiding the
perception of the native speaker to aspects of special cultural concern.
In an individual, it constitutes part of what Hofstede (1980, p. 14) calls
"mental programming." Being linguistically "programmed," however,
are we then also unwittingly imprisoned by our native language, as
Whorf (1956) would have us believe? Opposing this view, Chomsky
(1965) and Halliday (1971), each in his own way, both claim that languages are essentially more similar than different. To the extent that we
can at all "learn" a foreign language, we do not seem to be hopelessly
deterred from insight into other cultures. Obviously, each particular
language exhibits its own unique features; functionally, however, languages seem to differ mainly in the relative ease with which they can express concepts referring to phenomena that are deemed important in
each specific culture. As I shall try to demonstrate in this paper, Japanese is remarkably well suited to mediating culture-specific values in

3. JAPANESE VERBAL INTERACTION AND GROUP DYNAMICS

3.1. Basics of Japanese Grammar

What follows is a very brief outline of the structure of Japanese, to serve
as a background for the subsequent discussion.

Verbs constitute the most important class of words in Japanese. By
themselves, they can form complete sentences. In one sense, however,
they are ambiguous: they are inflected neither according to person nor
number. For instance, the verb *kaku* ('write') can have various meanings,
depending on the context:

· to write
· I write, you write, . . . they write

There are only two tenses: present (*kaku* 'write') and past (*kaita* 'wrote').
The present tense (*kaku*) can also imply a future action:

· I shall write, etc.

Nouns, too, are ambiguous: they do not take articles, and they are
unspecified as to gender and number. Thus, the noun *ronbun* ('thesis', or
'academic paper'), again depending on the context, could mean:

- a paper/papers; the paper/papers; my paper/papers, etc.

The noun *hito* ('person') could refer to:

- a person
- people
- somebody
- me
- personal disposition

The relation of the noun to the rest of the sentence is shown by means of post-positional particles. The particle *o*, for instance, indicates that the preceding noun is an object; thus, *ronbun o kaku* (lit. 'paper←object write') could mean:

- I (or you, etc) write a paper
- I write my paper
- I write papers (for a living)
- I shall write a paper

The clause *ronbun o kaita* (he wrote a paper, lit. 'paper←object wrote') by itself forms a complete sentence. However, it can also function as an adjectival clause:

- *ronbun o kaita* + noun, as in *ronbun o kaita hito* (the person who wrote a paper, lit. 'paper←object wrote person')

In a similar way, the particle *ga* indicates that the preceding noun is the subject:

- *hito ga kaita* (somebody wrote, lit. 'person←subject wrote')

The subject, however, is often omitted, together with all other parts of speech that can be more or less directly inferred from the context (verbal or situational). For instance:

- question: what happened?
  reply: *hito ga ronbun o kaita* (somebody wrote a paper, lit. 'person←subject paper←object wrote')
- question: what did he do?
  reply: *ronbun o kaita* (he wrote a paper)
- question: what did he do with the paper?
  reply: *kaita* (he wrote it)

Adjectives have a verbal "flavor": they have tenses and moods like verbs. Thus, the adjective *omoshiroi* (interesting, lit. 'is-interesting') can form a complete sentence:

- *omoshiroi* (it is interesting, he/she is interesting, they are interesting, etc)
- *omoshirokatta* (past tense: it was interesting, etc)

Used attributively, it precedes the noun:

- *omoshiroi ronbun* (an interesting paper, a paper which is interesting, lit. 'is-interesting paper')
- *omoshirokatta ronbun* (past tense: a paper which was interesting)

It can even be inflected to form a conditional clause:

- *omoshirokereba* (lit. 'if-is-interesting')
- *omoshirokereba, ronbun o kaku* (if it is interesting, I shall write a paper)

On the other hand, verbs have an adjectival "flavor"; they can be used to create an adjectival clause:

- *kaku ronbun* (the papers which I write, lit. 'write paper')
- *kaita ronbun* (past tense: the paper which he wrote)

Using the above words as building blocks, we can now elaborate a little (natural units are underlined to aid interpretation):

- _kaku_ (you will write)
- _ronbun o kaku_ (she writes a paper)
- _omoshiroi ronbun o kaita_ (they wrote interesting papers)
- _hito ga kaita_ (people wrote)
- _hito ga ronbun o kaita_ (somebody wrote a paper)
- _omoshiroi ronbun o kaku hito_ (a person who writes interesting papers)

Quite apart from the way Japanese is actually used in social interaction, we can detect, then, a certain degree of ambiguity already inherent in the grammatical structure of the language.

3.2. Group Dynamics and Linguistic Encoding

Organizations are networks of people who communicate, mainly through language. A substantial part of this communication takes place in face-to-face interaction. Goffman (1967, p. 2) assumes "that the proper study of interaction is not the individual and his psychology, but rather the syntactical relations among the acts of different persons mutually present to one another." This assumption would seem especially valid in the case of Japan, where group affiliation is more important than individual personality traits.

But what specific forms do they take in Japan, these "syntactical relations"; what kind of verbal "acts" do people perform when they are "mutually present to one another"? Lebra (1976), Nakane (1973), and Rohlen (1981) have well depicted interaction and group dynamics in Japan from a social anthropological perspective; Goldstein and Tamura (1975), Mizutani (1981), and Naotsuka, Sakamoto, Hirose, Hagihara, Ohta, Maeda, Hara, &Iwasaki (1981), from a cross-cultural, linguistic; Barnlund (1975) and Minami (1981) from a social psychological; and Doi (1981) from a psychiatric.

The level of politeness (*teinei*) is a linguistically encoded aspect of the Japanese language, and whenever two or more people meet face-to-face, even before starting to speak, they first have to determine what degree of politeness is appropriate to the occasion. There are three different levels of politeness: the *plain*, the *polite*, and the *deferential* (Dunn & Yanada, 1958). They all imply varying degrees of social distance, but, whereas the deferential level represents an extraordinary degree of formality, the other two are both in common use, although in different situations, or by different persons in the same situational context. The three levels are indicated linguistically by means of plain, polite, and deferential forms of verbs and adjectives (when these appear at the end of a sentence—in other positions in the sentence, plain forms are almost always used; this fact makes it possible to delay the choice of level of politeness until the very end of the first sentence, when some feedback from the listener may already be at hand). For instance, *kaku* ('write') is a plain form; the corresponding polite form is *kakimasu*—it has exactly the same semantic meaning, but indicates a somewhat greater social distance. Together with a number of other words and phrases, first and second person pronouns (if used at all) also differ with the various levels or politeness.

Selection of the appropriate level of politeness is not primarily dependent on social relationships or kinship ties. Instead, to be able to speak Japanese in a socially acceptable manner, the speaker needs to appraise the specific circumstances of each new *interaction situation* in view of two separate social psychological dichotomies (Lebra, 1976): inside/ outside (*uchi/soto*), and back/front (*ura/omote*). Thus, one must first classify the person one is addressing (as well as any other person who happens to be present) as an "insider" or an "outsider"; next, one must decide whether the occasion admits of any display of inner thought and feeling, or calls for a more or less tightly controlled "face."

It is precisely here that *meishi* (visiting cards) become almost indispensable—they are exchanged at the very beginning of a face-to-face interaction, and the information they convey has a direct bearing on the way each participant will deal with the other or others linguistically. In this context, group affiliation (e.g., company) is far more important than individual position or function. Combining the two dichotomies mentioned above, we get the following four types of situations, with their concomitant (most probable) behavior styles:

A.1.	inside/back	unrestrained, intimate, regressive
A.2.	inside/front	inhibited, intimate, regressive
B.	outside/front	restrained, formal, ritual
C.	outside/back	unrestrained, unabashed, anomic

Lebra (1976, p. 112) refers to situation A.1. above as "Intimate," B as "ritual," and C as "Anomic"; she assumes that situation A.2. is "unlikely to occur." Barnlund (1975, p. 144), however, discussing the results of his investigation of communicative styles in Japan and the United States, claims that, "In short, the findings support the hypothesis that the Japanese communicate significantly less [than Americans] of their inner feelings and thoughts even with their most intimate aquaintances." Lebra (1976, p. 117) points out that "The frankness expected in intimate interaction often leads to aggression"; thus, group unity and harmony might be disrupted by an excessive individual display of spontaneity, and the balance between unity and spontaneity seems to be quite delicate. Yet, according to Doi (1981), there is a ubiquitous psychological desire in Japan to get engulfed by a group, regressing (*amaeru* 'to behave like a child') into a dependency reminiscent of the symbiotic relationship between mother and child. Thus, independent adults interacting as responsible individuals does not appear to be a particularly cherished ideal in Japan. As Nakane (1973, p. 139) notes, "The general tendency of the majority of Japanese . . . is to seek security rather than autonomy."

Whereas the need for restraint (*enryo*) is a prime characteristic of situation B, in type A.1. situations it is actively discouraged (situations A.1. and A.2. are designated with the same letter because of their great similarity in other respects). Reminiscent of the "sauna" phenomenon in Finland, social nudity (*hadaka no tsukiai* naked association, in contrast to *hadaka no kankei* naked relationship, i.e., sex) is encouraged at an *onsen* (hot spring), to transform a type B situation into one of type A (converting "outsiders" into "insiders"). In situation C, again, restraint is not necessary, but for a different reason: the "outsider" is not important.

Although situations A.1. and C share some common features (the "back" aspect, and a lack of restraint), they differ completely with regard to one vital element: *ninjō*[1] (feeling of sympathy, humanity). A high degree of *ninjō* is taken for granted in type A situations; even in type B, some *ninjō* may hopefully imbue a *giri*, which Doi (1981, p. 34) defines as a relationship of interdependence (lit. 'duty', 'obligation'), caused by incurring *on* ('debt of gratitude'); by contrast, in type C situations *ninjō* may be deplorably lacking (cf. Mizutani, 1981, pp. 61ff.; Lebra, 1976, pp. 131ff.; Doi, 1981, pp. 40ff.).

From a social psychological view, the phenomena described above are well known as common aspects of group dynamics. What makes Japan a special case, however, is the particularly pronounced separation of different types of interaction situations, with their concomitant styles of behavior. Although the boundaries (inside/outside and back/front) may shift considerably from one moment to the next (making the inside, or "we" area, bigger or smaller, and affecting the need to preserve "face"), thus modifying the definition of the situation at hand, there is relatively little inter-situational overlap of (even linguistic) behavior. In fact, uncertainty about the definition of a situation (e.g., when two or more types of situations coexist) can cause considerable behavioral confusion. On such occasions, recourse is usually taken to behavior pertaining to type B situations (or sometimes type C, pretending that the other person is not really there).

Linguistically, plain forms (indicating short social distance) are used in type A situations, e.g., *kaku* ('write'); in type B, polite (e.g., *kakimasu*) or deferential forms; and, in type C, once again, plain forms (even though polite forms are also feasible, especially among women, it is doubtful whether, in that case, it really is a type C situation, as defined above; characteristically, the level of politeness decreases sharply between situations of type B and C). If politeness is not a distinguishing feature of type C situations, "social distance" is also short, in the sense that you may show your inner self more freely without fear of losing "face"; even a radical decrease in physical distance may be acceptable, e.g., in commuter trains. The inside/outside boundary may also be manipulated intentionally—one extreme example would be the quarrelling married couple, interacting very "politely" and with marked "social distance," by means of a redefinition of the situation and a concomitant change of linguistic forms (Mizutani, 1981, p. 77).

Even after defining a situation and having chosen an appropriate level of politeness, however, a speaker is not yet ready to start talking, since the level of politeness is but one of two (mutually independent but

---

[1] A dash above the letter indicates a long vowel.

overlapping) ways of showing respect in Japanese. Together, these two systems are called *keigo* (respect language). Whereas the level of politeness refers to the speaker's attitude to the person or persons *addressed*, the second system concerns respect towards the person (or thing) spoken *of*, by means of two different categories of forms:

1. *honorific*, or respectful (*sonkei*), referring to (and "raising") *the actions of a superior* (or of people associated with him or her), to whom the speaker should pay respect; this superior might well be identical with the addressee (but he or she need not be).
2. *depreciatory*, or humble (*kenjō*), referring to (and "lowering") *the speaker's own actions* (or the actions of people associated with the speaker), when (and only if) these actions in some way *relate to a superior* (who might, but need not, be identical with the addressee), to whom the speaker should pay respect.

This way of showing respect is applied primarily in type B situations, but also in type A (indicating respect, but short social distance); thus, in Japan, intimate interaction (in the family or other primary group) does not seem to be hampered by status differences among the members. There is an impressive variety of these honorific forms in Japanese, reflecting even very subtle differences in status. For instance, the sentence "I will do it for you" might be phrased in the following different ways (among a number of alternatives), depending on the situational context (*kaite* 'writing' is the gerundial form of *kaku* 'write'; the pronouns "I" and "you" are not required):

· younger person to older:

    a. plain form (informal, in type A situations)
        kaite ageru (lit 'writing give-upwards')
    b. polite form (in type B situations)
        kaite agemasu (same meaning)

· older person to younger:

    a. plain form
        kaite yaru (lit 'writing give-downwards')
    b. polite form
        kaite yarimasu

Using honorific/depreciatory forms can be quite trying, since it is vitally important to keep track of the perpetually shifting boundary between "inside" and "outside." This holds true, not just for verbs, but for any kind of word that implies relative status. For instance, consider the following verbal exchange:

1. Son to his father:	"Father (*otōsan*) may I . . .?"
2. Same son to his friend:	"My father (*chichi*) said . . ."
(his father is not present)	"What did your father (*otōsan*) say?"
His friend's reply:	"My father (*chichi*) said . . ."
	"But did your father (*otōsan*) really say . . .?"

Thus, the word *otōsan* is used when addressing your own father, or when talking about the father of the addressee, whereas *chichi* is used when speaking (to "outsiders") about your own father. *Within a group* (as temporarily defined by the inside/outside boundary), *status differences take precedence*: you speak "upwards" towards (and about) your superiors (with honorific forms), "lowering" yourself (with depreciatory forms), at the same time being more or less polite (plain, polite, or deferential forms). However, the moment you start interacting with *an outsider* (even though you may form a new inside group with this person), the members of all the other groups to which you belong *collectively* fall in line with your own relative status *vis-á-vis the person you are speaking of* (should he or she be an insider of one of your groups, he or she, too, assumes your status, and no honorific forms are used); if the person spoken *of* is *an outsider* (he or she might, but need not, be the addressee), and if he or she has *a higher status* (and, if not the addressee, is still a person to whom you should pay respect), you "lower" yourself and your group (with depreciatory forms) and "raise" the person spoken *of* (with honorific forms). At the same time, of course, you have to keep an appropriate *distance vis-á-vis the addressee* (plain, polite, or deferential forms). If the addressee is *a superior*, he himself or she herself will *not* use respect language in his or her reply (unless he or she is speaking *of* someone who has still higher status; in that case, the latter must *not* be an insider in any of the addressee's groups, unless the original speaker is *also* a member of the same group); if the addressee is a subordinate (and *not* the person spoken *of*), the speaker could still use honorific forms *when speaking of a superior* (if all three persons are in the same group), but he or she would probably use the *plain* level of politeness.

Names are not commonly used in Japan, especially not when addressing (or speaking of) superiors. In fact, the only person in a family who is called by name is the youngest child; all others are addressed (and spoken of) according to their relative position. The same holds true for society at large—people are addressed (or spoken of) according to *group affiliation* (e.g., *Maruzen-honya-san* Mr./representing/Maruzen Bookstore; *-san* stands for Mr., Mrs., or Miss) or *position* (e.g., *kachō-san* Mr. Section Head: this is the way he would be *addressed* by his subordinates within the company; the president would probably say just *kachō*). Goldstein and Tamura (1975) discuss family and category terms at some length, comparing Japanese and American usage.

We can now integrate what has been discussed so far, in the form of a table, depicting the relative importance of different characteristics between the four interaction situations (see Table 1):

Table 1. Characteristics of the Four Different Interaction Situations

Situation type: characteristics:	A.1.	A.2.	B	C
inside/outside dichotomy	inside	inside	outside	outside
back/front dichotomy	back	front	front	back
concomitant (most probable) behavior style	unrestrained intimate regressive	inhibited intimate regressive	restrained formal ritual	unrestrained unabashed anomic
priority situation	──────────────→ X ←──── →(X)			
on, giri (debt/duty)	yes, but over-shadowed by *ninjō* (see below)	yes, but over-shadowed by *ninjō* (see below)	yes	no
ninjō (sympathy, humanity), degree of	high	high	medium	low
amae (dependency), degree of	high	high	medium	low
enryo (restraint), degree of	low	medium	high	low
politeness (formality), degree of	low	low	high	low (medium)*
teinei forms (linguistic politeness)	plain	plain	polite deferential	plain (polite)*
use of *sonkei/kenjō* (honorific forms)	yes	yes	yes	no

*When politeness is called for, a type C situation transforms into a type B (th "outsider"becomes important).

To recapitulate, in order to select linguistic forms that are appropriate to each new interaction situation, the speaker must keep asking himself or herself the following kinds of questions:

1. Who am I talking to:
   a. an insider or an outsider? (i.e. type A or B/C)
   b. if insider, how intimate? (i.e. type A.1. or A.2.)
   c. if outsider, how important to me? (i.e. type B or C)
   Aim: to be able to determine type of situation
2. Regarding any other person who happens to be present:
   a. same as 1.a.
   b. same as 1.b.
   c. same as 1.c.
   Aim: the presence (or unexpected arrival) of a third party might necessitate a swift redefinition of the situation, to avoid inter-situational overlap
3. Who is the person spoken *of*:
   a. a superior (or people associated with him or her)? (honorific forms, but *not* if the superior is an insider and the addressee an outsider)
   b. I myself (or people associated with me)? (depreciatory forms, provided my/our actions relate to a superior, but *not* if the superior is an insider and the addressee an outsider)
   c. a subordinate? (no honorific/depreciatory forms)

Even though the speaker's definition of the situation is likely to prove ephemeral, he or she may now (at last!) feel confident enough to dare to initiate the verbal interaction proper.

3.3 Purpose and Content of Japanese Verbal Interaction

Becker (1975, p. 58) notes, "Fundamental to social ceremonial is the proper use of words; the actor must be able to deliver the lines correctly." An utterance is delivered in a social context, and what is "proper," even within one specific cultural setting, varies with the circumstances of each particular interaction situation. In Japan, as has been shown, group affiliation (inside/outside), degree of formality (back/front), and relative status (within a group and between groups) are all basic criteria in choosing "proper" linguistic forms.

An even more basic consideration, of course, is the question of the very *purpose* of the communicative interaction. According to Halliday (1973, 1978), a verbal message simultaneously can fulfil three different functions:

1. To convey factual information (the *ideational* function—"meaning as content").
2. To mirror interpersonal attitudes (the *interpersonal* function—"meaning as participation").
3. To refer to the verbal and situational context (the *textual* function—"meaning as texture").

In Japan, the main communicative emphasis in face-to-face verbal interaction is on the second rather than the first of these functions. To use a simile from the animal world, spoken Japanese seems closer to the identification signalling of ants than to the direction dancing of bees. Though the paramount aim of communication is always to reduce uncertainty (in one form or another), spoken language in Japan is used, not primarily as an instrument for logical analysis and information exchange, but rather as a mediator of social relationships, to dispel interpersonal insecurity. In fact, these two functions of language are regarded not as complementary but as mutually almost incompatible, a view which has led to characteristic and far-reaching repercussions in the way the Japanese use their language in verbal interaction.

Group unity and interpersonal harmony (*wa* harmony, reconciliation, unity; interestingly, *wa* is also an older denomination for Japan: *wakoku* 'harmony-land') are seen as potentially threatened by an overly explicit and direct exchange of factual information. Not merely a desire to avoid open criticism or quarrelling, this fear of disrupting social harmony actually permeates practically every aspect of verbal interaction: questions, requests, orders, directions, expression of personal opinion, discussion, and even compliments could all prove to be menacing, especially in a type B (formal) situation. Thus, language use is deliberately geared toward creating an interpersonal (and intergroup) nonthreatening "buffer zone" of linguistic ambiguity; by subtly manipulating the level of vagueness, potentially dividing disagreements and conflicts can be avoided, or at least kept at bay. As Lebra (1976, p. 124) notes, "The Japanese language, especially in its spoken form, allows subtle, implicit, open-ended, obscure understatement." And again, "By omitting subjects, verbs, and negatives, the speaker can avoid making a verbal commitment and thus risking a loss of face."

According to Mizutani (1981, p. 95), sometimes "a considerable gap exists between the linguistic form and the actual meaning of the utterance." There is, of course, also a corresponding inclination for listening beyond the words; the verbal actor will indeed need skill to navigate safely between the Scylla of explicitness and the Charybdis of confusion.

The Japanese understanding of the word "sincerity" (*seijitsu* sincerity, fidelity, honesty) should be easier to comprehend against this background: it does *not* refer to a truthful expression of personal conviction, but to being "tactful" and showing commitment and fidelity towards important others. Paradoxically, even though the overriding purpose of the interaction is to display the speaker's attitude towards the listener (and towards the person or thing spoken of), it is not a question of expressing his or her own personal emotions (which might threaten the desired state of social harmony) but instead a matter of choosing linguistic forms (of politeness) which are appropriate to the particular situation. In fact, even disclosing one's personal likes and dislikes (let alone being assertive) is considered proof of egotism and immaturity.

On the other hand, since information concerning a person's social standing (i.e., group affiliation and status) is a necessary condition for a smooth-running interaction, questions about this are considered quite legitimate (although a visiting card, *meishi*, usually provides the basic information needed). Consequently, there is little utilization of creative or individualized ways of expression in spoken Japanese; on the contrary, set phrases abound, and these are not only expected and acceptable, but actually seem to be preferred (because predictable and thus nonthreatening). Goldstein and Tamura (1975, p. 69) point out that, "Since Japanese speech formulas for standard situations are self-contained units requiring no additional explanations of personal circumstances to help the words ring true, the Japanese speaker will not hesitate to use the formula in the appropriate situation even if a number of people present have already made the very same identical statement." These "speech formulas," or situation dependent set phrases, encompass the whole gamut of greetings, apologies, and thanks; they are not applied in type C situations, however, since unimportant outsiders (outside/back) are not treated as linguistically significant (unless they become "absorbed" into a type B situation).

An interesting analogy is Haiku poetry: featuring a "set" form (a short, unadorned and matter-of-fact description of a concrete situation), the task of supplying any concomitant emotional content, or "meaning," is left to the reader or listener.

Even if there is scant wish to convey factual information explicitly, a certain amount of social talk is still required, by means of appropriate set phrases, especially in type B situations; this verbal behavior may well appear shallow and trivial, or even "stupid" and "robot-like," but it plays a crucial role in confirming interpersonal (and intergroup) relations. On the other hand, apart from the expected quota of set phrases, silence is not interpreted as an ominous sign.

There is, in Japanese tradition, a deep distrust of the power of words to convey any genuine "meaning" beyond the mere surface impression. This attitude was presumably inspired by Zen Buddhism, in which real understanding or spiritual enlightenment (*satori*, from *satoru* see, realize, understand) is taken to be uncommunicable, at least through words; to believe otherwise wold be tantamount to "mistaking a person's finger pointing to the moon for the moon itself." Rather than explicit, intellectual, brain-to-brain give-and-take, the ideal communication should be wordless and intuitive, a heart-to-heart understanding (or rather a stomach-to-stomach one, since *hara* 'abdomen' is considered the seat of human intuition, courage, and spirit), emulating the symbiotic relationship between a mother and her new-born child (cf. the discussion of *amaeru* in section 3.2).

A specific linguistic factor may also have contributed to this disenchantment with words: when the Japanese adopted Chinese pictorial characters (*kanji*) to write their own (very different) language, this led to a state of affairs which could well be described as mild "linguistic schizophrenia." Each pictorial character stands for a particular concept in Chinese. In Japanese, there was usually no single exactly corresponding concept, but instead several which only partly (more or less) overlapped with the Chinese concept; similarly, when trying to find an appropriate Chinese character to depict a Japanese concept, there were several possibilities, but only with approximate equivalence. In other words, a Japanese word (as opposed to loanwords) can be written with different Chinese characters, depending on what shade of meaning is emphasized; a Chinese character also corresponds to several Japanese words, its pronunciation and meaning depending on the verbal context. On top of this, each Chinese character also has one or (usually) many Chinese readings, adopted as loanwords at different times and from various dialects of Chinese; thus, there even exist *different* Chinese loanwords with the *same* semantic meaning. For example, the character for 'birth, life' has two Chinese loanword readings, and it is used to represent at least 18 Japanese concepts (all pronounced differently). This creation of a hybrid written language, with Chinese pictorial characters intermingled with special Japanese phonetic characters, presumably helped pave the way for a relativistic sense of linguistic "meaning"; paradoxically, there is also an obsession in Japan with the correct way to *write* each particular pictorial character—once again, we find a preoccupation with appropriate form rather than content.

3.4. Verbal Behaviour in Face-to-Face Interaction

Usually, verbal interaction is conceived of as an exchange of interrelated but self-contained utterances between two or more paticipants. Argyle (1967, p. 52) suggests that "Two people should speak enough for nearly all of the time to be filled with speech, for the duration of the encounter. If they speak more than this, there will be interruption and double-speaking; if they speak less than this, there will be periods of silence. When A has finished speaking, B should reply." In Japan, however, this notion of individual verbal actors taking turns in a polarized yet orderly manner is not a very realistic description of actual face-to-face interaction. Mizutani (1981, p. 86) offers an apposite simile, "English as tennis and Japanese as volleyball." In fact, Naotsuka, Sakamoto, et al. (1981, p. 88) suggest that the conversational ball tossed at the listener may not even be the same when it returns: "Japanese 'tact' emphasizes making the other person feel good much more than the relative 'truth' of the expressions used." Spoken language is a flexible medium, and the Japanese seem to have found a way around the usual type of polarized exchange between individual verbal actors; participants in an interaction tend to regard each other as partners rather than potential opponents.

Like any other aspect of social conduct in Japan, verbal behavior is highly dependent on the circumstances of the particular situation.

On very formal occasions (extreme type B situations) verbal behavior is quite ritualistic; each speaker, in descending status order (usually corresponding to age) delivers an uninterrupted monologue, while all the other participants silently wait for their turn—for a junior it might never arrive, since the verbal flow tends to come to an end if some senior member in the chain chooses not to speak. In such a context, seating arrangements underscore differences in status: the most senior person occupies a central position, with his retinue in ranking order.

By contrast, in less formal type B situations, verbal behavior is remarkably different. Here, after exchanging greetings by means of appropriately deep bows and the correct set phrases, one person intiates the interaction by uttering the first couple of words of what is subsequently likely to become a more or less collectively created monologue, where the roles of speaker and listener will probably be hard indeed to differentiate. The Japanese do not favor (and are not used to) a discussion in which A states his or her opinion while B is listening, and B then replies by way of offering his or her own opinion; this, being an individualistic type of interchange, could easily end in dispute and conflict. Instead, A starts by delivering what amounts to 'well . . .' (*ano ne*, or *ano nē* which is more emphatic); B then interjects what is known as an *aizuchi* (usually some form of 'yes': *hai, ha, e,* or *ē,* or perhaps just a grunt; *aizuchi o utsu* means to 'chime in with another' or 'echo another's words') to confirm that he or she is listening with empathy (*omoiyari* 'sympathy', 'compassion', 'consideration', or 'empathy'). *Aizuchi* are given, not just to prompt the speaker to continue, but also to indicate that the listener understands (but does not necessarily agree with) what the speaker says (not only the semantic content but also the contextual reference, both verbal and situational); they might, of course, also convey subtle indications regarding the listener's reactions. Depending on the feedback A receives by means of B's tone of voice when offering *aizuchi*, he or she may now either modify his or her utterance or go on as he or she had planned, until the next occasion for receiving confirmation; in fact, after each word with its concomitant post-positional particle there is a natural short pause, where *aizuchi* are more or less regularly proffered by the other interactors. Since the final verb or adjective is the most important part of a Japanese sentence (see section 3.1.), before reaching that point the meaning of the utterance is not really conveyed (although it may be anticipated); in fact, B may even take over from A and interject his or her own linguistic unit (i.e., a word and its concomitant post-positional particle, see section 3.1.). Then C, after giving his or her *aizuchi*, anticipates what B intended to say next, so he or she (C) now takes over instead (he or she may have sensed that the utterance was heading in a dangerous direction), only to surrender the conclusion of the sentence to D (or once again entrust it to A). And, even after having reached the final verb or adjective, as a last recourse there is an assortment of end particles that could help soften the tone and make the utterance sound less assertive: -*ga* ('but'), -*keredomo* ('although'), -*noni* ('though', 'while', or 'I wish . . .'), -*shikashi* ('but'), and -*kara* ('because'); but even before that, of course, the verb or adjective could easily be replaced with a less threatening one, or changed into negative form, or omitted altogether, leaving the sentence open-ended. Since Japanese questions are all in the form of a statement plus a question mark (the post-positional particle *ka*), a statement could even easily be turned into a question. If -*kashira* ('I wonder if . . .') is added instead, this turns the whole utterance into a rhetorical musing. In this way, two or more participants may collaborate in creating one single collective utterance; each contributes his or her confirmation of what the previous speaker has said, and modifies the sentence according to his or her own interpretation of the feedback received from the other interactors. Hinds (1982, p. 325) suggests that "Japanese conversational interaction can proceed for extended periods with overlapped speech."

This kind of verbal interaction, then, could hardly be called a dialogue or discussion, in the usual sense of those words. All members of a group participate in creating a joint utterance; nobody is left out, everyone gives his or her feedback, either verbally (through *aizuchi*), or nonverbally, by way of just nodding or smiling. Rather than an interindividual (or even inter-subjective) exchange, what ensues could perhaps best be described as an intricate web of "social meaning," a "collective monologue," or a "linguistic gestalt." As a matter of fact, this manner of co-operative verbal (and nonverbal) "intermingling" is even more characteristic of type A situations; not only is there a marked decrease in politeness distance (a transfer from polite to plain forms), but physical proximity is also more pronounced (even some bodily contact is permissible). There is a promise of relief, here, from the tensions that are likely to accumulate in type B (formal) situations. Talk of work will not be well received; instead one may disclose somewhat more of one's *honne* ('private self') as opposed to the *tatemae* ('rules' or 'etiquette') one is expected to conform to in type B situations; even some mild expression of criticism might be acceptable in such a setting, when everybody presumably will feel comparatively safe anyway. While, in a type B context, everybody would be likely to order the same dish at a restaurant, in the "inside" group (type A) they would probably be more individualistic in their choice (Mizutani, 1981, p. 134). Although people are generally much more talkative in a type A setting, being silent is also quite acceptable as long as one is obviously participating as a member of the group (offering verbal or non-verbal *aizuchi*); in fact, it is less reprehensible to fall asleep in the middle of a party, than to leave before the others. The closer a type A group is knit, the less is the probability that gratitude will be expressed among the members, since this would create "distance": it is only natural that you should do the other person a favor without expecting anything in return; (cf. Doi 1981, p. 88); in type B contexts, however, any service offered or received would immediately incur an *on* ('debt'), thus establishing a *giri* relationship (see section 3.2.).

A "creative" discussion is expected to engender new insights for the participants, quite apart from any consideration of social confirmation; in Japan, however, due to the fear of disrupting social relationships this aspect is comparatively neglected. Sethi, Namiki, and Swanson (1984, p. 38) point out that "If a member wishes to present an opinion, he does so by prefacing it with 'I happen to know someone who thinks that . . .' or 'Let me say this, but I'm just thinking out loud.' This gives him a way out if he sees that what he says is radically opposed by other members." Naturally, a verbal interaction could always develop in ways that are hard to predict, but in Japan there is always a check by means of *aizuchi*. Each new utterance is delivered (more or less collectively) and interpreted against a "safe" background of (presupposed) shared experence, and threatening information is not permitted to come to the fore, since it could disrupt the delicate state of social homeostasis; the semantic content of an utterance is mellowed with the help of a number of subtle linguistic devices, and the whole message is enfolded in appropriately soothing introductory and ending set phrases.

The Japanese have a tendency to use indirect forms of expression (for requests, refusals, or complaining) in order to avoid a direct confrontation; *atsui nē* ('it's hot, isn't it') would signal a desire that some subordinate open a window, the actual phrasing of the utterance (degree of politeness, etc.) indicating who is intended as addressee, even if no personal pronoun is used. Instead of a direct request, like *kore o shite kudasai* ('please do this', lit. 'this←object doing please-give'), the wish would probably be stated as a rhetorical question.

Ideas and suggestions are subtly hinted at, rather than stated explicitly; paradoxically, this holds true especially when trying to communicate something important (being at the same time potentially more threatening): *tokorode* ('by the way', 'incidentally', or 'well now') or *sate* ('well now') even though (intentionally) sounding casual, in fact indicate that something essential is to follow. Some words indicating 'about' (*-gurai, -hodo, -bakari*) are used even in situations where a n exact amount is implied, to make the speaker sound more polite and less assertive, *ringo o mittsu-gurai kudasai* (lit. 'apples←object three-about please-give'). Even in situations where a direct question is presented, *kono ringo wa ikura desu ka* (lit. 'these apples, how-much-are-they?'), the answer is likely to be indirect: "Yes, they are very fresh." (cf. Mizutani 1981, pp. 25, 88).

As Rommetveit (1974) points out, verbal communication can not be properly understood apart from the context in which it takes place. There is, in Japanese, quite a pronounced dependence on the specific circumstances of each particular interaction situation. What the speaker actually tries to accomplish with his or her utterance, delivered against the background of a unique set of verbal and physical contextual characteristics, constitutes the focus of the pragmatic level of linguistic analysis. Linguistically encoded "context-pointers" can explicitly denote physical objects or persons in the situational context, or refer back to what has been said before; they can imply a desire for *aizuchi* (by means of particles like *ne* or *nē*/more emphatic/ 'you see' or 'isn't it', or just a short pause), or indicate degree of politeness as well as relative status (see section 3.2.; there are also honorific particles, like *o-* and *go-*). Thus, words like *sore* ('that thing by you') are used not only in a "deictic" way, pointing to an object in the immediate situation, but also "anaphorically," referring back to 'that which you said before', i.e., the verbal context; similarly, *kore* means both 'this thing by me' and 'what I said before'. *Are* ('that thing over there, away from you and me') is an extremely frequent (and ambiguous) expression which could refer to *anything* that "we" (the interactants in the particular situation) supposedly all know about; interpretation is left to the listener, and nobody needs to feel threatened: *ano ne, are wa* ('well, thinking about that . . .'). Similar (very common) phrases are: *ano hito* ('that person', or 'he/she'), *sono toki* ('that time', 'then'), and *sore desu kara* ('because of that').

Even though Japanese is inherently a "dualistic" language, in the sense that extreme cases (e.g., 'yes' or 'no', 'good' or 'bad') are easier to express than intermediate, presumably more common phenomena (e.g., 'perhaps, but not likely,' 'relatively good'), in actual use there is a strong tendency to avoid polarization, and instead a continual attempt to attain an appropriate level of vagueness and ambiguity to preserve the faces of everyone concerned. In type B situations, since there is always (by definition) at least one important outsider (i.e., outside/front) present, protecting face (in the sense of social mask or repute) becomes a paramount consideration. As Goffman (1967, p. 14) notes, "the person will have two points of view—a defensive orientation toward saving his own face and a protective orientation toward saving the other's face." In Japan, if a person's face (or the collective face of a group) is challenged, the injured party will try to restore it, either defensively (the extreme case being *seppuku,* '*hara-kiri*', lit, 'bellycut') or aggressively.

Naotsuka, Sakamoto, et al. (1981, p. 135) note that "Japanese . . . give much more weight to the person's attitude, i.e., his friendly intent to please and his considerable reluctance to hurt, than to the actual words that he uses." The case is rather like that of a student who has learnt to anticipate what kind of answer the teacher expects. The intent is to please others, provided they are deemed important persons vis-à-vis oneself. In the Oxford Advanced Learner's Dictionary of Current English (1974), "empathy" is defined as the "(psychol)(power of) projecting oneself into (and so fully understanding, and losing one's identity in) a work of art or other object of contemplation." The Japanese use of *aizuchi* conforms remarkably well to this concept; it also bears some resemblance to Gordon's (1979) description of "active listening." Even if the Japanese seem to be quite good "therapists," however, they certainly are not equally willing "patients," since this empathy seldom leads to, nor is intended to elicit, an open display of inner feeling or opinion.

Expressions of assent/consent or denial/refusal offer an interesting illustration of this attitude: *hai, ha, e,* and *ē* ('yes') can all be used to confirm the truth of what someone else has just said: *"This is not an apple, is it?"*— *"Yes"* (= *'I agree* with what you just said: it is *not* an apple'); "No" here would indicate that it *is* an apple, after all (= '*contrary* to what you say'). Puzzling as this use of assent or denial may seem, still it is relatively straightforward. On the other hand, although derived from this habit of confirming the truth of what the other person has just said, the "echoing" (*aizuchi*) function of these expressions has an entirely different implication: the user just confirms that he or she is listening and tries to be pleasant.

As regards denial, apart from the "polite" use of 'no' (*ie* or *iie*), refusal is rarely expressed directly (except in trivial, nonthreatening situations); indirection, intentional ambiguity, and understatement are the rule, or the person concerned may try to divert the conversation to another topic. In extreme situations, nervous laughter, behavioral "freezing," or even trying to escape from the scene altogether, would not be unlikely reactions. In business contexts, a prolonged silence may indicate a negative reply, a loss of confidence, or an unwillingness to openly admit mistakes or difficulties; information flow is usually directed into the group rather than outwardly, *"iwanakute mo wakaru darō* ('they should understand it even if we don't mention it'). Some popular phrases with an ambiguous undertone are:

- *kekkō desu* means 'very well, fine, splendid', but is often used to imply: 'no, thank you', 'we don't want to do it', or 'it won't do'.
- *sō desu ne* 'it's like that, isn't it' or 'yes'; often used for 'no, I don't agree, but I can see your point'.
- *zehi sō shimashō* literally 'by-all-means in-your-way let-us-do', but used to signal '. . . some time, perhaps . . .'.
- *kondo ni shimasen ka* literally 'now not-do?', the ambiguous point being that *kondo*, apart from 'now', also means 'soon' or even 'another time'; the implied meaning is usually 'won't we leave it?' or 'let's drop the matter'.
- *chotto* 'wait a minute' could sometimes imply 'indefinitely'.

Mizutani (1981) well describes this tendency; Imai (1982) finds no less than 16 ways to say "no" implicitly in Japanese.

Apologies, too, could be used for evasive purposes, or just as a "social lubricant" (Naotsuka, Sakamoto, et al. 1981): *sumanai/sumimasen* (plain/polite forms; 'I am sorry', being the negative of the verb *sumu* 'be settled, be brought to a conclusion', ie 'it is not yet settled'; leaving work, subordinates are expected to say *shitsurei desu ga* to their superior, lit. 'impoliteness it-is but . . .').

In case some object belonging to somebody else breaks, even if one is not personally responsible, one is still expected to use the transitive form of the verb 'break' (i.e., 'I broke it') rather than the intransitive ('it broke') when reporting the incident to the owner (providing he or she is a person whose opinion one cares for), if there is even a marginal connection between the object and oneself; the important fact is not *who* caused the damage, but the *attitude of respect* towards the owner (Mizutani, 1981, pp. 116ff).

Becker (1975, p. 66) notes that "Joking carries the encounter along automatically, and also provides for release of tension." An interesting fact is that this only applies to type A situations in Japan, and then in a very specific sense. In a type B (formal) context, laughter usually indicates either confusion and perplexity as to the proper handling of a situation (as in situational overlap), embarrassment (if being asked an unexpected question), or just not understanding what the other person has said; in relating something sad, in order not to impose their own sorrow on the listener, people sometimes smile—another example of *omoiyari* (consideration) or *seijitsu* (sincerity). Mutual apology, rather than joking, is used to "lubricate" social contacts in type B contexts. On the other hand, in type A situations humor is permissible, but it mainly relates to basic bodily functions; there may even be some concomitant display of aggression and regression—according to Lebra (1976, p. 119), "Stupidity acted out on such occasions is actually considered a sign of manliness." In quite a different context, *manzai* comedians play at violating ritual code (*tatemae*); another kind of comedians, *rakugo*, tell set stories: it is not the stories in themselves that are important, but the way of telling them (cf. set phrases).

In Japan, face-to-face contact is crucial to get to know the other person intuitively (cf. section 3.2. *hadaka no tsukiai*, and section 3.3. *hara*); the size of Japanese expense accounts nicely illustrates this fact. Letters are less popular, for the obvious reason that you cannot modify your message in accordance with the reactions of the reader. Even when using the telephone, *aizuchi* feedback is used intensively throughout the call (substantially increasing the earnings of Japanese telephone companies).

4. IMPLICATIONS FOR DECISION-MAKING, WORK GROUP MOTIVATION, AND LEADERSHIP

Because of the long-term perspective regarding employment in Japan, smooth social relations within a work group become a necessity. We have seen above how spoken Japanese is put to use to accomplish this. But if it is true that the information-conveying function of language might stand in opposition to the social-meditating aspect, what possible consequences will this incompatibility bring to bear on decision-making and leadership?

4.1. Decision-Making

Hofstede (1980, p. 35) states that "Japanese has no equivalent for 'decision-making.'" There certainly are some words for 'decide', however:

- *kimeru* 'decide, fix, settle, agree upon, appoint, choose, resolve' (intransitive form: *kimaru*)
- *sadameru* 'decide, establish, lay down, stipulate, determine, appoint' (intransitive form: *sadamaru*)
- *kessuru* (Chinese loanword) 'decide, settle, vote on, judge'

But the process of forming decisions is specifically Japanese: it closely conforms to the general pattern of verbal interaction described in the previous section. Thus, there is a scarcity of frank, creative, and analytic debate of the pros and cons of various possible options. Instead, most important decisions are forged behind the scenes, with the help of what is known as *nemawashi* (lit. 'root-transfer', referring to the careful handling of the roots of a tree before replanting: a rather more poetic and suggestive term than its English counterpart 'spade-work'). *Nemawashi* implies a tactful (and indirect) sounding out of each group member (i.e., each "root") about his or her thoughts and feelings concerning a certain issue; it also functions as an instrument for subtle persuasion. The aim, of course, is to reach a unanimous decision, but the path to this goal is a precarious one: no group member should be led to commit himself or herself openly during these preliminary consultations lest he or she feel compromised later, should the final decision not be in line with his or her suggestion. In view of this, "decision by consensus" is a rather ambiguous denomination, implying as it does a group-discussion context for the actual decision-making process; instead, the really vital deliberations and compromises are handled very tactfully and discretely, by means of *nemawashi*, usually in several consecutive dyadic (or small group) interactions, to protect the face of everybody concerned. Go-betweens are often used in this context, to mediate among potentially conflicting interests.

Majority decisions are avoided, if at all possible; by being defeated, the minority would suffer an affront to their face, and their cooperation and commitment would be hard to enlist in the future (not only concerning the current issue). The coveted goal, rather than a coordination of individually held opinions, is a gradually emerging consensus, where individual differences of opinion (never even explicitly voiced) only very gradually (and thus in a nonthreatening manner) ooze out and blend into a pool of collectively created "opinion." There is a risk here, of course, that the price for social harmony could turn out to be no less than "inverted synergism" (as regards creativity and innovation). Although slightly reminiscent (in aim) of Gordon's (1979) "No-lose Method" of problem-solving, the Japanese way is considerably more oblique and implicit. Throughout any organization in Japan, even at the highest levels, *nemawashi* is constantly employed as a crucial tool in the decision-making process. The Japanese language seems particularly well suited for such delicate and subtle negotiations. Though this continuous consultation consumes a considerable amount of time, it is vital for securing invole ment, acceptance, and commitment. As Rohlen (1981, p. 192) notes, "to push for an early consensus or to fail to involve everyone can often lead to resentment and opposition." Even if urgent matters sometimes necessitate that a manager makes a unilateral decision, usually he or she[2] will endeavour to get post-facto general approval with the help of the same process of *nemawashi*. In a long-term perspective, quite apart from the consultation concerning the particular issue, these recurrent *nemawashi* interactions also have the important spin-off effect of helping to preserve group unity and harmony; in fact, they are often performed for this very purpose alone.

A formal decision-meeting (*kaigi*) is arranged only when all employees who will be affected by the forthcoming decision have been "consulted" repeatedly, and a general agreement seems likely. This gathering, then, is decidedly not intended as an opportunity to vent individual opinions about the relative merit of different options; on the contrary, it constitutes a formal confirmation that a consensus decision is already at hand.

Even the formal phrasing of the decision will often intentionally be kept vague, in order to permit flexibility and continued *nemawashi* during the implementation stage.

There is also a more formalized procedure of decision-making called *ringi-sei*, used especially in cases where the cooperation of different divisions is called for; initiated usually at the section level (and moving upwards), each (management) party concerned is expected to affix his or her personal seal (*hanko*) to a clearance form (*ringi-shō*) as a mark of approval. The drafter of a *ringi* proposal (usually a section head) does not work in isolation: he or she harbors a notion of what is expected of him or her by middle and top management, and at the same time it is his or her responsibility to ensure the unanimous support of his or her subordinates. Even here, as Noda (1981, p. 128) points out, "the essential decision is often made by the *nemawashi* process and the *ringi* is the formal procedure of writing and detailing the decision." Sometimes, however, the *ringi* procedure amounts, in fact, to no more than a purely formal ritual, an *ato-ringi* ('after-*ringi*'), where a post-facto approval is sought for a decision that has already been made at upper levels.

A conception we seem to cherish about our own decision-making style in the West is that we first define the problem and then search for a solution; Mayntz (1976), describing a study of policy development in the German federal bureaucracy, asserts that "Decisions in organizations are rarely taken by individuals," that they "are rarely triggered by preconceived goals," and that the decision-making process is "an iterative one" rather than a goals-means dichotomy. Noda (1981, p. 144) claims that "The top executives in a Japanese company prefer to avoid the cool ra-

---

[2]Even though the expression "he or she" is used below in referring to managers, in the vast majority of cases the Japanese manager is a male. According to the Statistical Handbook of Japan 1985, p. 105, the figure for 1984 was 93.9%.

tional presentation of options where advocates neatly present all the arguments for each option. They prefer that an obvious solution emerge from these long discussions with a broad range of company employees so that, when a decision is finally made, the overwhelming majority in the company can see why such a decision is desirable and necessary." In a similar vein, Hofstede (1980, p. 381) suggests that "In complex decision-making situations 'facts' no longer exist independently from the people who define them, so 'fact-based management' becomes a misleading slogan; intuition may not be a bad method of deciding in such cases. And if, for their implementation, decisions need the commitment of many people, a consensus process, even if it takes more time, is an asset rather than a liability." When comparing time consumption in different kinds of decision-making processes, we should perhaps consider the issue in a broader perspective:

- What is the total time needed from the first conception of an idea right up to its successful implementation, and
- what are the potential costs of *not* anchoring a decision extensively, before taking action?

4.2. Work Group Motivation and Leadership

Nakane (1973) distinguishes what she calls 'frame' (a specific locality, institution, or situation) from 'attribute' (by birth or achievement); in Japan, 'frame' rather than 'attribute' is the prime determining factor for human relationships. Rather than kinship ties or ability, then, the very fact of appearing in a particular context for an extended period of time, together with others, constitutes the main prerequisite for securing harmonious social relations and group unity. As shown above, there is even a linguistically encoded classification of people into concentric circles, with 'us' in the center and 'them' outside; group cohesion is forged, with the help of language, by defining 'them' as separate and different. As Mizutani (1981, p. 61) points out, "Attacking outsiders = strengthening group solidarity." Intragroup rapport and vitality, then, is bought at the price of severe intergroup competition, even within a company. Vogel (1981, p. xxi) emphasizes that, "Indeed, it is partly a reflection of the deep involvement of individuals in the organization that these rivalries are so intense." In fact, with section heads (*kachō*) being judged according to the performance of their respective groups, the prime concern of middle management is in trying to maintain close personal relations (by means of *nemawashi* consultation) with all competing group leaders (*kachō*) in an effort to preserve an acceptable degree of lateral coordination and co-operation. It is here, especially, that the *ringi-sei* procedure plays a potentially crucial role: Noda (1981, p. 138), describing organizational development efforts, notes that "The intention was to correct the drawbacks in an organizational format so heavily dependent on the *ringi*. However, it became clear that it was nearly impossible to define objectively the content or scope of administrative jobs."

A section is in fact the basic unit of a Japanese company (headed by a *kachō*). Since an organization constitutes a 'frame', the section head is likely to be older than his subordinates (i.e., he or she has appeared within the 'frame' for a longer time); he or she is not necessarily more competent (competence being an 'attribute'). Nor are his or her subordinates explicitly evaluated individually as to their merits or faults; it is the collective result of work group endeavor which is important, not individual ability—it could even prove a liability, in the sense that the exceptionally able individual deviates too conspicuously from the others, thus risking exclusion. This does not necessarily imply that his or her competence is not benefitted from, but only that he or she themselves, as individuals, are not allowed to stand out from the group. Yoshino (1981, p. 153) points out that, "In the best Japanese tradition, the demonstration of concern and effort is often as important as the results achieved." These work groups, although being discretely watched, are allowed some degree of autonomy; socially, as well, they form a self-contained unit (even if group members also identify with the company as such).

Seating arrangements within an office usually underscore the importance attached to face-to-face contact: the superior, sharing room with his or her subordinates (unless he or she is a member of top management), occupies a strategic position from which he or she can survey the whole scene at a glance; if possible, group members (usually less than 25 people, of various ages) sit facing each other, rather than in isolation.

Social relations at work mirror conditions in a family: the experience of rapport within a group does not eradicate status differences; instead, emotional bonds, reminiscent of parent-child dyads, often develop between younger and older group members. The formal roles of superior/ subordinate transform into relationships of mutual trust and interdependence: *senpai/kōhai* ('senior/junior) or *oyabun/kobun* ('parent-part/ child-part'). Though the older person plays the role of mentor, he or she is, himself or herself, in an equally dependent position vis-á-vis his or her protegé. There is a wish, ideally, for the same *ninjō* (feeling of sympathy, humanity; see section 3.2.) that is presumed to arise spontaneously between a parent and a child, to be evoked in this interdependent relationship as well; the status inequality, however, will still be preserved in their respective ways of addressing each other. In fact, to be 'friends' (*tomodachi*) is conceivable only between group members of the same age and sex (i.e., between persons having approximately the same status, since age and sex are the crucial criteria); all other relationships remain unequal. The *kachō* (section head), then, cannot expect to form friendships with members of his or her own work group, since he or she is probably their senior. Potential candidates for friendship are other *kachō* of his or her own age and sex; towards them, however, he or she is likely to feel some degree of rivalry, due to intergroup competition.

Even if he or she has developed *senpai/kōhai* relationships with members of his or her own work group, his or her position is nevertheless rather delicate; it is the classical case of double loyalties: each *kachō* is likely to be a *kōhai* (junior) vis-á-vis another *senpai* (senior) with an even higher status (who, in his or her turn etc . . .; the same pattern is usually duplicated throughout an organization, cf. Nakane, 1973). This relationship, too, is one of mutual trust and interdependence. Giving orders (*meirei*), direction (*shiji*), or guidance (*shidō*) becomes a precarious balancing act: if too direct, there is a danger that he or she will be gradually (even linguistically) excluded from group life, being transformed into one of 'them' instead of belonging to 'us'; if this happens, he or she will probably lose even the opportunity for subtle persuasion. On the other hand, if he or she is too oblique, his or her group will not perform properly, even if he or she remains an insider. In all likelihood, a considerable degree of mastery of the *nemawashi* process will be required in order to preserve smooth relations at both ends.

Since Japanese people often have few aquaintances outside the social networks of their family and work group, they naturally tend to expect satisfying social relations at work (since women are generally expected to abstain from a full-time career after they marry, their social networks tend to get even more restricted); they expect to be consulted, if only to feel then they are part of a socially "meaningful" context. Thus, whether a manager likes it or not, he or she is more or less compelled to find the time needed for *nemawashi, ringi-sei*, "discussions," meetings, parties, picnics, or excursions to *onsen* (hot springs). But no matter how much the manager exerts himself, his or her subordinates are likely to feel at least some degree of frustration at times, or even aggression towards other group members. What probably saves a group in such situations is the pronounced task orientation of Japanese work groups, encouraging purposeful action rather than passivity. Rohlen (1981, p. 200) notes that "Increased emphasis on ability in promotions, on character-building programs, and on penalties for poor performance are all aimed at the individual rather than the group. These attempts, although minor, are indications of management impatience with the inadequacies of the group-motivation approach." In fact, Cooper and Arbose (1984), reporting on the results of an *International Management* 10-country survey on executive stress, note that no less than 29.8% of the Japanese managers find interpersonal relations a stressful factor at work (this was the highest figure among the ten countries), and 34% experience job dissatisfaction (the second highest figure).

It would seem, then, that the Japanese management model has its flaws; the pronounced emphasis on social relations, in the particularly Japanese way—even subtly encoded in their language—has apparently not been successful in every respect; the reported negative effects on management well-being would merit a closer investigation.

5. CONCLUDING REMARKS

The Japanese seem to use their language in a paradoxical way: while on the one hand coveting an unequivocal vocabulary for social relationships, where any uncertainty as to group affinity and relative status would be intolerable, on the other, they crave a high degree of ambiguity concerning personal views and individual preferences. They lay emphasis on 'frame' rather than 'attribute'; they concentrate on appropriate form rather than information content; and behind it all, there is a basic distrust of words . . .

Somewhat surprisingly, spoken interaction—despite being such a commonplace and inevitable phenomenon in any organization—does not appear to be a particularly common topic in economic research. We seem to take language for granted. Even in linguistics, analysis of face-to-face verbal behavior is a relatively new—though rapidly developing—field of interest. Halliday (1978, p. 192) notes that, "After a period of intensive study of language as an idealized philosophical construct, linguists have come round to taking account of the fact that people talk to each other." The aim of the current paper was to demonstrate that analysis of verbal behavior patterns might well be a valuable research tool even in economics. Halliday (1978, p. 233) in fact suggests several possible applications, e.g., "How are decisions made, and how are they transmitted? What are the *linguistic* features of the decision processes?" and "Where are the *breakdowns* in communication, and why?"

Marvelling, from a safe distance, at the "peculiar" ways in which the Japanese use *their* language, we should perhaps take the opportunity to turn and look back:

· how would *a Japanese* tend to describe *our* way of behaving verbally? *Our* leadership styles? The way *we* form decisions?
· are they justified in their belief—or fear—that social harmony and information flow are incompatible aspects of language?

REFERENCES

Argyle, M. (1967). *The psychology of interpersonal behaviour.* Harmondsworth, England: Penguin Books.

Barnlund, D.C. (1975). *Public and private self in Japan and the United States: Communicative styles of two cultures.* Tokyo, Japan: Simul Press.

Becker, E. (1975). The self as a locus of linguistic causality. In D. Brissett & C. Edgley (Eds.), *Life as theater* (pp. 58-67). Chicago, IL: Aldine Publishing Company.

Berger, P.L., & Luckmann, T. (1967). *The social construction of reality.* Garden City, NY: Doubleday.

Chomsky, N. (1965). *Aspects of the theory of syntax.* Cambridge, MA: MIT Press.

Cooper, C., & Arbose, J. (1984). Executive stress goes global. *International Management: Europe, 39* (5), 42-48.

Doi, T. (1981). *The anatomy of dependence.* Tokyo, Japan: Kodansha.

Dunn, C.J., & Yanada, S. (1958). *Japanese.* Sevenoaks, England: Hodder and Stoughton.

Goffman, E. (1967). *Interaction ritual.* Garden City, NY: Doubleday.

Goldstein, B.Z., & Tamura, K. (1975). *Japan and America: A comparative study in language and culture.* Tokyo, Japan: Tuttle.

Gordon, T. (1979). *Leader effectiveness training L.E.T.* London: Futura Publications.

Halliday, M.A.K. (1971). Language structure and language function. In Lyons, J. (Ed.) *New horizons in linguistics* (pp. 140-165). Harmondsworth, England: Penguin Books.

Halliday, M.A.K. (1973). *Explorations in the function of language.* London: Edward Arnold.

Halliday, M.A.K. (1978). *Language as social semiotic.* London: Edward Arnold.

Hinds, J. (1982). Japanese conversational structures, *Lingua, 57,* 301-326.

Hofstede, G.H. (1980) *Culture's consequences: International Differences in work-related values."* London: Sage.

Imai, M. (1982). *Never take YES for an answer.* Tokyo, Japan: The Simul Press.

Lebra, T.S. (1976). *Japanese patterns of behavior.* Honolulu: The University Press of Hawaii.

Mayntz, R. (1976). Conceptual Models of Organizational Decision-Making and their Application to the Policy Process. In G. Hofstede & M.S. Kassem (Eds.), *European contributions to organization theory* (pp. 114-125). Assen, The Netherlands: Van Gorkum.

Minami, H. (1981). *Psychology of the Japanese people.* Tokyo, Japan: University of Tokyo Press.

Mizutani, O. (1981). *Japanese: The spoken language in Japanese life.* Tokyo, Japan: The Japan Times Ltd.

Nakane, C. (1973). *Japanese Society.* Harmondsworth, England: Penguin Books.

Naotsuka, R., Sakamoto, N., Hirose, T., Hagihara, H., Ohta, J., Maeda, S., Hara, T., & Iwasaki, K. (1981). *Mutual understanding of different cultures.* Osaka, Japan: Science Education Institute of Osaka Prefecture.

Noda, K. (1981). Big business organization. In E.F. Vogel (Ed.), *Modern Japanese organization and decision-making* (pp. 115-145). Tokyo, Japan: Tuttle.

Rohlen, T.P. (1981). The company work group. In E.F. Vogel (Ed.), *Modern Japanese organization and decision-making* (pp. 185-209). Tokyo, Japan: Tuttle.

Rommetveit, R. (1974). *On message structure.* London: John Wiley & Sons.

Sethi, S.P., Namiki, N., & Swanson, C.L. (1984). *The false promise of the Japanese miracle.* Marshfield, MA: Pitman Publishing.

Statistical Handbook of Japan 1985. Statistics Bureau/Management and Coordination Agency (1985). Tokyo, Japan: Japan Statistical Association.

Vogel, E.F. (1981). *Modern Japanese organization and decision-making.* Tokyo, Japan: Tuttle.

Whorf, B.L.W. (1956). *Language, thought, and reality*. Cambridge, MA: MIT Press.

Yoshino, M.Y. (1981). Emerging Japanese multinational enterprises. In E.F. Vogel (Ed.,), *Modern Japanese organization and decision-making*. (pp. 146-166). Tokyo, Japan: Tuttle.

7

The Japanese Culture of Organizational Communication

Edward C. Stewart

INTRODUCTION

Since 1945, the United States has been the dominant technological power in the world. With other major industries left in ruins by the destruction of World War II, American industrial productivity capacity provided the major means and resource for reconstructing from the devastations in the world. But by the 1970s, the American industrial plant was considerably older than those of West Germany or of Japan, losing part of its competitive edge as American productive performance declined. The Japanese industrial plant underwent far more drastic structural changes than either the American or European capital equipment. In industry after industry, the Japanese expanded capacity, improved productivity, and then used their economic capability to penetrate and saturate markets. The Japanese strategy of economic activity prevented capital equipment from aging to the same degree as in the American industrial plant, but, by the late 1970s, many Japanese industries had been compelled to contract sharply as the rapid expansion of their industry came to an end. The Japanese high risk strategy of economic development has resulted in the elimination of capacity in some industries, has been costly to the Japanese economy, and will require a restructuring of Japanese institutions to accommodate the shrinkage of its agricultural employment, to meet the needs of disadvantaged groups, such as women, and to adapt to the changing values of the successor generation, the one born since the war, as it gains access to power in the government and in the private sector. The future of the Japanese economy seems to rely more on social and cultural factors than on economic ones, in the same way that the success for the economic performance of the last 30 years generates from Japanese culture and society and not from its technology, which is imported from the West although perfected in Japan.

The Japanese people, living on crowded islands, lead a precarious life despite external signs of economic vigor. Japan must rely on imports for much of its foodstuffs and, in 1978, was dependent on foreign sources for 86.3% of its energy requirements. The economic success of Japan cannot be attributed to abundance of resources, as has been said of the American economy, nor to geography. Japan lacks a tradition of admiring merchants or businessmen, which might have produced the current state of modernization. An inquiry into the Japanese success must probe for cultural and social factors, which in the face of great odds have produced the contemporary Japanese economic state. Numerous studies exist on Japanese industry and modernization. Writing from the point of view of management, Pasoale and Athos (1981), or from the point of view of the economy (Allen, 1981), or sociology (Clark, 1979), include valuable information about the cultural base of the Japanese industrial system, but do not provide a firm foothold in culture. Others, such as Vogel (1979) in *Japan as Number One*, apparently intent on alarming and educating Americans while uplifting the Japanese, avoids a systematic cultural analysis. In all of these works, culture appears as a peripheral factor, leaving a gap between Japanese industry and economy, on the one hand, and culture and social systems on the other. Works on Japanese culture typically only suggest the connection with organizational communication, but do not elaborate it. The writers either did not intend to look at the cultural base of Japanese industry, or they used Western concepts to analyze it, with the result that the analyses are seriously flawed. Things Japanese become elusive when approached with Western organizing ideas and terminology (van Wolferen, 1982, p. 121). Before describing the Japanese culture of organizational communication, it is necessary to confront the conceptual barriers to understanding Japanese ways.

CONCEPTUAL BARRIERS TO UNDERSTANDING JAPANESE CULTURE

Diffuse Calculus of Belonging

Belonging is an attribute for Westerners. When we say that "Smith is with Kyoda," we speak at the level of psychology, and imply that Smith has a personality with identity and motivation, forming an absolute and independent person. Smith's beliefs, attitudes, and ideologies, not to mention contracts, form the link with Kyoda at the level of the organization. Kyoda, assumed by Westerners to be entirely separate from the individual, is understood to have a structure of substantive reality which can be analyzed in terms such as corporate culture, management, and personnel. At a more general level of society, Westerners speak of democracy, capitalism, and class, once more suggesting that integrated structures exist at the level of sociology. Analyses based on such concepts define and measure the attributes of individuals, groups, and society, and yield a center and stark clean lines of explication (van Wolfenren, 1982, p. 121). Although the validity of such structural analyses has been questioned (Shils, 1975, p. 111), they serve Western societies reasonably well, but fail to pass cultural inspection when applied to explain Japan. The structural concepts used by Westerners produce a distorted representation of what Japanese culture is like.

Belonging for the Japanese is *identity*—the words used for "I" imply "the representative of my house, Kyoda," rather than personality, society, or culture. The Japanese reference point is the network of membership (Yoshimura, 1986), and not the Western concepts of personality, organization, and society. The Japanese subject of analysis is the social context in which the individual lives and works. The Japanese representation is close to the Western notion of "network," in which neither individual behavior nor even dyadic links appear as significant structure (Whitten & Wolfe, 1973, p. 720). Its representation reaches the core of Japanese character. Japanese are reassured that, in the privacy of their own thoughts, they experience what is common to others. Thus personal introversion of shared experience composes Japanese individuality (Morley, 1985, p. 120). The Japanese acts, feels, thinks, and decides as if the network, and symbolically Japan, would act through him (Singer, 1973, p. 109). Cooperation in group life, active dedication, and self-sacrifice are the means for realizing the true self (Kyogoku, 1985, p. 7). Japanese respond to human relations as fish to water, and are borne by it as sea gulls by air currents. Lacking transcendental moral principles, actions are governed by a vague sense of appropriateness, accord (*wa*), and a drive to occupy the proper place within the network. The identity with members of the network is relational and it is expressed concretely as participation. Japanese culture is a civilization of everyday life (Hasegawa, 1965, p. 27).

Japanese belonging is more a calculus or a process than a structure; and identity is like polarizations or centers of gravity. Their chief characteristic is diffusion. Belonging by participation has little to do with beliefs. The Japanese are driven to improve and to sustain their social pride and ambition, and they often give evidence that they are clearer about what they are not than what they are. They leave little doubt about who are insiders and outsiders, but the critical attributes for belonging are often particular, not absolute, and they do not stick to Western standards of classification. They respond to persons rather than to abstractions, and they are much more sensitive to immediately present authority figures than to remote persons, systems of status, or abstract principles such as justice. Continuity and need are of greater importance then what is right and just (Singer, 1973, p. 57). The language does not provide a concept of public with the range of application and potential for creating political issues and parties (Morley, 1985, pp. 120-124). Perhaps even more than in the West, political leaders engage the consciousness and interest of citizens only at events such as elections or celebrations, or at times of crisis. Religion appears in life events and social occasions: birth, rites of passage, weddings, examinations, festivals, and death. There are no confessions to make, initiations to endure, or beliefs to accept.

> There is no ethic based on moral commandments laid down by a transcendent creator—god, nor is there the tradition of prophets who transmit the righteous anger of the creator—god to those in power. (Kyogoku, 1985, p. 7)

Religious commitment to Shintoism and Buddhism means appropriate participation in rituals and festivals and observance of customs and traditions. Besides the political considerations based on secular pragmatism, there is no moral restraint against the corruption of power.

Barrier #1:   American thinking is attributional; Japanese is relational. Individuals, groups, and even society are detached and relatively absolute for Americans, but relational for the Japanese. As a consequence, Americans consistently overemphasize the significance of the person, the group, and the social order; miss the criticality of the links, attachments, and relationships; and misjudge the significance of gifts, payments, favors, and other means used to create obligation and dependence strengthening relationships. (See barrier #11 of the analytical correlate of #1.)

Barrier #2:   Japanese belonging and identity overlap considerably, while American identity is relatively independent of belonging. Japanese belonging is primarily participation and action, therefore highly particular and contextualized, while American belonging has a conceptual base of belief, attitude, and ideology, usually understood as goal, reason, or purpose for joining a group. Participation is carried out on a narrow gauge for performing tasks and providing special outlets, as in a social club. Americans consistently misinterpret Japanese business conduct, are baffled by the time and nature of planning and decision making, and are constantly surprised by the quickness of implementation and capacity for changing.

Geometry of Japanese Thinking

In his book, reflecting on his experiences in Japan during the 1930s, Singer introduces the concept of geometry of social and mental space to characterize the general pattern of cultures (Singer, 1973, pp. 94–104). Japanese geometry displays two terrain features: vertical differentiation according to rank in a hierarchy, and the great horizontal divide between insiders and outsiders (*uchi-soto*). Although all societies to a degree make the two distinctions, unlike any other culture the distinction of *uchi* and outsiders is the hinge of the Japanese social order (Nakane, 1973, p. 7). Outsiders do not qualify for normal social amenities, explaining the callous Japanese treatment of strangers. Indeed, moral, ethical, and social regulation of behavior is restricted to those living as insiders.

Taut inside relations are often strengthened by the negative valence of exclusion of outsiders, and its power may exceed the positive one of inclusion of insiders. The camaraderie which develops within a group may be compared to the bonds developed among American soldiers in combat under fire, created and sustained by the danger of the enemy. Once the danger is past, the bonds slacken and may disappear. In a similar way, Japanese groups seem to require a real or imagined opposition from outside groups to retain identity. When the Japanese group travels to countries such as the United States, they risk disintegration, since American social organizations, built on attraction among group members rather than enmity toward outsiders, do not provide to Japanese groups the effective opposition required for them to thrive. The social pressures upon inside members of the group are severe. Efforts to escape the compression of groups feed the drive to negotiate the labyrinth of the organization and climb up the steps of the hierarchy.

The horizontal divide of Japanese culture is reflected in communication and in social values. It is on the inside that Japanese can display spontaneous behavior and reveal the inner identity of natural feelings and tendencies, *honne* in Japanese. Communication and social life follow well established forms so that relations within the family observe proper precedent, but, on the job and outside the immediate family, ceremonial and formal modes of expression, custom, and behavior take over. Westerners see this as maintaining face, which in Japan is *tatemae*. It takes precedence over inner identity, although it is *honne* that is the dynamism within the society. These two phases of Japanese identity represent the stress than the Japanese put on the social web of the society, and the relative neglect of talent.

Singer observes that Japanese life allocates less room to genius and intelligence than any other great civilization. In today's Japan, selection of personnel still slights intelligence and academic achievements. Demonstrated ability for integration in groups and known connections—such as being a graduate of the right university—are used rather than ability or intelligence, as favorable markers of a promising employee.

> With a unique determination and persistence, stress is laid on the harmony of the whole, on unbroken continuity, on jealous safeguarding of enduring patterns which are preferably enshrined in semiconscious automatisms. These qualities, while perhaps hindering Japanese civilisation from producing many men or many works or more than national significance, have helped to give the whole of Japanese civilisation a paradigmatic value. Japan has to offer few contributions to world culture except this signal one: to have given an example of a style of life subordinating everything to one value: duration. (Singer, 1973, pp. 94–95)

Unbroken continuity has a double significance. First, it refers to survival. Although duration might be associated with any culture, none observe it as scrupulously as the Japanese. For instance, the Japanese approach a first meeting warily, since each one understands that a permanent relationship may be established. Each one is on guard not to be caught in an unfavorable situation. When Japanese become acquainted, as in a classroom in college, the relationship becomes long lasting. Once started, continuity takes over as a value in addition to harmony, although Singer suggests that continuity takes precedence over harmony. The explanation lies with the identity for the individual provided by the relationship.

Relational belonging in Japanese life creates a mystique for personal exchanges. The focus of the culture on the interpersonal encounter is frequently described as orientation to immediate experience, and it is typical for Japanese to use the full powers of perception and mental concentration to guide the fulfillment of attachments and obligations in concrete events. Japanese behavior is contextualized to a degree incomprehensible to Westerners.

The withholding of fulfillment and the commemoration of incompleteness exercise a profound influence on Japanese sensibility and action. Unhappiness is much more finely articulated than happiness. Japanese pessimism is fatalism, becomes serene despair, and is transformed into a moral doctrine that canonizes unhappiness as a form of spiritual discipline, deemed desirable and even beautiful. The power of absent fulfillment imposes discipline for endurance but restraint on emotions in Japanese regulation of life (Morley, 1985, 179–180).

There is in Japanese communication and social relationships a hide-and-seek cadence which conceals the Japanese spirit. Japanese silence and meditation is implosive, poised on the brink of action. There is a raw sensibility of fate and fatalism in Japanese emotions. Thought and action appear molded by perpetual comparisons with others. Energy and learning spring from within, but competitiveness is closely regulated by the hierarchical social structure of seniority in age, rank, and position. Actions and initiative must be adjusted to precedents and rules to preserve harmony. The social discipline required for living and working suppresses the inner resources, and yet its web unalterably defines identity.

Perhaps the cadence of communication is the most revealing feature of the Japanese spirit. Speakers using the Japanese style of communication create the impression that they use language to retain information about their own immediate situation. The Japanese seem to prefer open-ended statements, in which implicit and indirect use of language, and omissions apparently serve to exclude outsiders. When judged as social participation, the Japanese language in use functions more for exclusion than for inclusion, for inner group solidarity (Morley, 1985, pp. 70–79). Communication is incomplete as sentences trail off, and subjects are omitted. Much is left unsaid. This style fits in with the Japanese appreciation of incompletion and insufficiency in the arts, crafts—with emotional restraint and effacement of presence (Morley, 1985, pp. 179–180). Nevertheless, even an absence is part of communication, and suggests a part of the field that is out of sight, the land beyond which completes the wholeness of the Japanese geometry; the concealed, the invisible and the disguised imperceptibly intrude into communication, and into the receiver's search behind spoken words for what was really meant. The insistence of the wholeness of life compels consciousness to span the known and the unknown and to include contradictions, as communication continues with hide and seek.

The land beyond is known in time as much as in space, but it is not the American time of measurement as in time and motion studies, nor of control as in deadlines. The Japanese

> are neither strongly built nor steadfast and unswerving, but after each disaster they are ready to begin a new phase of life without looking back; yet they carry into the future the whole past of their race, in minds incapable of forgetting. It is not space that rules this form of existence, but time, duration, spontaneous change, continuity of movement. (Singer, 1973, 147)

Japanese preoccupation is with origins more than with the past, with impermanence more than with passage of time, and with the innovation in technology rather than with antiques. The diffusion of belonging, the ambiguity of communication, and the sensitivity to what is not said or done precipitates a contradiction. Japanese belonging and identity are realized by participation; but how is coordinatoin achieved? Rather than accepting the uncertainty of this situation, in the business climate, the Japanese show one of the highest levels of avoidance of uncertainty (Hofstede, 1980, p. 165). This contradiction is resolved by restricting contacts and work to small groups that remain together indefinitely, and by searching back from origins and precedents, yielding rules and forms of conduct. It is not principles or explanations which the Japanese seek, but was it done or not, and how. Implementation of rules and the duration of social relations among small groups reduce the uncertainties of life which loom obsessively in the Japanese mind.

The Japanese spirit expresses itself in a holistic and flexible range of experience. The various dualities that we have reviewed do not appear as contradictions to the Japanese as they do to Westerners. In each case, the contradiction is resolved by the construction of a pragmatic intention which encompasses both ends of the polarity. This fusion of opposites is characteristic of the Japanese temperament.

Barrier #3: The two divides in Japanese society, vertical hierarchy and inside–outside separation, assure that virtually every judgment and decision contains a social base graduated according to rank in the society, in distinction to the greater conceptual base of equivalent American dispositions. This Japanese fusion is misinterpreted, since it lacks a Western conceptual term to represent it. What Americans see as social or affiliation is closer to the exercise of power disguised as a natural event. The presence of power is partly derived from the influence of exclusion of outsiders as the drive for cohesion in the group. The strength and function of exclusion is systematically misinterpreted by Americans who respond to attraction in forming groups.

Barrier #4: Americans systematically miss the Japanese dynamic of behavior in *honne*, separating it from *tatemae* in the way that motivation is separated from human relations in American culture. But, for the Japanese, outer social form is only another phase of the inner world of the individual. Americans respond only to the outer form and apparent conformity of the Japanese.

Barrier #5: Americans are blocked from understanding Japanese-directed activities by the influence of American decision making, particularly its conceptual base of deciding by anticipating consequences of the courses of action considered. The Japanese rely on precedents and rules which automatically introduce tradition, continuity, and power at the base of their judgment and commitments.

Barrier #6: Language and behavior seem to function to conceal and to protect insiders by excluding outsiders. Americans misinterpret and are baffled by this mechanism. Reliance on rules and precedents compensates for the ambiguity, frequently shared by the Japanese themselves, and avoids uncertainty.

Models, Medium, and Imitation

The dome of imitation suspended over Japanese behavior implies the presence of a model held in common, explaining the remarkable sameness of the Japanese sense of appropriateness (Morley, 1985, 54). The presence of the model is seldom appreciated by Westerners. Our interest resides in the consequences of the model, rather than judgments of it. Its presence indicates a Japanese approach to learning and to behavior, more profound in implications than the judgment of Westerners who see the influence of the model as a deficiency: as lack of originality and as conformity. Orientation to learning through imitation replaces Western models that are more functional and problem-solving oriented. Imitation and rote memorization and learning encourage attention to details and to perfect replication. In the absence of open ended initiatives on the part of the learner, the remaining field for personal expression is in the cultivation of form and style in what is learned. Imitation in learning and conformity in social affairs, both associated with the model, require judgments and evaluations based on matching and comparing particular things and events with the model.

The role of imitating, comparing, and matching in learning and judgment induces emotional restraint and creates the conditions for fatalism in which the person serves as the medium for the expression of natural and social forces. This capacity for displacing causes to external sources is of fundamental importance. For example, the Japanese part in World War II has been interpreted by some Japanese as a natural disaster and therefore as absolving the Japanese from any responsibility for it. The opposite face of this displacement is the ideal Japanese strategy for exercising power, in which human actions are interpreted as the force of natural events and not human intentions.

Barrier #7: Japanese make judgments by comparisons of like things and appear to avoid judgments by potential results or absolute qualities of things judged. This relational feature in judging is often ignored or trivialized by Americans, who also use comparative judgments but not so systematically as the Japanese.

Barrier #8:   Quality is conveyed by refined measurements of details presenting a barrier to Americans who, more than Japanese, assess quality as effectiveness or consequences.

Western-Japanese Analysis

To the Westerner, Japanese culture does not reveal its inner workings easily. Analysis is required to lay bare even the commonplaces of daily life. Western analyses typically take shape on a dichotomy which separates abstract theory or principles from their concrete manifestations. An explanation consists of showing the causal link between the principle and occurrences. The analytical strategy is potentially embedded in most Indo-European languages, which stress a separation of subject from predicate. Thus, English predisposes its users to describe fixed relationships between subject or things and their qualities or attributes (Fisher, 1972, p. 111). The statement, "The Japanese import few American cars," leads to explanations based on attributes of the Japanese market, 'it is closed'; or of American cars, 'they are of poor quality.' Relational explanations based on exchange rates, Japanese customer preferences, political considerations, or marketing strategies are overshadowed by the language's tendency to suggest that something is or is not. English is less effective in describing variable conditions of a process which are not exactly one way or another. These explanations become the objects of research analysis and usually conform to abstract ideas used to explain the concrete fact. English and American thinking are strong in their conception of action and events since English has the pattern of actor–action–result.

   The Japanese language does not place an equal emphasis on the dichotomy between subject and predicate, and therefore the language naturally combines abstractions and concrete manifestations. (The Japanese meaning of an American car imported to Japan is automatically associated with driving it.) Furthermore, the language is terminal; it leaps to the conclusions without carrying the user along in the process of reaching the conclusions as does the English language in the sequence of actor–action–result. Thus, Japanese predisposes its speakers to think in relational terms, since this is how the language classifies linguistic objects. For example, English separates an individual or a person from a group; these are distinct and separate ideas. When the individual joins a group and becomes a group member, the person is in a group but remains an individual. In Japanese, there is no clear synonym for group. "Guluupu" is the Japanese pronunciation for the English word group, and it is used to refer to the emotional involvement found in informal groups, but does not convey the idea of group cohesion or structure, the quality or attribute in which English is strong. A second word is used, *shuudan*, to refer to a set of people of a certain quality:

> For instance, a group of people who are graduates from renowned universities and working for distinguished companies is called "elite-'shudan.' " Apparently, these people do not necessarily share emotional backgrounds so that "shudan" does not have the quality which we want to analyze in order to understand the Japanese. (Yoshimura, 1986, pp. 33–34)

The word does not convey the connotations about structure and other attributes of the group. In short, the Japanese do not pick up the English dichotomy between the individual and the social order. The language, of course, has the capacity of suggesting the division, but not through the choice of single words, as in English, that connote both ends of a lineal dichotomy of individual at one end and group at the other. Words in Japanese serve more as prototypes than exclusive categories. In classifying, the Japanese avoid both the dimension and the separation of meaning. Their classification system is relational, not divisive as in English, combining both ends of what in English would be clear polarities. The abstract and concrete fuse, and, instead of concepts, images almost mythological in their foundation dominate in Japanese thought (Akiyama, 1986). Since the heart of Western analysis rests on separating abstract principles from concrete occurrences, and establishing objectivity, Japanese social reality eludes Western organizing and analytical concepts. A Western counterpart to the Japanese conceptualization would be a prototype which explains an idea and simultaneously stands for its concrete occurrence as a graph or picture.

The analytical block has been anticipated in the substance of preceding examples. The barriers block understanding at the abstract level as well as the concrete level of performance. Practicality for Americans implies specific performances to attain concrete objectives that are understood to be thing-like—technically called *object*. In view of Japanese ways with classification, their understanding of concrete and practical are different from the American. Concrete is not thing-like, but relational. For the Japanese, a concrete and practical suggestion would be one that identifies an effective and available human relationship for precipitating the action desired.

Barrier #9:   Images dominate Japanese thought. Japanese fuse opposites in the form of prototypes, dissolving contradictions, or contextualize opposites separately. Americans think more abstractly and separate opposites, forming dichotomies.

Barrier #10:   Japanese concentrate on details, measurements, and showing how these are related to their models. This orientation is an unsatisfactory explanation for Americans who focus on causes and analyze attributes of things.

Barrier #11:   American analyses of Japanese culture in English consistently overstate the thing-like quality, and understate the diffusion, the contextualization, and social naturalness of Japanese culture.

Surface and Deep Culture

For the purpose of this study, we make a distinction between two meanings of culture. How people dress, the expressions on their faces, and hand gestures are examples of surface culture, since they are observable. But much of culture lies below the surface and cannot be observed, but can be inferred from careful observation of behavior and of surface culture. The inferences made from the surface represent deep culture, comprising both values and patterns of thinking. The important aspect of culture can be defined as the values and orientations in a society and these can be seen as plans, rules, or "programs" (Geertz, 1973, p. 44). These can be summarized as "control mechanisms" that organize human diversity and govern behavior.

Japanese control mechanisms are social in nature, but the conclusion suffers from concept fatigue. In Japan, it is difficult to separate "political" and "social." The difficulty traces back to the Japanese social relational identity which prevents separating the exercise of power from the social structure. The sate is inseparable from the society, and laws are deemed legitimate by the Japanese people because they are administered by a class of persons who traditionally have held the right to do so (van Wolfenren, 1982, pp. 129–130).

Although surface vs. deep culture is a useful distinction in Japan, patterns of communication serve to illustrate a significant difference with the West. Japanese senders transmit symbols which serve to "signal" instead of "convey" their meaning, encouraging receivers to search behind the words used and the expressions perceived for the real meaning of what was said. Japanese psychology deals with consciousness and gives much less attention to the Western preoccupation with the unconscious.

Whereas Western psychology is better conveyed by a vertical distance, the Japanese fits a horizontal distinction between surface and deep culture, perhaps better put as "front" (*omote*) and behind in the "back" area (*ura*) (Lebra, 1976, p. 112). A good example occurs in the dispensation of favors in Japan, often confused with the exercise of power:

> What is in Japan popularly mistaken for the exercise of political power are the personal privileges, the ability to relay requests to the bureaucrats for favours on behalf of lobbying supporters. The most practical influence for the politicians consists of rewarding their constituencies with special building projects and subsidies. But their significance in the legislative process is almost totally ceremonial. Their Diet debates are elaborate democratically reassuring performances that have, with few exceptions, no influence on developments in the country's affairs. (van Wolfenren, 1982, 123)

In American culture, the surface is used to probe for values and purposes and patterns of thinking which make up deep culture, but in Japan a similar probe cannot omit a search for other people acting in the background.

Barrier #12: The exotic surface of Japanese society and behavior misleads Americans to base judgments on surface culture, assuming deep purposes where there may be none. On the other hand, Westerners frequetly misperceive. For example, visible dispensers of favors are frequently identified as power figures, which they are not. The power figures remain concealed.

Empathic Communication

Although some communicators have shown considerable interest in nonverbal communication, in comparison with the Japanese, Americans rely on language to convey the intentions of the sender. More so than the Japanese, American messages are plain, direct, and mean what they say. The words used serve as *conduits* for the meaning which the sender wishes to convey to the receiver, understanding the message is more or less reflexive, and its art consists of using the right words, capturing the attention of the listener, and adapting the message to the receiver's interest and level of understanding. Nonverbal communication gives an accent to the message.

Japanese communication is full of indirections, suggestions, and ambiguities. The course of communication seems to move in circles before swerving to touch lightly on the subject toward the end of the message. Words may be described as signals alerting the receiver about how to interpret what has been said. Quick, fleeting perceptions register stimulation from the sender's body language, tone of voice, smells, touches. The physical setting, the event, appearance, and expressions of the sender function as integral parts of the message. Thus receivers interpret behind and around the words, and notice subtle supporting signs. The process of understanding is empathic:

> Such understanding is not derived from external sources of stimulation but comes instead from memories, traces of language, images, emotions, and unformulated perceptions in the present. They may be fleeting sensations and experiences which lend their flow to empathic understanding. It is a knowledge obtained from the inside, constructed by imagination and memory, and it depends on participation to take root. It is a way of knowing . . . that assigns to memory, to imagination, and to the immediate apperception of human interaction and communication a modality of knowing which is radically different from thought formed as induction or deduction. . . . In an intercultural situation, empathy should generate regressions towards cultural assumptions, values, and patterns of thinking. (Stewart, 1981, p. 80)

Empathic communication becomes virtually impossible if the sender and receiver do not share the same style of communication. Japanese empathic communication is better understood if we build on the preceding discussion of culture and analysis, and make a distinction between two phases of the process of communication.

Americans typically understand communication as an exchange of information, but the exchange is not empty. In some form, the transaction of words and symbols is understood to transmit meaning. The relationship between words as symbols and what they mean provides the entry for separating communication exchanges from communication representations.

Before exchanges take place, the raw experience of perceptual and mental impressions must be encoded as ideas, emotions, skills, and information, and finally as meaningful symbols. In the final stage of encoding before transmission, the meaningful symbols are put into words, pictures, graphs, or figures. Transactional communication benefits if the separate levels of representation of the sender are congruent with those of the receiver. Empathic communication implies understanding at the level of meaningful symbols (metaphor, expression of the face, the sender arrived late, etc.) or interpretation of patterns of daily life to intuitively reconstruct the sender's emotion, intent, or disposition. Effective transactions require that the message be encoded in symbols or signals that share the same perception and response of sender and receiver. Language is by far the most comprehensive system of symbols.

The complete immersion of Japanese experience in social relations conceals that the dynamic of the society is communication. How else can social relations be actualized in the present moment? Over the centuries, the Japanese have developed styles of communication which rely on perception and interpretation of events, actions and people, placing emphasis on what is not revealed. Silence and absence execute their meaning and language is distrusted in matters of sincerity, loyalty, and commitment.

Empathic communication is so deeply embedded in Japanese experience that it has no single term to represent it (as the word "communication" in English). This diffusion of meaning does not appear to be accidental since the ambiguities of speech and communication, and the indirection for which the Japanese are known, function to exclude outsiders.

Barrier #13: The indirection and ambiguity of Japanese empathic communication creates an information gap which distracts, confuses, and excludes Americans from the inner circles of Japanese life.

American-Japanese Communication Gap

American managers occasionally are tempted, when considering the force of the conceptual barriers in the American–Japanese communication gap, to ask the ironical question of how intercultural communication can take place. A response to the doubt should point out that the position implicitly accepts a misconception that communication means only exchange of information for purposes of persuasion, and exaggerates the conduit feature of the message. It ignores the representational phase of communication which can operate as routine and as common fate. A brief explanation of these issues should bring a fresh look at the conceptual barriers and communication. We shall briefly explain the case in which persuasion is absent, or fails, but cooperation takes place within or between organizations, drawing attention to processes which support communication, but which neither persuade nor transact information.

The first explanation implies that much of communication is routinized exchanges that depend on the verbal and nonverbal habits of the organization. Deviations from simple communicative norms of American society illustrate verbal habits. For instance, in one organization, one of the managers was known to be insensitive to certain social amenities for conversation. Those dealing with him for the first time were carefully cautioned not to ask him how he was because "he will tell you." Most people know that "How are you?" is not an inquiry about feelings nor health. Its routinized status is similar to that of "Good morning." Most people know better than to question or challenge the greeting. Norms of conversation provide greetings, set responses and subjects of conversation, that permit people to carry on conversations without creating understanding or revealing one to the other. Routinization of communication is particularly marked with the Japanese.

The second explanation of cooperation with absence of persuasion—common fate—includes two contextual factors. The pressures of the organization impel managers to act cooperatively. What is required is a coordinated perception of the situation, implying a minimum compliance with the models, procedures, and principles of planning, decision making, and other aspects of managing. Perception of the situation shades off into the organizational culture. Members of the company undergo formal, informal, and subtle processes of acquiring ways of thinking and of doing that meet the norms of the company's culture (Jabilin, 1982). Coordinated perception and organizational culture construct a common base for cooperation without anyone actively persuading or transmitting information.

Returning to the communication gap, two examples should give a bite to the missed opportunities caused by the cultural barriers between Americans and Japanese. The first example is from the field of communication itself. Americans take pride in the practicality of their organizational communication, and make judgments based on results—they would claim—and quantified if possible. Research in the field, and the influence of MBAs, tend to conceptualize the issues of communication in abstract models. Such models appear to be increasingly remote from reality. There is accumulating evidence that Americans develop a prototype for the communicatively competent person in specific communicative situations (Pavitt & Haight, 1985, p. 238). Thus the veteran manager with his rules of thumb may be close to the "prototypical" concept of a competent communicator concealed underneath acquired models of human behavior. This view approaches the Japanese way of conceptualizing according to prototypes rather than dichotomies.

The second sample of the bite of the cultural barriers is the quality control circle movement. The inspiration for it came from the United States; but, in Japan, with quality control circles acquiring distinctive characteristics and enviable reputation, Americans have often studied them (Seelye, Stewart, & Sween, 1982). Researchers usually conclude that the quality control circles are deeply steeped in Japanese culture and therefore cannot be generalized to the American scene. This view is blinded by the conceptual barriers to the function of Japanese quality control circles. In Japanese industry, quality control is not isolated as a separate process. Japanese managers insist that the quality control circles have to do with human relations and not methods and procedures for improving or controlling quality, but Americans fail to grasp the point (Barriers # 1,8,11). Quality control circles are best described as a management strategy for securing low level participation and responsibility in managing and improving work performance. Sensitivity to American industry (Barrier #7), as well as Japanese experience, has transformed the original American invention into a tool for cultivating learning by experience instead of the usual method of imitating a model. Verbal communication is a second informal objective, and its cultivation brings about horizontal communication among quality control circles within the same company, and even with other companies through horizontal channels, to a degree breaking through the divide in Japanese society between inside and outside (Barrier #3). A third purpose is learning and using negative reasoning, the problem-solving approach which is so important in technology and safety. Looking at performance of products from the point of view of what is wrong or dangerous, and imagining a worst-case analysis, is unusual with the Japanese. But within the quality control circle, schematic designs are used, such as the "fishbone diagram," to identify factors which impede, disrupt, or lower the quality of performance and products. In some circles studied, the members are encouraged to transplant methods and ideas to their own work and lives, but for our purposes it should be stressed that the quality control circle provides a restricted group acting as a laboratory for transferring at least these three processes which lack dominant status in Japanese culture. In fact, the quality control circle movement seems to function for Japanese industry in the exciting role of an organic transfer mechanism of Western ideas.

Since the analysis of the conceptual barriers has been carried out in unchartered waters, the results should be considered tentative. Their speculations will be left behind. As we turn to an analysis of Japanese culture using Western concepts, we shall leave in place the thirteen barriers, and refer to them only occasionally to neutralize certain distortions of Japanese culture imposed by Western concepts.

JAPANESE REPRESENTATIONS OF EXPERIENCE: DEEP CULTURE

The conceptual barriers discussed above reveal the inadequacy of Western concepts to explain Japanese behavior. In this section, we turn to the theme of this study: the culture of organizational communication in Japanese industry. The values selected for review below are the ones that seem to be the most important.

1. The Polarization of Japanese Deep Culture

The Japanese identity, unlike the thing-like quality of the American self, is diffuse, resembling a center of gravity or polarized field of forces. Boundaries between the Japanese self and nonself exist, but they are permeable to the influences of situations and others; hence, they seem to shift. Social involvement is the major and, at times, overbearing focus for identity. To relieve its compression, Japanese culture provides a safety valve in the selfhood of the individual which allows for the suspension of social involvement, to which the individual self is polarized. Emotional relief occurs during the temporary state that has been called a "social moratorium." During these sanctioned periods, the individual gains isolation through introspection, meditation, and self-reflection. The pursuit of these solitary inquiries, when carried to extremes, produces an awareness of one's immediate feelings and emotions undisturbed by social norms. The truth is revealed in deepening awareness of the world of emotional subjectivism, and the enjoyment of emotional anarchism. For the Japanese, truth is associated with what might be called "mental exorcism," whereby one is supposed to eradicate all the inner pollution that is clouding the true self. The self that emerges in introspection through exorcism is thought to be the source of great potency (Lebra, 1976, pp. 161, 163).

Many Japanese find satisfaction in work deriving from energy expenditure, and attach value and moral significance to a steady flow of physical or mental energy, to perseverance and to endurance, reaching the point of masochism. The commitment bordering on excess relies on an optimistic belief that single-minded effort and concentrated discipline can achieve anything one undertakes.

> Familiar proverbs say that "A shaft can pierce a rock if pushed by a concentrated mind," and "Single-minded faith can reach heaven." (Lebra, 1978, p. 163)

Reliance on concentrated inner resources is a basic value of Japanese culture. It appears as *kokoro gake*, pervades the culture of which it can be said to be the dynamism. Mobilization of the self, particularly through mental exorcism, may be traced to the beliefs and rituals of Shinto, centering on ideas of defilement and purification, both physical and spiritual (Lebra, 1976, p. 163). The center of Japanese identity has been proposed to be based on the concept "*kami*," a word of uncertain derivation (Keane, 1980). The celebrated scholar of the eighteenth century, Motoori Norinaga, defined "*kami*" as spirits that abide in shrines and are there worshipped. Human beings, birds, trees, plants, mountains, oceans—all may be *"kami."* Norinaga observed that ancient usage called *"kami"* whatever seemed strikingly impressive possessed excellence, or inspired a feeling of awe (Keane, 1980, p. 4). This view of *"kami"* is amplified by the Shinto scholar, Jean Herbert, for whom *"kami"* represent a sacred entity:

> ["Kami"] is the deification of life-force which pervades all beings, animate and inanimate. Kami is the invisible power which unites spirit and matter into a dynamic whole while it gives birth to all things without exception. (Herbert, 1967, 25)

In his study of the *"kami"* concept, Keane concludes that the basic meaning of *"kami"* is the "core" or the "substructure" of Japanese culture. Although *"kami"*-faith cannot be clearly expressed, it has been retained without change, transmitted from generation to generation without support of dogma, reason, or logic. Intuitively and emotionally grasped, *"kami"* remains the elusive spiritual center of Japanese identity.

The Shinto concept of *kami* began as nature-worship and had become more secularized as energy or spirit. It is easily misinterpreted in the West. First, *kami* is associated with concrete and particular physical and living things and places. It is a faith that the ultimate form of the world is animism, combining abstract and concrete qualities. Second, Shintoism is an earthbound religion which addresses the anxieties and frustrations of man in this world. Shinto shares with Christianity and all other religions the common core of idealization of human relationships. Shinto gods and goddesses are human, and display all the foibles and temperaments of men and women. When Shintoism is described in English, the Western background of Christian beliefs in transcendentalism and revelation endow English translations of spiritual and *kami* with an otherwordly meaning and abstract connotation not implied in the Japanese (Barriers #1, #11). Shinto does not take the transcendental leap of Christianity, remaining firmly rooted to this world and lacking a clear vision of another world and life. Spiritual and *kami* are better interpreted to stand for the essence of the world and of life in the form of energy and power inseparably invested in concrete things. At the daily level, Shinto ideas lead the Japanese to think of process in contrast to structure, opinion rather than belief, and perspectives for perception and attitude rather than trait.

In the practical context of groups and organizations, the Japanese identity possesses a psychological or attitudinal center in contrast to the American centering on performances and skills. In addition, Americans place stress on technology as instruments for the worker and manager, while Japanese managers tend to place a strong emphasis on loyalty, attitude, sincerity, and other similarly vague and unobservable qualities of the individual which suggest attitudes to Americans, who are likely to pass over them lightly and concentrate on behavior and events. Thus, American managers will speak of social and technical skills and competencies, often in the context of hardware technology, and consider how these contribute to performance. In instances where Japanese managers make selections on the basis of attitudes, the American managers' selections are more influenced by observable skills and performances. The psychological focus in Japanese industry is illustrated by a recent study conducted by the writer (Stewart, 1982).

A plant located southwest of Tokyo was studied to determine how the plant personnel were implementing the safety system which had been adopted from an American corporation. The safety system, designed and developed by Americans in the United States, was transferred by American technicians to the entirely Japanese plant, which was working well since the safety record of the plant personnel was very good. The purpose of the safety study was to gain greater understanding of the interaction between an American system and the values and operational procedures of the Japanese personnel. Since the safety record of the plant was very good, the study did not aspire to solve problems. Given the conditions under which the study was carried out, it is believed that the managers and workers participating in the study reported accurate information and conveyed true attitudes.

The results of the study showed that the personnel of the plant identified three features of the safety program: first, technical devices which made the machinery safer. Second, the skills taught to and required of the workers operating the machinery to make their operations safer. Third, the organization of work space and the analysis of conditions contributing to accidents. The Japanese accepted fully and admired the system, particularly the third feature. They also appreciated the concern of management that took the initiative in implementing and maintaining the safety system. But several of the workers, when asked for suggestions and proposals, offered ideas contrary to the conceptualization undergirding the safety system, which relied on technology, skills, and analysis of production operations in time and space. Workers suggested the need for mental discipline and training, and understood the causes of accidents to be the failure, for reasons of fatigue or preoccupation of some kind, of concentrated discipline, a translation of *kokoro gake*. The study reveals the two centers in American culture, behavioristic and technological, and, in the Japanese, an appreciation of the same features, but still an inclination to preserve the spiritual center of the individual.

Throughout this study, we shall combine the qualities that make up the Japanese spirit. No single term is satisfactory. "*Kami*," as god or spirit in English is too abstract and absolute; "spirit" is too mystical for American pragmatism, and "energy" and "power" are too restricted, and at the same time too vague, in meaning. We shall arbitrarily coin a term from *Nihon*, Japan, calling the essene of the Japanese way and spirit the *Nihon spirit*.

2. Distinctive Influences of Japanese Deep Culture: Man and Nature

The value orientation that describes the relationship between man and the world has important implications for many activities in the arts and crafts, as well as in technology and the sciences. For the Japanese, when the world is interpreted as Nature, the values are clear. Japanese culture provides a special status to forms and experiences which are natural and recall the asymmetry and even the imperfections of natural beauty, as if man himself can remove the imperfection by integrating in complete harmony with nature, not only in spirit, but in acts which refine the appearance of natural manifestations. Refined appreciation is significant for understanding the Japanese love of nature revealed in miniature gardens (*hakoniwa*), miniature trees (*bonsai*), flower arrangement (*ikebana*), the tea ceremony (*ohanoyu*), short poems called *haiku*, and even in the art of cookery (Watanabe, 1974, p. 279). These objects and activities, although naturalistic, reveal careful control and precise articulation to accommodate Japanese perception and values of man rather than any naturalistic qualities of heaven and earth, the three forming the three principles of *ikebana*, representing Japanese cosmology. But in the Japanese traditional view, there was no absolute division of heaven and earth, not an absolute "oneness" of time. There existed beings and seasons, and everything came and went in cycles (Watanabe, 1974, pp. 280–281). Despite the pessimistic teachings of Buddhism and the direct experience of violence of nature, the Japanese still turned to the natural world for respite from suffocations of the group and for refuge from toils of life. For the Japanese, nature was an object of his appreciation and even his best companion, and not an object subject to mastery (Watanabe, 1974, p. 280). Even today, nature occupies a privileged position in Japanese thinking, appearing to function as a metaphor for the social network which comprises Japanese identity. The boundary between man and nature is fuzzy, since man is perceived as a continuous part of the world and integral with it.

> The Japanese regard this world, with its diverse phenomena, as in itself absolute, and tend to reject viewpoints that seek the absolute in some realm beyond phenomena. (Nakamura, 1977, p. 61)

The absoluteness of the phenomenal world originated with the indigenous Shinto religion. The ancient Japanese, believing that all things were invested with spirit, personified even nonhuman spirits and deities, *kami*, but considered human *kami* the primary entity. When Buddhism came to Japan, the original Shinto commitment to the phenomenal world prevailed over the Buddhist concept that there exists a realm of ultimate enlightenment transcending the phenomenal world. The Japanese interpreted the lofty concept of *hongoku* to mean "innate Buddhanature" of "origin of Buddhahood," retaining it within the scope for the phenomenal world, since nothing was intrinsically hidden from man (Nakamura, 1977, p. 61). Watanabe (1974, p. 280) writes about the same idea with a discussion of flower arrangement, *ikebana*, which represents the unity of nature, and man lives in it as part of the unity. The phenomenal integration of man and the world prevented the Japanese from developing an objective and detached view of the natural world, and, as a result, the Japanese did not initiate studies of nature. The world was not an object of study, even though life on the Japanese islands was often threatened by natural disasters. Although often visited by earthquakes, the Japanese did not initiate their scientific study. Seismology began only after Japan was opened to the West and Western visitors were exposed to earthquakes (Watanabe, 1974, p. 281). The Chinese, experiencing a similar value of man coexisting with nature, studied earthquakes at a very early date, and seem to have invented a machine to study them (Bloom, 1974, p. 850). Thus, coexistence of man and the world does not seem sufficient to explain the different developments of science and technology in China and Japan. The critical factor seems to be the phenomenalism of the Japanese, which the Chinese did not share to the same degree. Chinese intellectual history provides examples of absolute concepts, of good and evil for instance (Lebra, 1974), which are strange to the Japanese sense of phenomenal relativity. The Japanese sense of continuity with nature found expression in techniques of perfecting trees and gardens, and in crafts such as swords and pottery, but did not launch the study of the world. A second fact helps explain the difference. Chinese culture ascribes a special status to man by developing particular qualities to deities, recognizing historical figures and producing writings, but the Japanese indigenous faith of Shinto has no absolute being in its pantheon of deities, no founders, and no sacred scriptures (Maruyama, 1977, p. 75). Thus, the Japanese people did not develop a philosophical or intellectual tradition, but remained constantly open to foreign ideas.

The Chinese approached the Western position more closely, but did not attain the concept of man's special station and of the objectivity of the world and its separation from man, which appears to subsume the development of science.

> In the Western idea, man was not an ordinary part of nature. He was a specially privileged creature, and nature was subordinate to him and even to his sin. He was the master of the natural world, which was at his disposal to analyze, examine, and make use of. (Watanabe, 1974, p. 280)

Protestantism accepted the study of nature for the improvement of mankind, giving religious sanction to man's objective inquiry of the world. The separation between man and the world occurred early in Western history. Pythagoras, in the fifth century B.C., writing in the vein of a tradition already long, divided the internal world of the subjective and mystic mind from the external, objective world that could be treated with mathematics. This view permits man to imagine the detached and objective realm of scientific principles and laws which can be applied to independent technology derived from research. Lacking these values in a significant way to develop science and independent technology, the Japanese have relied on field dependent technology, evolved slowly, developed from consistent opportunities mixed with some need, stimulated by the symbiotic relationship between man and his physical and social environment, and guided by the Japanese talent for craftsmanship and design. In addition, and particularly in modern times, the Japanese have relied on the transfer of science and technology, which provides models which are imitated and improved in the direction of adapting them to the Japanese context.

During the post-war period, Japanese scientific and technological development have taken giant strides. In science, and including nuclear physics, the Japanese have substituted brainpower and craftsmanship for lavish use of capital and natural resources (Campbell, 1964, p. 776). In 1975, Japanese manpower in scientists and engineers was 399,842 for a research and development budget of 10,022 million U.S. dollars. Assuming that all the scientists and engineers are engaged in research, the difference between the two countries diminishes somewhat when additional factors are considered. Americans have more concentration on the basic research end of the spectrum, while the Japanese stress the development end, where engineers are more important. Furthermore, a large proportion of American research and development is for defense, of which the Japanese have almost none. Finally, the United Sates conducts much high-energy physics research which is capital intensive by necessity, while Japan avoids it. Thus, the two research and development enterprises are not strictly comparable on the basis of their budgets and number of scientists and engineers. Despite these reservations, qualitative differences still remain in the opinions of most observers.

3. Social Relativism

Diffuse identity makes it difficult to elaborate the deep culture of the Japanese. In searching for its "thematic distinctiveness," Lebra uses the concepts of ethos (1976, p. 1), perhaps first used by Bateson in the sense of the characteristic spirit of a people (Bateson, 1958, p. 2). Later Bateson identified ethos as the emotional emphases of the culture (p. 32) and the "standardized system of emotional attitudes" (p. 119). The choice fits Japanese culture, where emotion rather than reason or cognition serves as the cultural binder.

Lebra (1976, pp. 2–6) discusses Japanese social preoccupation in the concrete form of people. The commitment is profound, but the people are always seen in a relationship, so that in Japanese culture it is understood that the member of a relationship merges with a social medium flowing among members of the network. As a consequence of the merger with the medium, it is impossible to locate prime movers or causes, since these are a part of the social medium. This phenomenon Lebra (1976, pp. 6–9) calls interactional relativism. The combination of social preoccupation and interactional relativism yields social relativism (Lebra, 1976, p. 9). The concept suggests the definition of the self in Japanese society as a part of the social nexus (Nakamura, 1964) guiding behavior along lines of conformity and of imitation of models. This view of course neglects the enter of gravity in the *Nihon* spirit, but both the idea of *kami* and of social relativism combine in the concept of "*jen*," the Confucian value of human-heartedness. Adopted as "*jin*" by the Japanese, the concept carries the meaning of psychic love (Hsu, 1966, 62). Although *jen* refers to a cosmic principle among the Chinese, it conveys for the Japanese an abstract idea of relationship. The Japanese *jin* implies the concrete recognition of others as human beings identical with the self. The individual is conceived to be a member of a group, institution, or society as a whole, and to occupy an appropriate place fulfilling all social obligations attached to the position. (The term best illustrating this social orientation is *bun*, and even the term for self is a *bun*–compound noun, *jibun*.)

The *jin* as the individual aspect of the network comprises what is expressible of the consciousness and the intimate aspects of the society and culture. This view of the individual makes no room for the Freudian unconscious or other structural aspects of deep personality found in the West. Japanese analysis of behavior is horizontal and not vertical. *Jin* replaces the Western concepts of personality, ego, and even of self in Japan (Hamaguchi, 1980, p. 67). *Jin* is more suitable for clustering human experience around relationships. Although the network represent abstractions, Japanese culture avoids empty categories, and thus the relationships are seen in particularistic settings. Actual contacts are important in Japanese culture. Without them, relationships wither.

Jin summarizes a difficult and critical aspect of Japanese culture which has played a major role in Japan's modernization. The commitment which Japanese managers and workers deploy in their work-places traces to social relativism, which has been mobilized in Japan to form the substructure of industry. Historically, the social relations of *jin* were modelled on the family. In Japanese society, the dominant relationship is found between the father and son, which provides the prototype of the corporation. The family relationships of unigeniture—the eldest son inherits the household head, and the markedly hierarchical and binding ties between the heir and brothers are carried over into the company and form its social organization (Hsu, 1975, p. 232). The primal bonds among the members of the company form the strength of the Japanese corporation.

The *jin* model perhaps may be reinterpreted in the form of a technical metaphor which may provide to Westerners a more persuasive analysis of mechanisms of control and the role of outsiders on the operations of a network. The Japanese pattern of social organization seems to fit the model of a *hologram* principle. Its features are as follows:

> In a hologram the information in a scene is recorded on a photographic plate in the form of a complex interference, or diffraction, pattern that appears meaningless. When the pattern is illuminated by coherent light, however, the original image is reconstructed. What makes the hologram unique as a storage device is that every element in the original image is distributed over the entire photographic plate. (Pribram, 1969, p. 73)

In Japanese groups, the interference pattern is met in the incentives for group cohesion and performance. These often emerge from negative sources, from the exclusion of others. Thus each network exists in a potentially dangerous competition with others, and its members are armed with the inextinguishable desire to exceed the competition. The interference from the competition is the coherent, or "resolving," light which provides direction and purpose to the group. (A crisis which challenges or threatens the group's survival often also serves as a resolving light.) The loyalty and the dedication directed toward the group provides the Japanese with a social safety zone of security for their sense of identity (Yoshimura, 1986, pp. 54–67). Japanese often lead a life contained within narrow social boundaries. In the organization, power tends to be diffused over many semi-self-contained, semi-mutually-dependent bodies which are neither responsible to a central authority nor ultimately subservient to one another (van Wolfenren, 1982, p. 129). The system presents a picture of infinite complexity of aggregated mosaics, in complex balance, with none holding final power or authority. Thus, patterns of performance and striving fit the model of the *hologram*. Of signal importance is the necessity of external influences, the resolving light, to guide and direct the group.

The control mechanism in the organization refers to the use of power. Japanese control mechanisms differ from American. The control in American organizations ideally is localized in the decision maker or the leader, who takes pride in deciding. In the Japanese organization, the ideal is to conceal the locus of control. Thus, decisions in Japan seem to happen; they are delocalized and purposefully appear to be mere accommodations to existing realities (Weisz, Rothbaum, & Thomas, 1984, p. 956). The Japanese exercise secondary control over existing realities, usually acting through a medium rather than directly. Americans, in contrast, exercise primary control and influence over existing realities. The Japnese approach to power, using secondary control, is more subtle than the direct American approach. The Japanese distinguish several different ways of yielding to power (Azuma, 1984, p. 970). As might be expected, both the American and the Japanese control mechanisms are adaptations of fundamental values. The Japanese secondary control is adapted to the Japanese self always in an interdependent relationship with the environment. Thus, Japanese power can be associated with the value of social relativism in Japanese organizations, and explained according to the holographic model.

4. Japanese Management

Resembling American management in some ways, but differing from it in others, Japanese management will be contrasted with American to heighten understanding of the cultural base of Japanese industry. In their study of Japanese management, Pascale and Athos (1981) identify seven factors in the 7-s Framework which will be used to organize information about management. I shall depart from their approach by assigning a separate section to structure, the organization of firms. I disagree somewhat with their conclusion that the ensemble of "hard" factors, strategies, structures, and systems, are the same in the hands of both Japanese and American managers. Generally, it is true that the culture of Japan predictably encourages the cultivation of the soft ensemble, staff, style, skills, and superordinate goals, while Americas, admiring the tough, decisive, objective, and macho executive, assign lower priority, if not neglect, to the same soft factors (Pascale & Athos, 1981, 204).

Strategy

This factor refers to the plans and procedures used by the firm to allocate service resources and to attain success. At least two major but subtle differences exist between American and Japanese strategies, reflecting emphases rather than discrete differences. Both Japanese and American cultures have been described as stressing process rather than structure—how to get things done, rather than things themselves. But the Japanese attunement to persistently flowing processes is remarkable. Lebra (1976, p. 163) discusses the high value placed on the steady flow of physical or mental energy. Japanese culture also values repetition and imitation in learning and in performance. These values of deep culture may well surface in the organization of supplied and raw resources in Japanese industry, stressing more so than American industry the constant flow of input to the assembly line, which minimizes stockpiling. Although the explanation for the emphasis invites reasons of space and facility, the process emphasis seems natural to all areas of Japanese life. Discussion groups, committees, and plans lack clear starts or ends, flowing and proceeding interminably.

The second major but subtle difference refers to the debate of profit versus market. Using profit for an objective in Japanese culture carries negative implications in Japan. Secondly, the Japanese orientation of social relativism leads us to expect that strategy in business will give priority to the development of human relationships, and give attention to markets before pushing products and profit. Of even greater interest is the cultural expectation that domestic systems of distribution will be stubbornly defended, and that customers and their networks will receive concentrated attention. These strategies in business reflect cultural factors, particularly social relativism and *jin*.

Structure

This second factor refers to the characterization of the organization of the firm, such as features of centralization and functions. Since the subject of structure will be given a section to itself, it suffices to mention the vertical organization in Japanese groups built around the frame, which is the particular, localized working situation (Nakane, 1970). The competitive drive among Japanese groups, and the hostility reserved for other parallel groups, resulted in the necessary centralization in the figure of a leader who occupies a vertical position relative to contending groups and persons (Nakane, 1970). The primal bonds among members of the group includes the distinctive Japanese form of reciprocal dependence (*amae*), and concentrated energy, derived from both internal cohesiveness of network members an d hostility engendered from exclusiveness.

Japanese groups run the risk of fission and then establishing groups within groups. This social tendency usually prevents horizontal cooperation on the basis of equality. An equal balance of power between peers is an unstable situation in Japan that can provoke ruthless competition. Social stability always resides in imbalance between powers where one dominates the others (Nakane, 1970, p. 55). Seniority and the hierarchical structure of the Japanese organization curb the competition between networks. The relationship between the individual and the group in Japan was established in the dim past, so that the social norms have a long history (Hasegawa, 1965, pp. 11–13). The unity and identity of the people of Japan, constantly reinforced by primordial bonds of language, ethnicity, race, religion, region, and custom, provide an idealized cohesiveness unmatched by any other major nation in the world.

Systems

Systems are defined as the procedural reports and routinized processes used to move information around and, in an organization, to make decisions and to implement change (Pascale & Athos, 1981, pp. 35-36, 81). This American category breaks down when it is applied to Japanese culture since it assumes a universal definition of information, a similar function for communication, and independence between the system of flow and the nature of the information which the systems moves. Americans differentiate more so than other people among data, images, impressions, facts, gossip, and other forms of what can be called information, in the technical sense of interpreted or "meaningful" facts. The Japanese do not make similar distinctions, insisting that all forms of "information" must be collected; and perhaps more so than anyone else, the Japanese believe that quantity of "information" is good, and that no clear distinction exists between common sense "information" and the technical meaning of information, verified and interpreted as facts.

The Japanese cultural orientation toward information raises significant issues about the role of communication in Japanese management. Three points deserve mention. One, the Japanese language is best suited for hierarchical communication. Two, Japanese displays its power when communicating emotional tones and social feelings. The language itself is ambiguous, leaving understanding open to interpretation.

Three, the verbal message spoken in Japanese relies on nonverbal communication to a degree seldom appreciated by the English speaker. Verbal communication is inseparable from nonverbal communication, from vertical social relations and from Japanese experience. In its uncertainty, the ambiguity of the Japanese style avoids developing an adversary relation, placing instead the burden of understanding on the receiver. The Japanese way compels the receiver to concentrate on the meaning presumably conveyed by the sender, while the sender, bound by indirection and vagueness, becomes equally attentive to the receiver. Communication improves if all communicators know each other well and can anticipate what each will say or do. Thus the ambiguity and vagueness of communication contribute to team work and group cooperation.

Communication in the field of technology raises the additional problem of probability thinking and of coping with uncertainty. Japanese managers seem reluctant to avoid reaching conclusions based on probability. Hofstede (1980) reports a high avoidance of uncertainty on the part of Japanese business, and reliance on rules and precedents as one way of reducing it. In dealing with uncertainty, Japanese show what can be compared to a craftsman's criteria: accuracy of measurement, inclusion of all variables, and perfect performance rather than anticipation of consequences. Despite the wide use of statistical control in industry and business, Japanese managers seldom derive ideas or conclusions from statistical analyses. In quality control, Japanese typically insist on quality for each individual unit produced and reject the American practice of inspecting a fixed percentage of all units and projecting to the entire lot. In production figures, the same difference appears. The Japanese report the actual count, while Americans typically estimate it on the basis of the percentage of capacity at which the plant operated. Japanese technology has stronger roots than American in the arts and crafts than in work or economic motives.

Japanese attitudes toward probability, models, and uncertainty are brought together in some case studies collected in a research project with Scandinavian shipping interests which had contracted with Japanese shipbuilders. The Scandinavians report that the shipbuilder assumed, once the blueprints had been formally approved, that the ship would be built precisely according to its specifications, and, therefore, that there was no need for sea tests. In one case, the Japanese blueprints were rejected and a structural change suggested that would strengthen the frame and help prevent fissures developing in the metal caused by metal fatigue if the ship were exposed to extreme conditions of waves such as occur in the North Sea. The Japanese responded with evidence that the same design has been accepted 8 years earlier. They also presented an enormous amount of data supporting their design. They were not willing to modify the design to accommodate speculations of worst case analysis.

Along with these observations, we should mention the Japanese preference for adapting to and adopting existing conditions. It is considered a sign of maturity to accept the phenomenal world in all of its imperfections and impermanence. This orientation seldom leads to inquiries into causes. In compensation for accepting imperfection, the Japanese manager is open to suggestions and accepts the objective of endless improvement. He places his ultimate trust in personnel and not in ideas or analysis.

Staff

Japanese industry since the Meiji Restoration accepted the Confucian value of practical knowledge, with the result that Japanese managers drew abreast, by 1928, of the educational attainments of European businessmen today (Clark, 1979, p. 36). Professional training, however, was assumed by the companies and not by the universities, with the result that attaining the status of a member of the company, of a citizen, and of a professional person became part of the same process of belonging to the company. Education of the employee is carried out in part by moving him to various positions within the same company, resulting in a manager who becomes a specialist in his own company, but at the same time does not develop specialization in finance, marketing, or some other specialty. The manager consequently becomes more firmly entrenched in his own company, and less marketable to other companies. A final point to be borne in mind is that future managers typically enter the company at the bottom and work their way up the hierarchy. These qualities combined endow resilience to a good Japanese company, permitting it to change and adapt to a surprising degree when viewed from the point of view of American management and labor. Since the foreman on the line may in fact have a degree in engineering, adapting a new process or making a change can be done quickly and efficiently without having to give special training to the work force. The high level of training and the cohesiveness and dedication of the staff give Japanese companies a strength which would be difficult to export to and replicate in countries that prefer the posture of adversaries in business and litigation in solving problems.

Style

Style provides considerable insight of the cultural aspects of Japanese industry. Pascale and Athos (1981, p. 81) define it as the characterization of how key managers behave in achieving the organization goals. Although the Japanese and American styles of doing business overlap, there are critical differences consisting of combinations of values and patterns of thinking which produce different points of views, objectives, and ways of operating.

The Japanese make judgments by comparing like things with each other in a style that is unrelentingly comparative. In his own mind, the Japanese is likely to decide by comparing one course of action, or one person with another. The Austrian or German judgment provides a better contrast to the Japanese than the American. These Europeans typically consider the appropriateness or the goodness of a course of action, assuming an ideal standard to guide their actions in applied areas. This style employs absolute judgments in decision making. The American business judgment resembles the Japanese, since it is comparative. But when applied in decision making, Americans show traces of absolute judgment, more like Europeans. The essential quality in which Americans differ from both Japanese and Europeans is to stress reaching decisions by comparing the anticipated consequences of comparable courses of action.

In its ideal form, American decision making is time-bound, reflecting the American time orientation toward the near future. American decisions typically rely on a conceptual base that anticipates future events, usually described as objectives and goals. Americans develop time-binding, as in time-motion studies, deadlines, objectives, and goals, to a refined level of managerial art. Relying on the conceptual structure of decision making, Americans establish theory, policy, and select courses of action. The process of decision making passes through a mental analysis of positive and negative factors, alternatives are carefully weighed, and then a choice is made—which is the decision. The decision maker is an individual or it may be a group, but, typically, the conceptual nature of the decision and the adversarial process used in reaching it reveal the major sources of it. For Americans, utility is the decision criterion, and it refers to a future event, not a present one. The employment of the future is the critical aspect of American decision making, and perhaps explains the optimistic cast of American decision makers, often presuming greater control over the world than experience gives reason to expect. In the East, including Japan, we lack the information for reaching conclusions about similar systematic errors. Managers in Japan are uneasy in accepting any one decision as final, or "finalized." They also resist the American preference for one-dimensional criteria, such as profit in business. Instead, the Japanese are likely to perceive a continuously unfolding train of events to which they accommodate (Pascale & Athos, 1981, p. 110). The notion of controlling events, in the sense of the

American systematic error, is much more likely to become an adaptation to the situation and even an avoidance of decision making, allowing events to take their course. Thus the American desire for closure, for finalizing, in the Japanese company is more a matter of flowing with events. These differences in decision making follow from the conceptual nature of American decision making, on the one hand, and the organizational aspects of the Japanese company on the other. Japanese decisions are more like discussions conducted among various people, and lack the formal qualities of alternatives, predictions, and other qualities which punctuate American discussions.

Japanese managers are more likely to devote attention and time to building support for a decision than in organizing the conceptual structure of alternatives. Thus, decisions are reached in an organizational or social field, in distinction to the conceptual field of the American decision. The Japanese manager feels obligated to include other people in the decision-making process. Although individual decisions sometimes occur, group decisions are much more characteristic of a Japanese organization. But this simple comparison obscures the important difference of the patterns of thinking and the nature of judgments that distinguish the two styles of decision making. The Japanese obligation to include others insures that the process of decision making matches the Japanese patterns of identity which, unlike the American, is anchored to the group, treated as *jin* or the social nexus (Nakamura, 1964). Thus, the process of touching base with many people, redundant to Americans, acculturates the decision and establishes support for its eventuality, which comes after interminable talk. The discussions focus on feasibility, rather than theory, policy, or profit. Each course of action or each alternative is talked through in terms of its "implementational feasibility" (Pascale & Athos, 1981, p. 111). The decision is assumed to require reconciliation of competing interests, all of which would be included to insure a proper balance between substantive options and feasible implementations. Though a process which may be described as "discussion attrition," the alternative with the best all-around prospect of success emerges as the decision. A formal decision making session often provides a ceremonial consensus to an issue already settled behind the scenes. Unanimity may only mean that the group backing the decision is too strong for other groups to oppose; therefore, the others choose not to object for the lack of power to successfully oppose the decision. A unanimous vote is probably a ceremonial performance most of the time.

It is doubtful if the Japanese ideal way of attaining consensus qualifies as an example of decision making. The exercise of power in Japan is social, political and typically concealed. Power figures avoid making conceptual decisions. They prefer to remain out of sight, waiting for events to overtake and resolve issues. The ideal exercise of power is to convey the impression that issues are resolved by the inevitable forces of events. A study of this intricate process—the equivalent of American decision making—opens to view significant features of Japanese culture. When striving for a consensus, Japanese managers regularly reflect on their own experience, but after withdrawal. In the social context of the workplace, the manager is preoccupied with obligations, duties, and protocol surrounding his own position. Psychologically, it is essential for the manager to escape from the suffocation of the group, come to a fesh face-to-face with his own experience, and allow his thinking to percolate through his own emotions free from the pressures of the work social nexus. Pascale and Athos, discussing the Japanese company, Matsushita, describe the need for acceptance time which gives managers the opportunity to come around to a point of view in their own way.

> Acceptance time is a powerful antidote to conflict in Japanese organizations. The things a person believes in are often more important belongings than physical possessions. People die for their central beliefs as well as for their important possessions. Even less compelling beliefs reach back into a person's past and forward into his future. When new ideas or facts come along, however, compelling they may be, it is felt that people need time to let go gradually of the old before they can accept the new. Despite the pressures and intensity, acceptance time is built into the Matsushita way of doing business. (Pascale and Athos, 1981, p. 48)

Acceptance time leads to aspects of Japanese deep culture in the areas of identity and learning. Although the Japanese identity is relational with others, the focus of social involvement exists in a dialectical relationship with an inner core of the self, emotional and meditative, which is in touch with experience, its roots leading to Zen, which insists that a person experience the thing in itself, the reality, not the empty abstraction. The central perception of the truth of Zen sees all things as things in themselves and at the same time sees the one in the many and the many in the one. Zen rejects the intellect—verbalization, logic, conceptualization—and accepts intuitive understanding as knowledge which comes from deep within the being of the person. Zen, a religion of the will, is simple, direct, self-reliant, and self-denying. Traditionally linked to the military classes, Zen is now widely dispersed throughout all classes of Japan (Suzuki, 1977, pp. 46–49). Withdrawal of the individual to the Zen center of his being, for the purpose of communing with his own experience, is an aspect of the central concept of Zen which has spread throughout Japanese society, deeply influencing strategies of learning and of change. This quality of Zen generates strong internal reserves in its Japanese practitioners, but often leads to serious misunderstanding of the outside world (Aida, 1977, p. 67). The bent of Japanese thought toward experiential self-immolation points to values governing learning that are deeper than those suggested by acceptance time. Withdrawal in time, if not in space, as a condition for learning and accommodation to change, refers to assimilation rather than acceptance time. The reality of assimilation time and the development of inner reserves does not remove the need for a concrete model which is imitated before it is improved. Japanese, in comparison to Americans, are excellent listeners, attentive to the "model" communicated.

The factor of style which we have been discussing overlaps with the other factors. The common ground is particularly apparent with the factor of systems, discussed previously, and the one of skills.

Skills

By skills, Pascale and Athos (1981, p. 81) mean the distinctive capabilities of key personnel or of the firm as a whole. This factor is more suitable for comparing specific companies than for the analysis of organizational communication, but skills serves the purpose of drawing attention to a distinctive capability of Japanese industry, the incremental improvement of a product or a service. This distinctive feature can be illustrated with a brief discussion of the Japanese orientation toward technology.

Japanese industry and business have developed and modernized by acquiring abroad technology which is transferred to Japan, where, in the course of events, it is improved and perfected. Generally, Japanese industry has avoided committing too much of its resources to theoretical research which could be used to develop a research-driven technology. Since industry's budget for research and development is likely to be allocated for the improvement of existing products, the best index for gauging the commitment to a research driven technology is the research and development budget of the government. In 1975, the government financed 29.7% of R and D, lower than any other major country. Just above Japan was Italy, with 41.4%; the United States was 50.7%, and France was the highest at 53.5%. Recent figures on patents seem to dispute the assertion that Japanese technology is transfer- rather than research-driven technology, but in fact an examination of patents issued confirm the Japanese genius for improving rather than inventing. The controversial figures refer to U.S. patents for inventions issued to foreigners. In 1966, Japan had issued to them 1,122 patents, for 8.1% of all patents issued to foreigners, but, in 1976, the number had risen to 6,542, for 25.1%. The shift to research-driven technology is not supported by the figures, if one accepts the explanation that a team of Japanese technical personnel maintain a close watch on all patents nearing expiration, and change selected ones enough to qualify for a new patent when the old one expires. The close observation of the situation in the U.S. patent office, and the prepared response to expiration of a patent, seem to be in the mainstream of the Japanese approach to business, and do not indicate a shift to research-drive technology. This quality of Japanese industry is well illustrated by the Matsushita Electric Company.

Pascale and Athos provide an analysis of Matsushita from which we extract the following comments supporting the features of Japanese industry discussed above:

> The third element of Matsushita's strategy is followership. From the outset, Matsushita (the founder and CEO) did not attempt to pioneer new technology but emphasized quality and price. . . . To this day, Matsushita rarely originates a product, but always succeeds in manufacturing it for less and marketing it best. . . . At the heart of Matsushita's followership strategy is production engineering. An executive from RCA sates, "If you watch where Matsushita puts its resources, their success through followership should come as no surprise. They have 23 production research laboratories equipped with the latest technology available. Their concept of 'research and development' is to analyze competing products and figure out how to do it better." (Pascale & Athos, 1981, pp. 30–31)

Matsushita is a great Japanese company, and therefore not typical, since greatness deviates from normative features of all companies, but some features are typical in an ideal sense. The authors point out unusual aspects of the company's strategy, but, with respect to the need for a model, Matsushita represents the ideal of a fundamental thrust in Japanese technology.

Superordinate Goals

Superordinate goals include "significant meanings," "shared values," and "spiritual fabric" which function as the guides imbued in its members by an organization (Pascale & Athos, 1981, pp. 81, 177–178). The meaning of superordinate goals seems a bit inflated, and also culturally biased. Placing superordinate goals at the center of the managerial molecule (Pascale & Athos, 1981, p. 202) raises the operations level for competing objectives to an idealized, integrated level. The information reflects a decision-making style of thinking in which future events (i.e., goals) serve to organize the data for the decision maker. Choices made among alternative courses of action to reach the goal rely on a set of values, including a clear idea of the future, lineal time, and the capacity to clearly differentiate among alternatives. Conceptual clarity and logical relations undergird the decision-making process. The formulation aptly reflects American management thought, but bears little resemblance to Japanese way of thinking. Superordinate goals, first, refer to a hierarchy of objectives, with the one at the pinnacle, the superordinate, resolving conflicts among competing objectives which can now be treated as instrumental under the guiding influence of the superordinate goal. This rephrasing of the superordinate goal, with the deliberate exclusion of the temporal aspect of goals and objectives, lends itself to application to Japanese organizations.

The Japanese organizational structure is hierarchical, with communication and relationships reinforcing vertical rather than horizontal bonds. The Japanese group, bound together by emotional processes, compresses a high potential for splitting info factions and subgroups. Fissions are prevented, or at least contained, by the vertical relationship of positions in which allegiance is given upward to only one leader until the top man in the organization is reached. Promotions on the basis of seniority also help to curb destructive competition. Personal allegiance in a large group extends beyond the span of personal *jin*; hence, an extension is needed to encompass all members of an organization. The firm belief systems are described by Pascale and Athos (1981, pp. 49–52, 81) as spiritual values and identified as superordinate goals. Belief systems provide concrete examples of what functions as enfolding cognitive and emotional games for reaching judgments and making decisions. The frames may also be described as deductive thinking, in which general and abstract ideas (in the case of the Japanese, these are vague and emotionally laden) provide the beginning of a train of thought which moves toward more concrete and particular ideas. It is necessary to remember the Western bias to attribute more influence to a conceptual base than is justified in the case of the diffuse and participatory belonging of the Japanese (Barriers #1, 11).

Pascale and Athos use Matsushita to fill in the abstract ideas posed by superordinate goals, since both founder and company are superb examples of the Japanese approach. It is customary for business leaders and government officers in Japan to frame their observations implicitly, if not explicitly, within a moralistic and ethical frame that provides a deductive but essentially emotional tone to their statements. For Matsushita, people needed a way of linking their productive lives with their membership in the larger society. He developed a managment philosophy which linked business profits to the social good within a Darwinian paradigm. The concept is very similar to the Protestant ethic, in which the saved shall be known by their good works, and, therefore, success in the secular pursuit of business becomes a sign of grace. For

Matsushita, the religious motive existed, but the end is societal and collective rather than individual and sacred. Profits become a vote of confidence from society that what is offered by the firm is valued. When a firm ceases to turn profits, it should be permitted to die, since it wastes the resources of the society (Pascale & Athos, 1981, p. 49). The philosophy of the company is implemented in a song, sung each morning, and in a code of values. Employees of the company are exposed and trained in the code from the beginning, and conformity to the company's basic principles is strictly required. These principles commit the employees of the firm to recognize their responsibilities. The commitment is made to progress, the general welfare of society, and to the development of world culture. The employees' creed approaches a litany of social values—of progress, development, combined efforts and cooperation, and continuous improvement of the company. The third aspect is the seven spiritual values: national service through industry, fairness, harmony and cooperation, struggle for betterment, courtesy and humility, adjustment and assimilation, and, last, gratitude (Pascale & Athos, 1981, p. 51). These principles provide little guidance for workers on the production line or for decision making by groups discussing technical issues. The power derived from implementing the Matsushita management philosophy resides in the enfolding and centripetal emotional frame established around each member of the company, drawing each to each. The conflict which is present remains latent, and competition is sublimated after attaining its goals, to allow for a harmonious community.

The Japanese cultural features of Matsushita can be compared to two American firms, IBM and ITT. The appeal of Matsushita was emotional, but that of IBM was cerebral, celebrated by the THINK sign hung all over the factories and offices. During the second World War, PEACE joined THINK all over the company, reminding everyone of the war situation and the potential effect for IBM's expanding international business (Pascale & Athos, 1981, pp. 180–183). In these practices, IBM displayed a pragmatic and rational appeal lacking the emotional bond of the principles of Matsushita linking the company and the society. The beliefs of IBM stress the individual, the customer, and excellence. Fundamental principles place priority on business and technology, then on the people working for IBM; then stockholders appear, and then the principles note the communities where the facilities are located and end with the need to accept responsibility as a corporate citizen of th U.S. and all the countries in which IBM operates (Pascale & Athos, 1981, pp. 184–185). The American corporation, unlike Matsushita, has committed itself to the cutting edge of research, witnessed by THINK signs.

Another American corporation closely resembles Matsushita—ITT. As a matter of fact, it can be considered the American counterpart of the Japanese firm (Pascale & Athos, 1981, p. 59). ITT never excelled in basic or applied research, and there are no basic products associated with its name, such as with IBM, Xerox, or Polaroid. Its CEO between 1959 and 1979, Harold Geneen, built a management system based on unshakeable facts. An intricate web of checks and balances, a system of rewards and punishments, carefully staged personal confrontations, and an elaborate system of information collection and management permitted Geneen to ensure the veracity of the data and feed his hunger for facts, on which his style of managing relied. The approach permitted him to exercise his superior abilities of reading, recalling, and thinking in the domain of numbers (Pascale & Athos, 1981, pp. 70–74). This rational, cold, and impersonal approach, in which negative motivation drove managers to contribute through the mechanism of grinding confrontation, contrasts sharply with Matsushita emotional envelope, constructed to endow the company with meaning.

5. Japanese Social Systems

By the time of the Meiji Restoration, Japanese visitors to the West confirmed what was already evident, that the strength of a nation laying its manufacturing industry, and that the means for attaining it was through the joint stock company (Clark, 1979, pp. 27–29). The challenge was how to start up for modernization. Japan perceived the West to have primed the pump of materialism with individualism and avarice, but this strategy flouted the Confucian Ethic and its contempt for material things. But the governments and semiofficial entrepreneurs appealed to nationalism and public spirit in an early example of a superordinate goal. In the early years of Japanese industrialization, private enterprise was supported by the state, as the government adopted the view that internal motivation was necessary for modernization. This opinion, still current (Cho, 1966, p. 40), aptly describes the Japanese character in the Meiji Period and today, with its inner motives for change as well as a spirit of resistance against cultural impact from the West. In the period from 1868, the Japanese people clarified a distinction between public and private, and drew upon it as a standard of accountability for their political figures (Kelly, 1985, p. 245).

The Japanese merchants during the Meiji Period relied on the institution of the family to form their businesses. The family in Tokugawa Japan consisted essentially of a group called a "house" (ie). The word refers to a physical entity and to the people associated with it (Clark, 1979,

p. 14). Japanese group consciousness goes back to the concept of house-hold. In the words of Nakane:

> The essence of this firmly rooted, latent group consciousness in Japanese society is expressed in the traditional ubiquitous concept of *ie*, the house-hold, a concept which penetrates every nook and cranny of Japanese soci-ety. The Japanese usage *uchi-no* referring to one's work place indeed de-rives from the basic concept of *ie*. The term *ie* also has implications beyond those to be found in the English words "household" or "family." (Nakane, 1970, p. 4)

One of the implications suggested by Nakane is developed by Clark, which is that the *ie* institution endowed the Japanese company with two of its ideal values: that employees should stay with one organization for life, and that their relations within the company should in some sense resemble those within a family (Clark, 1979, p. 17). The process by which a new employee is "adopted" into the company illuminates the critical relationship between a member of the company and the com-pany itself. Facets of the process of introduction have been described by Rohlen (1978), who participated in a training program for new recruits to Uedagin Bank (a fictitious name for a regional bank in Japan).

The high point of the men's training program, lasting over 4 months, was a 25-mile marathon walk scheduled as the last special event. The en-tire group of over 100 recruits walked the first nine miles together as an entire body. The stroll, begun in the coolness and freshness of the morn-ing, was pleasant. The recruits talked and joked before breaking down into squads to cover the second nine miles of the course. Competition increased among the squads as some groups quickened their pace. Heat, fatigue, blisters, and stiff muscles began to take their toll. Young men from the bank tempted the walkers with offers of cold drinks, which the recruits had been forbidden to take. Some recruits sank down by the wayside, sucking salt tablets, as the time approached noon and "the park baked under the heat of a June sun" (Rohlen, 1978, p. 27). The training staff, also walking the course but in the opposite direction, instructed the squads to break up and continue walking the last seven miles in single file and in silence.

> Soon a long line of slowly moving trainees stretched along the circumfer-ence of the course. Having already covered 18 miles, the last nine at a gru-eling pace, we found the excitement and clamor of competition gone. We pushed forward, each individual alone in a quiet world, confronted with the sweep of his own thoughts and feelings. (Rohlen, 1978, p. 27)

The episode described by Rohlen, coming toward the end of the training program, provides a remarkable symbolizatoin of Japanese psychology. First, the first nine miles of the walk, all together, symbolizes the group affiliation which is the centerpiece of Japanese identity. The second phase, conducted in squads, stands for the specialized work unit, which generates hard work and fierce competition. Learning from harsh experience, reflection upon it is preserved for the third phase, when each individual walks alone, locked in silence. Earlier in the program, about one third of the way through, the recruits had received Zen training, learning to meditate and experiencing the spartan rigor of Zen. Other parts of the program emphasized the values of the company, associating its superordinate goals with the welfare of Japan. The training provided the resources for the ordeal of the hike, what the Japanese call spiritual strength (Rohlen, 1978, p. 28). The program overall can be considered as a rite of passage for the recruits, and consistent with the initiation rites that promote internal unity in communities throughout the world (Rohlen, 1978, pp. 29–30).

The extensive company training described by Rohlen is not a traditional part of Japanese business. It represents a traditional Japanese reaction, which attempts to neutralize cultural changes brought about by the imposed education reforms of the American occupation and the westernization of popular culture. The cultural contradictions created by the foreign influences, which were needed but not entirely held at bay from nonessential areas of Japanese society requiring their use, have created schisms such as the one separating the world of business and the world of universities and intellectuals, which have grown apart and become hostile to each other (Rohlen, 1978, p. 29). The gap between the two sectors has not been planned, since the Japanese, infused by the Confucian valuation of knowledge of how things are done, accepted as early as 1871 curricula established by the Ministry of Education for industry and commerce. As a result, the proportion of Japanese managers with college degrees rose from 8% in 1900 to 55% in 1928, a rate comparable to European industry today (Clark, 1979, p. 36).

The schism between industry and education in Japan suggests that the pattern of industrial organization has characteristic tendencies. Clark identified four of these. The first one and perhaps the most important is that the company in Japan tends to be

> an elementary unit, a clearly defined cell of industrial or commercial activity, rather than merely one of a number of industrial organizations whose memberships overlap. (Clark, 1979, p. 49)

The Japanese company serves as the elementary unit of Japanese industry, and at the same time provides the social nexus of membership and even identity for its employees. The second characteristic is a tendency for the company to be narrowly specialized and engage in one line of business or perhaps a few closely connected ventures.

The third tendency deserves elaboration. Japanese companies are arranged in a hierarchy in which the bigger the company the better its standing. Large firms engage in capital-intensive modern industries, achieve high productivity, and pay high wages. Small firms, on the other hand, sometimes in traditional industries, use less capital, achieve lower productivity, and pay lower wages. The differences existing between large and small firms have been called "industrial dualism" and "dual economy."

The fourth tendency is for the company to be associated with other companies in some form of group. This and the preceding three tendencies decry a society of industry, in which a company takes its place according to what it does, whether it is dominant in its particular line of business, how it is allied with prestigious companies and so on. The society of industry influences the inner workings of each company, and the company has an effect on the wider community of industrial society (Clark, 1979, pp. 44–50.) The same principle of reciprocal fusion that exists between the individual and his social network is repeated among companies and groups of companies. Furthermore, the government assumes a major role with private industry, sometimes blurring the distinction between public and private sectors. Indicative planning, as it is done in Japan between government and private industry, gives a brief glimpse of the relationship between government and industry. The functional aspect of uniting government and private industry provides an abstract parallel to the training of recruits for a company. Whereas the physical training of the long march symbolized the transformation of the recruits into members of the company, indicative planning abstractly shows the union of government and industry for the economy of Japan.

Indicative planning in Japan is associated with the actions of Morozumi Yoshihiko, who was one of MITI's first officers to be assigned abroad after the war, to the Japanese Embassy in Paris. In France, he became acquainted with the planning in which the French were engaged as a condition of Marshall Plan aid. He returned to Tokyo to urge MITI to adopt indicative planning, described by him with terms such as "consent economy" and "mutually determined national targets" (Hadley, 1975, p. 9). Japan adopted indicative planning, which

> has been a significant factor in the economy's extraordinarily (good) postwar performance, (Hadley, 1975, p. 1)

The governments of all major economies today provide some direction to the economy by employing the tools of monetary and fiscal policy. In indicative planning, these tools are used, but, in addition, the planning process addresses itself explicitly to resource allocation for the economy as a whole. Indicative planning supplements market forces (it does not supplant them) by fusing explicitly enunciated goals with reliance on market mechanisms. Unlike centrally planned economies which substitute market mechanisms with planning,

> Indicative planning uses market signals, the lure of profit, or market share to pull resources from where they are in the market into areas where it is believed there will be greater long-run advantage for the nation (Hadley, 1975, p. 4)

When the government planners sit down with industry, the government officials have the economy as a whole in mind as they use input–output analysis for tracing through the resource allocation consequences of changed investment patterns. Industry is neither ordered nor commanded to comply with the plans of the government; instead, the message from the government rests on "it will be to your advantage to follow this course." When industry does not see the advantage, they do not follow the advice. Incentives offered by the government have taken the form of tax treatment, credit at preferential rates, credit availability, facilitated imports of technology, bars against manufacturing and bars against marketing of foreign imports in Japan. When a company reached the export stage, additional benefits were provided, but they were conditional on export performance: the stronger the performance, the larger the benefit (Hadley, 1975, pp. 14–15).

The long time frame of Japanese planning Hadley (1975, p. 9) attributes to the tradition of dynamic economics instead of the static economics of the Anglo-American school. This assumption of economics, as well as the features of indicative planning, seem to fit Japanese deep culture. The integration of private industry and of government have contributed significantly to Japanese modernization. At the same time, indicative planning and the preferential treatment given to strong performance tend to concentrate exports in a few products; cars, transport equipment, electric goods, steel, and chemicals (Clark, 1979, p. 246). The resentment created in Japanese trading partners has weakened Japan's position in the world and at the same time made the economy vulnerable to structural conditions, political or economic, which will change the favorable economic picture of exports.

CONCLUSIONS

On the road seeking Japanese organizational communication, we have passed by a wide range of subjects. In conclusion, we shall attempt to draw together the many strands touched upon around the concepts of representation of experience, transaction of messages, and Japanese empathic communication.

1. Summary

Communication is the base of Japanese organizations, and yet the Japanese language lacks a standard term to represent the meaning of *communication*. Like water for fish, communication for the Japanese is inseparable from organizational activity of all kinds. For this reason, the analysis of Japanese communication lacks a thing-like center even more than American communication, which already is diffuse enough. For Americans, communication is a problem separate from other kinds of organizational activities such as decision making, motivation, and innovation.

Thirteen conceptual barriers were identified that obstruct objective American interpretations of Japanese culture. The quality of representation revealed in language assumes a significant role in miscommunication when we consider the prototypical quality of Japanese concepts, in comparison to the dichotomies formed by those in English. As the Japanese go from prototype to prototype, the American perceives a series of jumps, lacking continuity of logic or purpose. Japanese prototypical leaps are products of representation. On the American side, experience is represented in dichotomies, ideally with only two poles widely separated in binary opposition by a single dimension. This mental formation, well represented in language, encourages the description of attributes and a continuity in thinking favoring causal assertions. It also encourages the adversary relationship as a strategy in thought, and it is linked to adversary relations in communication and social relations. (For their part, the Japanese show a strong aversion to adversary formations.) Americans canalize thought along narrow paths, using judgments of practicality to search for a one-dimensional principle that serves as the criterion of success, such as profit or efficiency.

The major causes of the communication gap occur with representation of experience as patterns of thinking and values, i.e., deep culture. In Japanese culture, values of identity are diffuse and require participation. They are more like belonging-in-action, and, in the Japanese cultural scheme of things, their realization is governed by concentrated consciousness. The nature of the individual as a member of mankind is not sharply differentiated from nature, which serves as a metaphor for depicting the overarching interest of the Japanese in human relations and in its key concept, the network. These critical patterns of deep culture supplied the base for analyzing Japanese corporate culture, using the concepts of strategy, structure, systems, staff, style, skills, and superordinate goals. The interlocking of all components of the Japanese way in industry led to a short excursion into the society and into the historical antecedents of Japanese business.

The treatment of Japanese organizational communication applies to interpersonal relations but also to American–Japanese relations at the international level, supplying insights into the current friction between the two countries. From the American side, the tension begins with the American attitude toward the Japanese. Westerners, including Americans, when Japan was opened to the West, held a romantic view of Japan (Wilkinson, 1983, pp. 41–56). Today, their images of things Japanese provide little room for accepting Japan's attainments in technology and business. On the Japanese part, quiet penetration of foreign markets and empathic communication make it difficult to represent Japan's genuine interest to the rest of the world. As a consequence, history records that the present tension between the United States and Japan follows an old script. The West was caught off guard by the Japanese defeat of Russia in 1904–05, by the attack on Pearl Harbor, by the economic surge of the '60s and '70s, and by the current trade imbalance. These surprises indicate that the old images are still in place. Americans are slow to give the Japanese full credit for their technology, their business, or their attainments as a modern nation. Contemporary Japan is often dismissed as an economic miracle or as that brilliance which is distant enough to be safely dismissed. The danger of this pattern is that problems such as the current trade imbalance are allowed to reach the boiling point before they are seriously confronted. By then, damage has been suffered and negative public attitudes have congealed, demanding that government make draconian solutions. Thus there is urgency in the air for American and Japanese to commit themselves to filling the communication gap between the two nations. The threat is one not of doomsday prophecy but rather the need for a brisk accommodation between the two countries that will allow them to separate mutual and competing interests, and to remove cultural barriers, allowing negotiators to arrive at the most advantageous arrangement for the two countries.

2. Filling the Gap

The cognitive analysis of the communication gap naturally canalizes any recommendations that can be made toward education, training, planning, and policy. The assumption underneath the following recommendations is that, more often, Americans should become students and the Japanese teachers. This turn-around in roles is not likely to occur easily. When the Japanese are given credit for their achievements, as in business, Americans are likely to conclude only too quickly that the Japanese attainment is intimately a product of Japanese culture and not transferable to the United States, and that Americans have little to learn from the Japanese. Americans find it easier to pursue their usual patterns of communication, persuading people and explaining facts, and allow the Japanese to slip comfortably into the role of learners instead of themselves. Yet Americans have a poorer understanding of Japan than the Japanese have of the United States. Based on this analysis, the recommendation is to develop a third culture for communication that combines the best set of values from both cultures for a given purpose. The representation of experience for intercultural negotiations should strike a bargain between the American and the Japanese patterns, first capturing American problem solving, decision-making, and conflict resolution. Mathematical and other technical approaches used with these formulations of experience should make them more congenial for Japanese communicators. Second, these techniques, particularly problem-solving, should be analyzed to identify their components and to modify them where needed.

One of the most important lessons that Japan can teach the West is how to assimilate a new idea, using it for an express purpose and restricting its influence to those areas where it has been decided the idea should be implemented. For example, negative reasoning is a foreign pattern in Japan, but it has been imported and it is practiced by members of quality control circles, insulting the culture at large from negative reasoning. The social device of a transfer mechanism, illustrated by the quality control circle, is an important contribution to controlling the fear of and the dislike for innovations from abroad.

The center of emotion and human relations of Japanese culture leads to reliance on concentrated discipline in situations where Americans would put their trust in hardware or in technical skills. The difference reflects profound values of deep culture, but does not appear to introduce insuperable difficulties. Both Japanese and Americans appreciate efficient operations, but it is necessary to establish a balance between reliance on human factors or on technicism to perform a particular task. The burden of adjusting to this difference should be on Americans. In recent years, the development of technicism in American society has outstripped the ability of managers to apply it realistically.

Perhaps the most difficult difference contributing to the communication gap is in styles of communication. In negotiations, Americans prefer adversary relations and a rational approach. The Japanese, on their side, avoid confrontations, plead misunderstanding, and are reluctant to enter the iron cage of rationality. Given these pervasive differences, it seems desirable to rethink negotiations and to divide the process into two phases. The first phase would include substantive negotiations for the purpose of establishing reasonable positions for both parties. This aspect of negotiations should conform to Japanese practice, but it should also receive the technical attention which Americans have given to the process of negotiations. The second phase should be more routinized, in keeping with Japanese expectations. When the actual negotiations take place, a tight agenda should be observed, with the intent of ritualizing the proceedings to some degree. Within the scope of the agenda, the American style of negotiating issues should be followed. The overall pattern would become a blend of the Japanese and American practices.

The recommendations made above are general, in the sense that they are free floating and unattached to actual programs or organizations, lacking a place and context in which they should be carried out. They are specific in that they focus directly on what causes the communication gap.

They begin with actual problems and proceed to examine and to derive recommendations from the analysis itself. At this point, they can be made more concrete, if employed to develop training programs, materials, and methods which will address the issues raised by the communication gap. What has not been done is to bring to bear upon training and educational programs, or bring to the attention of policy makers, the existing resources and insights in a deliberate and concentrated way to fill the communication gap.

REFERENCES

Aida, Y. (1977). Anatomy of the Japanese consciousness. In M. Hyol & E. G. Seidsensticker (Eds.), *Guides to Japanese culture* (pp.65-68). Tokyo: Japan Culture Institute.
Akiyama, S. (1986, June). Analyzing Jungian Japan. *Japan Times*. p.8.
Allen, G.C. (1981). *The Japanese economy*. New York: St. Martin's Press.
Azuma, H. (1984). Secondary control as a heterogeneous category. *American Psychologist, 39*, 970-971.
Bateson, G. (1958). *Naven*(2n ed.). Palo Alto, CA: Stanford University Press.
Bloom, I. (1974). Letters: Japanese conception of nature. *Science, 184*, 850.
Campbell, L. (1964). Science in Japan. *Science, 143*,, 776-782.
Cho, K. T. (1966). Japanese ideologies and cross-cultural understanding. *Business and Government Review*. University of Missouri.
Clark, R. (1979). *The Japanese company*. New Haven CT: Yale University Press.
Fisher, G. H. (1972). *Public diplomacy and the behavioral sciences*. Bloomington, IN: Indiana University Press.
Geertz, C. (1973). *The interpretation of cultures*. New York: Basic Books.
Hadley, E. M. (1975). *Japanese indicative planning*. Paper presented at Southeast Region Conference, Association for Asian Studies. January 23-25.
Hamaguchi, E. (1980). Basic problems in the study of anthropology. *Personality, 8*.
Hasegawa, N. (1965). *The Japanese character*. Tokyo: Kodansha International.
Herbert, J. (1967). *Shinto: The fountainhead of Japan*. New York: Stein and Day.
Hofstede, G. (1980). *Culture's consequences*. Beverly Hills, CA: Sage Publications.

Hsu, F. L.K. (1975). *Iemoto: The heart of Japan*. New York: John Wiley.

Hsu, F. L. K. (1966). *Confucianism*. Pondicherry, India: Sri Aurobindo International Center of Education.

Jabilin, F. M. (1982). In M. E. Roloff & C. R. Berger (Eds.), *Social cognition and communication* (pp.255-286). Beverly Hills, CA: Sage.

Keane, J. (1980) *The Kami concept: A basic for understanding and dialogue* (Oriental Studies, No. 16). Tokyo: Orient Institute for Religious Research.

Kelly, W. K. (1985). *Deference and defiance in nineteenth-century Japan*. Princeton, NJ: Princeton University Press.

Kyogoku, J. (1985, October). Modernization and modern ethos: Japan in the twentieth century. *The Japan Foundation Newsletter, 3*, 1-8.

Lebra, T. S. (1976). *Japanese patterns of behavior*. Honolulu, HA: The University Press of Hawaii.

Maruyama, M. (1977). The intellectual tradition in Japan. In M. Hyol & E. G. Seidensticker (Eds.), *Guides to Japanese culture* (pp. 77-79). Tokyo: Japanese Culture Institute.

Morley, J. D. (1985). *Pictures from the water trade*. London:Andre Deutsch.

Nakamura, H. (1977). *A history of the development of Japanese thought*. Tokyo.

Nakamura, H. (1964). *Ways of thinking of Eastern peoples: India-China-Tibet-Japan*. Honolulu, HA: East-West Center Press.

Nakane, C. (1970). *Japanese society*. New York: Penguin Books.

Pavitt, C. & Haight, L. (1985, Winter). The "competent communicator" as a cognitive prototype. *Human Communication Research, 12* (2), 225-241.

Pascale, R. T., & Athos, A. G. (1981). *The art of Japanese management*. New York: Simon and Schuster.

Pribram K. H. (1969). The neurophysiology of remembering. *Scientific American, 220*, 73-86.

Rohlen, T. P. (1978, January). The education of a Japanese banker. *Human Nature*, 22-30.

Shils, E. (1975). *Center and periphery: Essays in macrosociology*. Chicago: The University of Chicago Press.

Seelye, H. N., Stewart, E. C. & Sween, J. A. (1982, July). *Evaluating quality control circles in U.S.A. industry: A feasibility study*. (Research Rep. No. ONR-82-1). LaGrange, IL: International Resource development.

Singer, K. (1973). *Mirror, sword and jewel*. Tokyo: Kodansha International.

Stewart, E. C. (1981). Cultural sensitivities in counseling. In P. P. Pedersen, J. G. Draguns, W. J. Lonner, & J. E. Trimble (Eds.), *Counseling across cultures* (pp. 61-86). Honolulu, HA: The University Press of Hawaii.

Stewart, E. C. (1982, July). *Adapting to deep structure of business in Japan*. Paper presented at the 20th International Congress of Applied Psychology, Edinburgh, Scotland.

Suzuki, D. (1977). Zen and Japanese culture. In M. Hyol & E. G. Seidensticker (Eds.), *Guides to Japanese culture* (pp. 46-50). Tokyo: Japan Culture Institute.

van Wolferen, K. (1982, Winter). Reflections on the Japanese system. *Survey, 26* (1), 121-150.

Vogel, E. F. (1979). *Japan as number one*. Cambridge, Massachusetts: Harvard University Press.

Watanabe, M. (1974). The concept of nature in Japanese culture. *Science, 183*, 279-282.

Weisz, J. R., Rothbaum, F. M., & Blackburn, T. C. (1984). Standing out and standing in: The psychology of control in America and Japan. *American Psychologist, 39*, 955-969.

Whitten, N. E. Jr. & Wolfe, A. W. (1973). Network analysis. In J. J. Honigmann (Ed.), *Handbook of social and cultural anthropology* (pp.717-746). Chicago: Rand McNally.

Wilkinson, E. (1983). *Japanese versus Europe*. New York: Penguin Books.

Yoshimura, N. (1986). *Japanese corporate culture*. Unpublished senior thesis, International Christian University, Tokyo, Japan.

PART IV

Teaching and Practicing
Communication "Competence":
Two Views

8

Communication Competence in the Information Age: Praxis, Philosophy, and Pedagogy

David A. Bednar
Grant T. Savage

An undergraduate walked out of his managerial communication class after completing a language competency test. The course was required for all business majors, and covered a balance of written and oral communication skills. The competency examination was administered early in the semester to provide both the professor and student feedback about the student's basic language skills.

The young man pushed the door shut behind him, stepped into the hall, and began talking about the exam with two of his friends. They commiserated together for a few minutes about what lay ahead for them in the course. Finally, one of the students summarized his initial impression of the course in the following statement: "This class is going to be a real pain in the ---!"

From a student's point of view, this assessment probably had merit. The course syllabus outlined a series of demanding written and oral assignments, the grading standards were rigorous, and considerable time and effort would be required to earn a satisfactory semester grade. Moreover, the assignments challenged students to think critically about managerial communication theories and practices. For a student with a short-term, grade-oriented perspective (and perhaps the hope of passing the class with a minimum amount of effort), the course truly would be a "pain."

From another perspective, however, the student's statement may reflect a much larger problem. Several recent reports about the decline and devaluation of education in the United States indicate a lack of basic skills among many high school and university graduates. Thomas H.

Kean (1985, p. 128), governor of New Jersey and chairman of the Education Commission of the States, reports: "Our colleges and universities are the next targets of education reform. Many of them have ample reason to feel like targets. Several reports critical of undergraduate education have appeared in the last year, and more are in press. We will soon have no shortage of information about academe's deficiencies or of ideas to correct them."

The following excerpts are representative of the findings, conclusions, and recommendations presented in these reports:

> The educational failures of the United States are emerging as a major concern of the 1980's. The abundance of reports diagnosing and prescribing for our schools and colleges, the urgency with which they are argued, the evidence that they summon, and the analyses that they offer are persuasive evidence that there is a profound crisis.
>
> Evidence of decline and devaluation is everywhere. The business community complains of difficulty in recruiting literate college graduates. Remedial programs, designed to compensate for *lack of skill in using the English language*, abound in the colleges and in the corporate world. (Our emphasis; from the *Report of the Project on Redefining the Meaning and Purpose of Baccalaureate Degrees, 1985, p. 1*)
>
> University business schools must revamp their curricula to train managers who are more broadly educated, flexible enough to cope with change, and *better able to communicate*. The core curriculum at most business schools should be expanded from the basics of marketing, finance, production, and accounting to include the political, environmental, ethical, and technological aspects of management.
>
> *Business schools should also seek to insure that their graduates are competent in oral and written communication.* Too few business schools teach the interpersonal skills that effective managers need. The rigor applied to financial and quantitative techniques can, and should, be applied equally to people management. Courses should emphasize the skills of interviewing, coaching, counseling, negotiating, motivating, and disciplining. (Our emphasis; from *America's Business Schools: Priorities for Change*, 1985, p. 5.)
>
> Schools are failing to stress the "invisible curriculum" of teamwork, honesty, reliability, and learning how to learn. Young people who have not learned discipline and mastered basic skills, *and especially mastery of English*, are doomed to failure and unemployability in later life. (Our emphasis; from *Investing in Our Children: Business and the Public Schools*, 1985, p. 2.)

Even though these reports evaluate a wide range of educational institutions (i.e., elementary, high school, university) and processes, one sobering finding is emphasized in each of the reports: *many of today's graduates are deficient in the basic communication skills of speaking, writing, reading, and listening.* Dealing with this problem is a major challenge for educators, administrators, and students, particularly at the dawn of the information age.

The importance of successfully meeting this challenge cannot be overemphasized. In a rapidly changing world, basic language and communication skills are essential and provide the foundation for personal, social, and economic development. However, basic skills alone cannot improve existing interpersonal and organizational behaviors—knowledge and critical thinking are needed as well.

Students should learn not only "how" but also "what," "when," "where," and "why." Students must also learn to think critically, examining the means and ends effected by skills and knowledge. By examining the basic assumptions underling praxis and theory, students learn how and why various communication practices initiate, destroy, maintain, change, or enrich interpersonal relationships and organizational systems. Critical thinking reveals the bridges between theory and practice—and the chasms.[1] U.S. students especially need to think critically in light of the widespread introduction of participative management techniques from Japan and Europe (Herrick, 1983; Zager & Rosow, 1982). Many of these participative practices are designed to create and sustain open communication among and within autonomous work groups residing in organizations. These practices emphasize not only efficiency and technical advancement, but also harmonious personal, social, and economic relations.

In an attempt to help the previously mentioned student understand both the necessity and importance of enduring the "pain" of his managerial communication course, we prepared the following letter:

Dear Mr. _____

We overheard your comments the other day about the "pain" you are experiencing in the managerial communication course. We thought some additional background information about your discomfort and its treatment might be useful.

In a complex and rapidly changing world, competence as a communicator is essential. The ability to effectively send and receive messages is the foundation upon which successful personal lives and careers are built. Communication competence is not just a term you need to memorize for an exam; it is an essential aspect of your career preparation and development.[2]

---

[1] We are using the term "critical thinking" in a much broader sense than it traditionally is used (see, for example, Katula & Martin, 1984). Our use of the term emphasizes how an informed critique can radically question taken-for-granted assumptions and beliefs.

[2] For examples of how the concept of communication competence has recently been applied by communication scholars, see Cegala (1984); Cegala, Savage, Brunner, and Conrad (1982); Norton (1978); Wiemann (1977); and Wiemann and Backlund (1980). Some of the theoretical controversies involving the notion of communication competence are discussed by Cupach and Spitzberg (1983) and McCroskey (1982).

Albert J. Simone (1985), President of the University of Hawaii, recently presented some facts and illustrations that underscore the importance of communication skills in international business:

1. Engineering and science students at the Tatung Institute of Technology in Taiwan must demonstrate speaking, writing, and reading fluency in at least *three* languages before qualifying for graduation. Two of the languages must be Chinese and English, and the third is selected from among Japanese, Spanish, and German.
2. It has been estimated that there are more than 10,000 English speaking Japanese business men and women in the United States. The number of Japanese-speaking American business men and women in Japan is *less* than one thousand.
3. There are more teachers of English in Russia than there are students of Russian in the United States.
4. Only 4% of American public school students study more than 2 years of a foreign language. Approximately 8% of American colleges require a foreign language for admission. (In 1966, 34% of American colleges required foreign language for admission.)
5. Patent applications are *83% higher in Japan* than in the United States, and almost four times higher than West Germany.
6. Approximately 90% of all Japanese scientific papers are published *only* in Japanese.

So what does all of this have to do with the pain you are experiencing in managerial communication? What is the implication of these statistics and trends? Many nations, the United States in particular, are experiencing a transition from an industrial and product-based economy to an information- , knowledge- , and service-based economy. This transition creates a need by businesses for the latest information, theories, knowledge, and technology made available through research. Countries such as Germany and Japan have developed and significantly improved their capabilities for conducting basic research. To the extent that the United States is to be a major partner in business and technology transfer, it must stay current with the latest innovations and technological breakthroughs.

For example, East Asia represents a major population block, accounting for approximately one-third of the world's population. It includes Japan, the second largest market economy in the world. The rapid industrialization and development of Japan since World War II has been described as the "economic miracle of the century" and is explained in part by the transfer of technology from the West. Today an increasing number of technological breakthroughs are occurring in Japan. Is it possible that the flow of new technologies from Japan to the United States could be impeded because of our inability to read and study the Japanese language? (See items #4, #5, and #6 above.) Business, government, and academic leaders are concerned about the lack of significant progress in improving American access to the Japanese technical literature in electronics and electrical engineering (Amatniek, 1985). To keep up with those fields, in which the Japanese are the acknowledged leaders, the United States must improve its capacity to understand the Japanese language.

Will you, as a future manager, miss important business opportunities in East Asian markets because you or your company do not understand or are not sensitive to people from different cultures and backgrounds?

More and more, business men and women must understand and operate in global markets and communicate effectively with people from many different nations. As indicated above, students in many nations are preparing for the international world of business that will exist in the 1990s and beyond. The major point is this: *the development and progress of these countries is occurring at the very time that major deficiencies in our own educational system are just being recognized.* Tatung Institute of Technology graduates engineers proficient in Chinese, English, and German. In contrast, many graduates from colleges and universities in the United States cannot spell or write a coherent memo or report in English.

"But," you say, "someone else can correct my spelling and clean up my memos. After all, I'm going to be hired for my business savvy, my knowledge of finance, accounting, management, or marketing. My secretary will handle all the writing chores; I'll just tell her or him what needs to be said."

The strength of this argument is rapidly being chipped away by two important trends of the information age. First, secretaries with the skills needed to repair your memos and reports are now in scarce supply. These women and men have discovered that their skills are needed in the managerial and professional ranks of almost all organizations.

Secondly, many businesses are learning that lower- and middle-level managers can more efficiently perform a variety of communication tasks themselves on microcomputers and word processors. Rather than spending 15 minutes dictating a letter—which will then take another 45 minutes to type, proofread, and correct—many managers are writing and producing letters in 10 minutes or less. Presently available microcomputer software allows a manager to "call up" a form letter, modify it for the particular situation, check its spelling, and print it on letterhead stationery in a matter of minutes.

The availability of such computer technology not only means that you will be expected to write and produce much of your own work, but it also means that you will have access to extensive data bases and sophisticated data analyses. You'll be faced with a very modern dilemma: how to make sense of an abundance of information. Your skills as a sense-maker and interpreter will be sorely tested.

An abundance of information increases the complexity of any problem. The questions you'll be asked will not have simple, easily understood answers. Multiple avenues of choice will emerge as you analyze each problem, and you'll have the unenviable task of communicating these complicated decision alternatives and recommendations to others.

Yet fuzzy problems and complex answers will not be your only worries. The media you use to communicate have also grown increasingly sophisticated in the information age. Traditional documents such as the letter, memo, and report are being transformed by new business media: electronic mail messages, video-laser disks, and computer graphics. Writing is being inscribed in new ways, sometimes with unforeseen consequences (Electronic Mail, 1985).

Even the process of person-to-person communication is being changed by technology (Gratz & Salem, 1984). From video teleconferencing to computer-to-computer conferencing, business people are using electronic media as substitutes for expensive and time consuming face-to-face meetings. Such technologies cut travel costs, but they also challenge the communicative competencies of business people. Every gesture you use and every word you say during a video-conference retains the aura of theater and television, encouraging participants to interpret seemingly insignificant remarks and movements as important.

Certainly, the computer and other electronic technologies herald an information age (Harris, 1985). But an information age does not necessarily mean an age in which more data and information will result in better decisions, or an age in which new ways of communicating will lead to better understandings. Decisions are choices. Understandings are the grounds of agreement. Neither decisions nor understandings emerge from information. You must transform that information, interpreting and expressing it. Your oral reports, your memos, your letters, your presentations, your recommendations—all are your interpretations expressed through your rhetoric to create choices and understandings.

Your sense-making and interpretive ability will be only as good as your understanding of the organizational context in which information is gathered, transmitted, and used. You'll need to be aware of how both the formal chain of command and the informal "grapevine" affect the flow of messages and information within an organization. You'll also need to understand how networks provide access to information and affect organizational decision making. Forming alliances and coalitions, bargaining and negotiating with groups inside and outside of the organization—all of these activities will require both an *understanding* of the organizational context and the *application* of basic communication skills. In short, theory and practice must interpenetrate.

Spectators at a football game can enjoy the sport whether they possess a rudimentary or sophisticated understanding of the rules, strategies, and tactics of the game. The spectators' foreknowledge or theory about the game provides the structure through which the spectator can vicariously experience each play. Hence, sophisticated spectators can more fully appreciate the nuances of the game. Yet, however knowledgeable a spectator may be, knowledge alone cannot ensure that he or she will be able to competently play the game. Specific skills such as running, tackling, blocking and throwing must be learned and practiced in order to execute plays successfully. Even the most talented athlete, however, will be a dismal failure on the playing field without a theoretical understanding of the game. Rookie mistakes will negate the athlete's skills *if those skills are learned without any general conception of how they relate to the rules, strategies, and tactics of the game.*

The rules of the game played in the business world vary from industry to industry, and the tactics and strategies also vary. But some of the general forms of the game remain the same, and generic strategies and tactics can be learned. Such strategies, once learned, become the avenues whereby communication skills are brought into play.

Human motivation is the catalyst for combining knowledge and skills. Your competence as a communicator is as dependent upon your desire and emotion as it is upon your cognitive and physical abilities (Hyde, 1984; Spitzberg, 1983; Spitzberg & Hecht, 1984). You choose which game to play, you choose which strategies and tactics to use, and you choose the ends and the means. Communication, as the ground where theory and practice interpenetrate, is not just the means for carrying out business as usual. It is also the wellspring from which new understandings emerge, potentially changing not just the tactics and strategies of a business, but the very rules that constitute it (Gray, Bougon, & Donnellon, 1985).

As a student preparing yourself for a career in a information age, you must be concerned about your communicative competence. Will one course make a difference? The answer can be "yes," if you accept the personal challenge to begin to gain new skills and insight about the communication process. Should you choose to ignore this challenge and rely only on your present skills and knowledge, the answer will be "no" and this course indeed will be a "pain in the ---."

EPILOGUE

The communication challenges facing students in an information age are matched by the practical, philosophical, and pedagogical challenges facing the educators of those students. These challenges include not only instruction in basic speaking, writing, reading, and listening, but also instruction about the broader organizational and managerial functions that are accomplished with and through these essential skills.

Students need to know the rules and skills of interviewing to obtain a job; to retain a job, they need extensive presentational, interpersonal, and group communication skills. None of these skills can be effectively applied, however, without an adequate theoretical grounding in organizational, group, and interpersonal communication. A student skilled in communication techniques, but lacking a conceptual framework or theory that guides the use of such techniques, is like the rookie quarterback with a superb throwing arm: although the quarterback can cover plenty of territory when passing, the ball often ends up in the wrong hands, going in the wrong direction.

Faculty and administrators in many colleges and universities already are working to meet these challenges through enriched curricula and innovative teaching techniques. For example, the American Assembly of Collegiate Schools of Business and the European Foundation for Management Development in their jointly sponsored book, *Managers for the XXI Century: Their Education and Development* (Walton, 1981), offer the following vision of what managerial communication education should attain.

Graduates are to be:

well grounded in communications, with new capabilities for listening, interpersonal interaction, negotiation, bargaining, and arbitration.
affectively mature as well as cognitively astute.
prepared to participate in and lead decision making that uses appropriate qualitative as much as quantitative methods.
practiced in connecting detail with principle, theory with practice.
socially responsible and international in orientation, holistic in their knowledge, well grounded in both liberal and professional wisdom, fundamentally more generalists than specialists.
imbued with self-confidence, and entrepreneurial spirit, persistent in seeking truth, and empathy.
versed in decentralized decision making and creative approaches to problem solving, based on mutually defined and accepted goals.

Faculty are to:

de-emphasize individual specialties in favor of holistic approaches, worked out through collaboration among liberal, professional, and "real world" colleagues, each of whom has been selected based on his or her "portfolio of abilities."
conceptualize courses as part of a continuing education, mixing experience or internship with studies.

incorporate into their teaching the means for affective development.

accept qualified management practitioners as fulltime accredited colleagues in the classroom.

move back and forth between "real world" managerial experience and academe.

be recognized for applied as well as "pure" research.

Students entering the world of work in an information age need to learn communication theories and skills in an holistic fashion. This is not the only challenge, however; the objectives outlined above also highlight concerns about students' affective development and social responsibility. These concerns emphasize the students' need to develop critical insights and the instructors' need to bear ethical responsibility for their teaching.

Praxis

Communication teachers and students are reflexively related by their own praxis to the very object of their joint study, and bring to the class-room assumptions and beliefs about organizational life (Light, 1979). Such assumptions both facilitate and inhibit learning.

To the extent that these assumptions allow students and instructors to question and explore organizational and communication practices, learning is facilitated. Conversely, when such assumptions unconsciously suppress the critical examination of organizational practices, learning is inhibited.

For example, many students and instructors assume that "blockages" in communication channels negatively affect the coordination of organizational activities. Such an assumption may lead to a better understanding of informal networks and to the redesign of formal organizational channels. At the same time, an unquestioning acceptance of this assumption about efficient communication may blind both students and instructors to the underlying reasons for channel blockages. In other words, students and professors may not question how such blockages support particular power structures in the organization, affecting access to information and influencing organizational decisions.

Noncritical thinking about communication blockages may lead to organizational change efforts with latently negative effects. Such seems to be the case with some quality circle programs that have failed in U.S. organizations (Seelye & Sween, 1983; White & Bednar, 1985). QC programs frequently bypass the traditional hierarchical communication channels through middle management, threatening the power of these managers. As a result, unless otherwise rewarded by upper management, middle managers are likely to sabotage the program. Moreover, union stewards may also be vehemently opposed to QC efforts, viewing the circles as a direct threat to the union's representation of workers' interests (Kilroy & Romano, 1984). In both instances, noncritical thinking blinds one to the sectional interests of other organizational stakeholders (Mitroff, 1983).

Noncritical thinking about organizational life, what phenomenologists call the "natural attitude" (Stewart & Mickunas, 1974), may lead to unquestioned support of technical over practical interests. Deetz (1985, pp. 124–125) explains,

> The technical interest is the drive for control, instrumental gain, and material/economic growth. The practical interest is a natural complement to this. It focuses on the meaning of existence and the fulfillment of social and symbolic needs. Technical and practical interests generate different types of reasoning and decision making. Technical reasoning is instrumental, tends to be governed by the theoretical and hypothetical, and focuses on the future and means-end chain. Practical reasoning is based on consumption, tends to be governed by the practical and immediate, and focuses on the goodness of the means as ends in themselves.

The nuclear arms race is a sobering example of the crisis arising from the conflict between technical and practical interests. Very few people would (we believe) object to eliminating all nuclear weapons if they could be assured that all nations would actually eliminate such weapons and destroy the means of manufacturing future weapons. Such is the practical interest.

But how have the arms talks proceeded? Through the play of technical interests, each nuclear power carefully counts missiles, busily develops new defenses and awesome offensive capabilities, and speculates about how a nuclear holocaust might be survived (Mitroff, 1985). Intent upon verifying every move, mistrusting every offer, and testing every contingency, each nation exacerbates the crisis.

On a smaller scale, and with stakes—though not nearly as perilous—involving central aspects of most persons' lives, labor and management negotiate about wages and benefits, working conditions, and the quality of work life. Here, a similar domination by technical interests may undermine the legitimacy of practical interests (Habermas, 1975). And the day-in and day-out decision making practices within organizations tend to support the domination of technical interests. Concerns about profits, productivity, and market share often overshadow practical, social concerns such as environmental pollution and quality of work life (Moskowitz & Byrne, 1985).

The successful integration of knowledge, skills, and motivation can effect an emancipatory interest which examines both the assumptions underlying instrumental, end-governed actions within the organization, and the means applied to fulfill social needs. Such an interest strives to integrate the needs of organizational stakeholders. An emancipatory interest values the balanced representation of sectional interests, and values the complementarity of practical and technical interests (Habermas, 1972).

Philosophy

The values of organizational members permeate their every act. Similarly, the values of professors and students color their interaction. Educators—professors, instructors, and teaching assistants—bear an ethical responsibility to their students (Freire, 1970). This responsibility is threefold.

First, educators should clearly articulate their own value orientation: what ends they seek and the means they use to achieve those ends. For example, an instructor who strongly believes in "the ideology of intimacy" in interpersonal relationships (Parks, 1982) should identify for students those occasions when he or she is advocating rather than explaining the concept of intimacy. Second, educators should attempt to explicate the basic values and assumptions that underlie various theories and techniques of managerial communication, exploring with their students the implications of key assumptions within each theory and technique (Redding, 1979). And third, educators should reflexively examine the praxis of the classroom, assessing how well the skills and theories students learn actually aid them in critically exploring current organizational practices. The values implicit in methods of presentation, assignments, testing, grading procedures, and evaluations of class participation should be disclosed to students and subjected to ongoing review.

These three ethical responsibilities, though seemingly simple, are difficult to fulfill. Each responsibility, however, is crucial in developing students' understanding of how their own desires, knowledge, and skills may be used in socially responsible ways. As role models, educators clearly should know what values they embody. To articulate these values requires more than merely expressing certain beliefs. Actions within the classroom speak more resoundingly than words. How the educator teaches may say as much or more than what the educator teaches.

Pedagogy

The pedagogical challenge offered by this philosophy is not easily met. Basic writing, speaking, listening, and reading skills are needed to empower students seeking to enter the world of work. And, although desire and knowledge alone cannot enable a person to competently communicate, neither can basic communication skills devoid of theory and ethos.

The transfer of technology throughout the world, the diffusion of computers, and the widespread use of electronic media herald an information age. This era highlights the crisis of cognitive and sectional interests. On one hand, the computer is the ultimate vehicle for furthering technical interests, advancing at the same time the interests of those controlling the production, distribution, and use of computers. On the other hand, the computer can be a means to promote an emancipatory interest, if educators can encourage students to critically evaluate the ends and means to which computers and electronic media are used in organizations.

Calls for basic communication competence, for computer literacy, for foreign language training, and for the integration of theory and practice frequently are heard in academic and professional circles. Calls for competence and literacy tend to further a technical interest, widening the chasm between theory and praxis. How theory and practice are integrated thus determines whether technical interests will dominate practical interests. Critical thinking is needed to ensure a balance between technical and practical interests. Such thinking not only should be directed at the body of knowledge and techniques used in managerial communication, but should also be directed at the pedagogy used to teach this vital subject.

Such innovative approaches as organizational simulations (Lederman & Ruben, 1984), organizational internships (Hanson, 1984), and experiential exercises in negotiating or interviewing (Mier, 1982; Seibold & Meyers, 1985) are aimed at integrating theory, skills, and practice. These innovations, however, can gain additional value if reflexive techniques are used to critique the ends and means embodied in these approaches. For example, Kreps and Lederman (1985, p. 361) indicate how reflexivity can be introduced in organizational communication case analyses:

> The instructor can facilitate effective in-class case analysis as a discussion leader by drawing attention to neglected facts, asking questions about points raised by participants, questioning the impact of different courses of action suggested, encouraging the group to ask questions and provide detailed commentary, and discouraging vague generalizations and ready made solutions.

Without the dialogue that facilitates such critical analysis and insight, the best that simulations, internships, and experiential exercises can attain is merely a continuation of the status quo.

Critical thinking can also be developed through traditional pedagogical techniques such as mass lecturing and testing. By asking challenging questions that require students to think and seriously consider their answers, mass lecturers can encourage open discussions of organizational theories, strategies, and values. And testing can be recast in a variety of ways to encourage student participation in and responsibility for learning. For example, computer tests of content areas can include electronically recorded "comments" from students about the ambiguity of test questions, the rationale for various questions, and the omission of particular content areas. Each of these techniques engages students in dialogue and creates a more transactive learning experience.

Microcomputer image projection, the ability to display computer produced images to an entire class, can also transform traditional didactic learning into transactive, dialogical learning. Just as with transparencies or slides, images can be pre-selected and sequenced by the instructor. However, at any time the instructor can interact with students and use their input to change the project image. By keying into the microcomputer suggestions from students, the instructor can immediately project their ideas for all to see. Or, by using a network of microcomputers linked to a large screen projector which is jointly controlled by the instructor and the student, various solutions to a problem can be developed simultaneously and used as a basis for discussion.

Transactive instructional techniques present advantages analogous to the use of musical instruments versus taped music to demonstrate various styles and techniques. Instructors using musical instruments can interact more effectively with students than can instructors relying on a limited, taped repertoire. The former can innovate at will; the latter must stick to a set agenda. Moreover, students who actually play the instruments experience directly the different musical styles and techniques. Similarly, innovative pedagogies can enable students of organizations to learn by doing, by emulating, and by reflexively examining their experiences.

SUMMARY

Recent reports about the state of education in the United States highlight a lack of basic skills among many high school and university graduates. Foremost among these deficiencies is a lack of basic communication skills. This problem is a significant challenge for students, educators, and administrators; how it is addressed and resolved will have far reaching implications for our society as we move into the information age.

In a rapidly changing and increasingly sophisticated world, communication competence is essential. New technologies and media are making available large amounts of information and increasing the complexity for the decision making process. Managers in contemporary organizations must be able to (a) critically analyze multiple avenues of choice and communicate to others complicated decision alternatives; (b) understand how the organizational context affects the processes by which information is gathered, transmitted, and used; and (c) engage in both technical and practical reasoning.

Innovative pedagogies and instructional methods can help to meet this challenge and prepare students for the information age. The ultimate objective should be the integration of knowledge and skills, philosophy and praxis. Transactive learning situations can foster critical thinking, provide opportunities for skill development, and encourage the responsible application of those skills.

REFERENCES

Amatniek, J. C. (1985, July 10). Access to Japanese technical literature concerns many. *The Chronicle of Higher Education,* p. 10.

America's business schools: Priorities for change (1985). Washington D C: The Business-Higher Education Forum.

Cegala, D. J. (1984). Affective and cognitive manifestations of interaction involvement during unstructured and competitive interactions. *Communication Monographs, 51* (4), 320-338.

Cegala, D. J., Savage, G. T., Brunner, C. C., & Conrad, A. B. (1982). An elaboration of the meaning of interactional involvement: Toward the development of a theoretical concept. *Communication Monographs, 49* (4), 229-248.

Cupach, W. R., & Spitzberg, B. H. (1983). Trait versus state: A comparison of dispositional and situational measures of interpersonal competence. *Western Journal for Speech Communication, 47,* 364-379.

Deetz, S. (1985). Critical-cultural research: New sensibilities and old realities. *Journal of Management, 11* (2), 121-136.

Electronic mail said to promote a 'confrontational style' (1985, October 2). *The Chronicle of Higher Education,* p. 32.

Freire, P. (1970). *Pedagogy of the oppressed.* New York: The Seabury Press.

Gratz, R. D., & Salem, P. J. (1984). Technology and the crisis of self. *Communication Quarterly, 32* (2), 98-103.

Gray, B., Bougon, M. G., & Donnellon, A. (1985). Organizations as constructions and destructions of meaning. *Journal of Management, 11* (2), 83-98.

Habermas, J. (1972). *Knowledge and human interests* (J. Shapiro, trans.) Boston, MA: Beacon Press.

Habermas, J. (1975). *Legitimation crises* (T. McCarthy, trans.). Boston, MA: Beacon Press.

Hanson, J. (1984). Internships and the individual: suggestions for implementing (or improving) an internship program. *Communication Education, 33* (1), 53-62.

Harris, C. L. (1985, October 14). Information power: How companies are using new technologies to gain a competitive edge. *Business Week,* pp. 108-114.

Herrick, N. (Ed.). (1983). *Improving government: Experiments with quality of working life systems.* New York: Praeger Publishers.

Hyde, M. J. (1984). Emotion and human communication: A rhetorical, scientific, and philosophical picture. *Communication Quarterly, 32* (2), 120-132.

Investing in our children: Business and the public schools (1985). New York: Council for Economic Development.

Kean, T. H. (1985, September 11). What states should do (and not do) to improve undergraduate education. *The Chronicle of Higher Education*, p. 128.

Kilroy, B. J., & Romano, R. J. (1984, March). *Quality circles: A case analysis of program failures.* Paper presented at the annual meeting of the Eastern Communication Association, Philadelphia, PA.

Katula, R. A., & Martin, C. A. (1984). Teaching critical thinking in the speech communication classroom. *Communication Education, 33* (2), 160-167.

Kreps, G. L., & Lederman, L. C. (1985). Using the case method in organizational communication education: Developing student's insight, knowledge, and creativity through experience-based learning and systematic debriefing. *Communication Education, 34* (4), 358-364.

Lederman, L., & Ruben, B. D. (1984). Systematic assessment of communication games and simulations: An applied framework. *Communication Education, 33* (2), 152-159.

Light, D. (1979). Surface data and deep structure: Observing the organization of professional training. *Administrative Science Quarterly, 24* (4), 551-559.

Mier, D. R. (1982). From concepts to practices: Student case study work in organizational communication. *Communication Education, 31* (2), 151-154.

McCroskey, J. C. (1982). Communication competence and performance: A research and pedagogical perspective. *Communication Education, 31*, 1-7.

Mitroff, I. (1983). *Stakeholders of the organization mind.* San Francisco, CA: Jossey-Bass.

Mitroff, I. (1985). *Talking about taboo topics within organizations: From corporate tragedies to nuclear war.* Paper presented at the annual meeting of the International Communication Association, Honolulu, Hawaii.

Moskowitz, D. B., & Byrne, J. A. (1985, October 14). Where business goes to stock up on ethics. *Business Week*, pp. 63, 66.

Norton, R. (1978). Foundations of a communicator style construct. *Human Communication Research, 4*, 99-112.

Parks, M. (1982). Ideology in interpersonal communication: Off the couch and into the world. In M. Burgoon (Ed.), *Communication Yearbook 5* (pp. 79-108). New Brunswick, NJ: Transaction Books.

Redding, W. C. (1979). Organizational communication theory and ideology: An overview. In D. Nimmo (ed.), *Communication Yearbook 3* (pp. 309-342). New Brunswick, NJ: Transaction Books.

Report of the project on redefining the meaning and purpose of baccalaureate degrees (1985, February 13). *The Chronicle of Higher Education*, pp. 12-30.

Seelye, N. H., & Sween, J. A. (1983, February). Critical components of successful U. S. quality circles. *The Quality Circle Journal, 6* (1), 14-17.

Seibold, D. R., & Meyers, R. A. (1985). Co-participant perceptions of information-gathering interviews: Implications for teaching interviewing skills. *Communication Education, 34* (2), 106-118.

Simone, A. J. (1985, May). *The role of universities in business and technology exchange in the Pan-Pacific.* Paper presented at the Pan-Pacific Conference, Seoul, Korea.

Spitzberg, B. H. (1983). Communication competence as knowledge, skill, and impression. *Communication Education, 32*, 323-329.

Spitzberg, B. H.,& Hecht, M. L. (1984). A component model of relational competence. *Human Communication Research, 10*, 575-599.

Stewart, D., & Mickunas, A. (1974). *Exploring phenomenology: A guide to the field and its literature.* Chicago, IL: American Library Association.

Walton, C. C. (Ed.). (1981). *Managers for the XXI century: Their education and development.* St Louis, MO: American Assembly of Collegiate Schools of Business.

White, D. D., & Bednar, D. A. (1985, Winter). Locating problems with quality circles. *National Productivity Review,* pp. 45-52.

Wiemann, J. M. (1977). Explication and test of a model of communicative competence. *Human Communication Research, 3,* 195-213.

Wiemann, J. M., & Backlund, P. (1980). Current theory and research in communicative competence. *Review of Education Research, 50,* 185-199.

Zager, R., & Rosow, M. P. (Eds.). (1982). *The innovative organization: Productivity programs in action.* New York: Pergamon Press.

9

Planning as Self-Enhancement

Henri Broms and Henrik Gahmberg*

SELF-DECEPTION AS A FACT OF LIFE

It is commonly believed that, in business communities, if anywhere, hard facts overrule every kind of wishful thinking. But in actual practice in the business world, this hard-facts attitude seems to dissipate somewhere into the realm of imagination.

In business corporations, the boards of directors usually have set up certain standards for proposals, such as major investment projects, to be presented for decision. The crux in these cases is regularly the expected return on investment (ROI), say 25%. The lifetime of an investment in machinery is normally not much more than 10 years. Within the decade, then, the investment should bring the company a profit up to the expected level.

This is an illusion, however, for in most cases the shareholders can be satisfied if the ROI comes to half or ⅓ of the target figure. There are several reasons for this. For instance, slack periods are not normally taken into account correctly. In capital-intensive industries running at ⅔ of optimum capacity, heavy losses are sustained in a few months—not to mention a recession of several years. Very often, these original projects do not consider all the later needs to improve the factory infrastructure, communications, power service, etc. These are normally presented later to the board as "necessary, nonprofitable investments."

All this means that investment decisions regularly miss their mark. This also means that the predictions of the firms are usually erroneous. It further implies that, if the board of directors realized the general fact that investment decisions do not correspond to realistic profit expectations, most of the investments would not be undertaken. Further, this

* Thanks are also due to Chancellor Klaus Waris, and Research Fellow Osmo Kuusi. An earlier version of this paper was prepared for the First International Conference on Organization Symbolism and Corporate Cultures, June 26–29, 1984, Lund, Sweden.

means that investments have to depend on plans that are a priori wrong. This self-deception is a socially accepted fact.

Another aspect of imaginary planning is the policy of growth. On the average, the growth of business firms is about 2%. However, firms in their annual reviews set growth targets of 8%–10%. If this could be achieved, after 10 years there would be only one business firm in Finland. There would be no room for any others. If some hypothetical firm succeeded in cornering 25% of the market, it could go on to conquer the whole market area and the rest of the companies would be left empty-handed.

Much government planning is also notoriously ill-fated, missing the mark not by tens but by thousands of percentage points. The question then arises: Why are such plans made? Perhaps many of the famous planning disasters suggested a vision, a picture of the future, one that sometimes needs to be produced, even at great risk, to sustain a nation's vitality and keep hope alive. After all, there are also planning successes.

Perhaps a case can be made for planning that might not be implemented in its original form, but under some other guise, a planning that opens new horizons and gives a sense of direction.

FAMOUS DISASTERS

This can be sometimes costly. Peter Hall's *Famous Planning Disasters* (Hall, 1980) gives stunning examples. The Anglo-French Concord airliner was planned to cost £170 million, but in reality it cost more than ten times more, £2 billion. The undertaking is running at a loss of £17 million pounds a year for both participating countries, and the chances of Concorde sales seem to be nil. The production lines, at least in England, have been discontinued.

However, at one time, the Concorde was the pride of Britain and France. The start was propelled by a grand view of historic concord and the integration of two European nations. The economic side on the undertaking did not matter. We read in Peter Hall's book (1980): "Later before the House of Commons Expenditure Committee Aubrey Jones was disarmingly frank: 'In retrospect I have to admit that my Department and I had no knowledge at all and had made no attempt at all to estimate the size of the potential market'" (p. 90). Still, the Minister of Aviation said at that time, "Space beckons us with a golden finger." So it did, but was the beckoning golden finger worth the 2 billions inpound sterling? The French still seem to think it was. A recent number of the *Paris Match* had a feature article on Concorde, which described the unhappy product in glowing terms.

The latest development is that American, English, and French entre-preneurs are planning a newer Mach 2- or 3-type supersonic plane. There now again seems to be a true market need for it.

Let us take another case of planning disasters, the spectacular Opera House in Sydney, Australia. Hall points out: "Sydney's new Opera House belongs to a select group of buildings that became immediately a popular symbol. The Opera House *is* Sydney, just as the Big Ben is London, the Arc de Triomphe is Paris, and the Empire State Building is New York City. It could thus be argued that it put the city on the mental map of great world cities."

Even this proof of ingenuity, boldness, and imagination was and con-tinues to be a planning disaster. As Hall remarks, it set a record against any other modern building project in time delay and cost escalation. But Sydney got its landmark, its "Arc de Triomphe." It is extremely difficult to estimate what such mental images and symbols are worth in terms of money.

"PURE" DISASTERS

The Concorde and the Sydney Opera House produced symbols and in-tangible values (in the case of the Concorde, skills) hard to measure. There are other types of disasters which leave us really with nothing in hand.

We may take a more recent example of a spectacular planning disas-ter in Finland. In 1974, the Finnish television factory, Salora, and the leading Social Democratic Party undertook factory production of televi-sion tubes in Finland. It was expected to be a triumph of high tech plan-ning. Japan was the new home of high tech, so Hitachi was asked to par-ticipate by subscribing 20% of the shares. The Japanese partners also contributed a task force of 17 engineers and foremen.

But nothing seemed to work out. Production failed to take off at the speed calculated in the plans. For reasons of government employment policy, dictated by party politics, the factory was built in an area lacking trained workers. The project was supposed to break even with an output of 300,000 tubes, but after the first year of operation a production ca-pacity of only a few thousand tubes was achieved. Sales lagged; costs soared. Material losses were high. According to the company's own figures, faulty tubes amounted to 50% of the total by the end of the year, when the factory closed down.

In 1978, rumors started to circulate that VALCO was ready to declare insolvency. In the autumn of 1979, the Board of Directors, made up mainly of Social Democratic politicians, sharply denied all such rumors. General elections were coming up in a few weeks' time. Immediately after the elections, VALCO went bankrupt. The hunt for culprits started. The difficulties of opening a new field of technology had apparently been underestimated. Hitachi's analysts said that the locality where VALCO was set up had no tradition of technical know-how in any branch of manufacturing. The trade union disputed the charge that the low production rate was due to the workers' lack of skill.

The planning of housing in Finland seems to prove the old maxim that "well planned is half done," since the implementation of such projects has constantly fallen short by 50%.

Plans can be classified according to their degree of implementation. Some, like short-range budget plans, are implemented often; long-range ones sometimes; but some, like the ones drawn up by political parties, as a rule, never.

There seems to be a deep-rooted need to engage in planning and making decisions, which, were the deciding body capable of soul-searching, would run every risk of failing partially—in some cases even 100%. The aforementioned investment plans, or instance, must inevitably fail. What is the mechanism of this irrational process? Or is there any mechanism at all?

A COMMENT ON METHODOLOGY

Right now, the study of organizational mythology and symbolism is at its apex. Symbolic action really needs to be explained for the apparently self-deceptive element of planning to be understood.

Traditionally, even to this day, businessmen tend to be rather more inclined to heed the hard-headed fact—even if they might act mostly, as Pareto (1968) maintains, on instinct. Talking about leading by instinct, the first (and still one of the best) strategists of modern times, von Clausewitz (1976), wrote that decision consists of boldness of judgment, of scarcity of time, of the necessity to guess, and also—let's not forget—of exact information. Decisions have to be made in a hurry and under duress; there is not way out of *not* making them. Wittgenstein told us to leave alone the irrational things about which we can get no exact information. But practical life and our daily routine will not let us leave them alone. Decisions that have been made by instinct can then, a posteriori, be given fine rationalistic reasons.

Many eminent scholars (like Vilfredo Pareto in his *Rise and Fall of the Elites*, 1968) have remarked on the primacy of feeling in decision making. Edzard Reuter (1985), a member of the board of directors of Daimler-Benz, in a recent thoughtful article described the methods of "scientific" management as based on dangerous superstition.

Von Clausewitz is strict in stressing the need for personal courage in the making of decisions. By some mental gymnastics, executives often confuse boldness with realism in the quantitative sense of the word. One can also be bold and a realist—in the Clausewitzian sense—by trusting one's own judgment of the irrational. This is actually the basic thesis of Reuter's article.

Regardless of all this, many managers would still like to think all their decisions are based on facts. Organizational culture is now a widely studied subject. The teaching of management has vogues that change like business cycles. For a while, people may listen to the mumbo-jumbo about symbols, but before long may come a time when symbolism won't sell anymore.

This is because the theories on the symbolic and unconscious are difficult and hazy and therefore somewhat suspect to many, who demand oversimplified answers. There are still quite a few good academics who do not believe a word of what Freud or Jung said. The same goes for the linguistic theories about the unconscious, which are exalted by some and spurned by others.

If symbolic learning were exact, we would not resort to the word symbol. The product of metaphorical knowledge must also be metaphorical, vague, and carrying many senses, because there the object of the act of knowing has many meanings.

At the Second International Congress of Semiotics in Vienna, René Thom defined well the two kinds of knowledge: (a) Causal: "From A follows B," and (b) Metaphorical: "A resembles B." Knowledge of the second kind cannot be made unequivocal.

As for the theories of the unconscious, we present one, which is based on communicational sciences. This theory has a rather wide currency in Eastern Europe, but it is less known in the United States.

TWO MODES OF LINGUISTIC COMMUNICATION

Perhaps half of all planning is directed toward one goal, but then, suddenly, quite different phenomena emerge. Generally taken, one can be happy if anything at all emerges from the planning as a whole. Much planning work is self-educational.

There is an interesting theory to decscribe self-educational planning—Yuri Lotman's autocommunicational theory.

Lotman's idea is that there are two basically different modes of verbal communication: In one, man speaks to other people; in the other, he speaks to himself, meditates, tries to absorb wisdom, etc. Both modes have specific linguistic features (Lotman 1973, 1977). Based on earlier studies by Buehler, Vygotsky, Whorf, and Jakobson, Lotman's ideas therefore have a fairly solid linguistic basis. Russian linguists studied the internal language of monologue at some length, and found that it is a language without vowels and with a syntax gone astray. The study of monologue and internal speech represents in itself a whole school within the science of linguistics.

The "usual" mode of verbal communication was described orginally by Karl Buehler in 1933, but was effectively put forward by Roman Jakobson (1972). It assumes that there is a verbal message:

Sender ---------------> Message ---------> Receiver

This form of linguistic communication is used when we tell somebody something he or she does not know. We wish to add to his or her present knowledge. But what kind of linguistic communication or tone do we use when we read to ourselves an Indian meditatoinal phrase, a seemingly meaningless mantra? When we repeat such a mantra a hundred times in transcendental meditation, we do not add any new information to our store of knowledge. We are using these words to reconstruct our psyche, or to enhance our ego. The same is true of prayers, battle cries, diaries. When we say a prayer, we know that it is a prayer and not a telegram or news item; in other words, we are using a special speech code. Proponents of Transcendental Meditation have remarked that oriental meditation does not enhance the ego but rather effaces it to let creative forces appear. But other views also exist: the national philosopher of Pakistan (well known also in other Islamic countries) was Muhammad Iqbal. He died in 1938. He said, in *Secrets of the Self* (1911), that the task of meditation was to strengthen the Self. His ideas were based on the classic al-Djili, dating from the 12th century.

According to Lotman, there is a special tone, code, or voice for speech addressed to oneself. It might be called by many names, such as a hope code, a prayer code, a mantra code or an artistic code; but he calls it "autocommunication." In it, the following process takes place:

```
Sender ------------------->  Message 1 ------------------->Message 1 -------------------
("I")                        Code 1                        Code 2                     I
                                                                                      I
                                                                                      I
                                                                           Displacement
                                                                            of Context
                                                                                      I
                                                                                      I
    Receiver <----------------- Message 2 <------------------------------------------- I
    ("I")
```

Lotman's findings were later followed by articles by S. Zolkiewski and Boris Oguibenine (1979), Osmo Kuusi (1984), and the present authors

(Broms & Gahmberg, 1981, 1982, 1983, 1987). As Lotman (1973) points out, artistic language is by its very nature autocommunicational. When we read *The Great Gatsby*, we do not read it to acquire more knowledge about the motor highway system of the '20s, but for self-enhancement.

THE QUALITATIVE AND THE QUANTITATIVE

The "I"–"He" system of communication makes it possible to transmit quantitative information, when quantity is seen as central. In the second system of communication "I"-to-"I", a qualitative change takes place in the person or group in question, leading to enhancement of the ego of the individual or of the team spirit of the group. This change leads to a displacement of context and thus to the introduction of a code, which turns the original message into a new one. When the transmission of information to oneself is paticularly strong, the result may be a reconstruction of the inner self.

The "ego" in this sense may be an individual manager or a corporate board of directors. In the corporate environment, a message, e.g., a strategic long-range plan, may be transmitted to other levels of managment by top management in order to be implemented, but the plan always has another purpose as well.

The second purpose, often carried out unconsciously, may be to enhance the CEO's ego or that of the strategic planning team or to improve the corporate image during the planning stage.

American authors, like Barnlund (1971) and Thayer (1968), actually also deal with a kind of autocommunication when they speak of *intrapersonal* communication. In his textbook *Communication and Communication Systems*, however, Thayer notes (1968, p. 337) that we do not know yet what happens intrapersonally in a communication situation. Lotman's important idea is to shed new light on this area and to link this intrapersonal communication with meditative methods, thus connecting the communication theory with 1000-year-old traditions that have been neglected.

Lotman thinks that any text can become meditational. When we read literature, the process is a re-shaping of our own minds. When we communicate with a novel, with whom do we communicate? With the author, of course, but also wit ourselves! But what makes Lotman's idea interesting, and actually raises it to the level for a far-reaching theory, is precisely the thought that the autocomunicational, "mantra" code can be added to any text.

Lotman writes that autocommunicative practices can be met with on all levels of life, in all texts, not only in art or religion. Every text can become a reshaping of the mind; even a plan can serve this purpose. It is man's orientation towards hope that brings to the fore the second code or a second mode of speech. Speaking of planners, when they hear the word "future," their imagination is instantly activated; it is given freer leeway. The second code is added, and man deepens his own experiences with free associations.

THE CODE OF HOPE

In autocomunication, a piece of information is taken up and a second autocommunicational code is added to it; then the infomation acquires a new content, a mythologically enhancing, make-believe content. The first code might be called the "usual" one. When someone reads a congressional report and understands it as a congressional report, he then uses the first code. If he starts feeling good about it and relates it to his present situation, then he is using a second code.

Artistic language almost always lends itself easily to this kind of enhancing reading. The reader says to himself: "This novel is not an historic text; it has a code in it that tells me it is verbal art." This is easy to understand, for a novel is not a history book. But, in line with Lotman's thesis, readers can add an enhancement code to any kind of text. Any text can be changed in subject matter by applying a new, second code to it. In such a case, the following process takes place: When we use any text as a code, we say to ourselves, "This touches me, this is meant for me." In fact, we then take up the text as a personal challenge, or identify ourselves with it. Kuusi (1984) writes that, if the text charges up or impassions the reader, it is justified to speak of autocommunication. When we read about the fate of Anna Karenina, we say, "This could be my life."

The text in question may also be a congressional report, but if one applies a new code to it and tells oneself, "This touches me," the text serves as autocommunication. The reader may then see himself as a great achiever or as the hero called to attain the goals of the report.

The I-to-you code means adding to one's fund of information. The I-to-I code means finding rich, new associations. Planning is autocommunicational if it gives a wide range of possibilities, wide associations, more worlds to conquer.

While planning, we can give to the future a thousand names. But a relationship to the present is needed. If one lays out the future, even the near future of organizations, as a hodge-podge of loose images, one takes on the role of a planner in the same sense as Saint John was a planner in the Apocalypse. The art of planning means finding many relationships, but still adhering to coherence.

Too much fussing with quantitative and statistical methods may also hold back the free flow of associations. In organizations, there are two types. There are those that understand long-range planning as a kind of budget planning, something that can be carried through unflinchingly. The other planning gives the imagination a chance.

There is a difference between normative, or long-range, plannnig and operative, or short-range, planning. Long-range planning almost of necessity becomes a workshop of imagination, an associative process, where those values that are already present or imminent in the organization are used as building bricks. The hopes of the planning group are given a concrete form.

MENTAL ASSOCIATIONS AND ORGANIZATIONAL LEARNING

Osmo Kuusi has made interesting linkages between autocommunication and organizational learning. In his article "How and Why to Communicate with Oneself" (1984), he has divided autocommunication into two types, according to its application:

Mythical tasks:
To strengthen beliefs (or visions)
To state the beliefs (or visions)
To search for a common feeling

Tasks related to learning:
To find new combinations
To memorize new combinations

He writes: "In order to bring to one's mind a thought, it is not necessary to repeat all the thinking processes that brought about the thought. Only a cue suffices. Such cues produce a jargon, which is used while looking for those who belong to the same coterie or outfit." Kuusi refers to the importance of finding new combinations in futurology and suggests that futurology is a typical autocommunication situation (p. 2).

Futurological books often present plans of the future as artistic images. Futurologists are using autocommunication and its second code profusely. Eric Wahlfors, for example, in his futurological work about Scandinavia, *Norden år 2030*, paints color pictures of the houses of the future. He has lately continued his task by hiring a ship which is a live show of futurology, a future trip. Bellamy had this same idea at the beginning of this century: he presented an image of one day in the future world.

Futurologists, like prophets, usually take their material from present-day realities. That is why the rockets of Jules Verne appear so outdated. Prophets who do not use the current vocabulary or imagery are not considered very interesting because they are unintelligible to us. St. John's

Apocalypse and the soothsayings of Nostradamus are examples of such difficult, long-range planning. Here, the ability to form mental associations has been cut loose from the present.

TWO KINDS OF CULTURE

Lotman distinguishes between two kinds of culture. The culture that concentrates on autocommunication concentrates on enhancement codes. In our experience, self-enhancement through autocommunicational planning is a fact of life in the Middle East. There, planning is a big deal, but in that area there is still much less follow-up and implementation of plans than in the West. It might be remarked that this sounds like "back home," but there are great differences of degree. Self-enhancing planning in the Middle East resembles meditational techniques, as we shall see.

Lotman maintains that the Western cultural attitude again is closer to the linear "hypodermic-needle" model, the "I-to-Him" type of communication. We mostly demand that plans be considered "real" messages, and we call them "good" only if a swift implementation is foreseen. In the West, we do not speak of planning as a meditation technique, even if it were, purely meditational.

Delahaye (1979) asserts that, in the West, it would be a disaster for a businessman to admit openly any relationship with the mythology of everyday life. Still, he shows how mythological the speeches of three major European leaders were. For example, in a speech about the economic future of France, Jacques Chirac described how France would take part in an "alchemistic rebirth," in which there would be a submersion into a cyclical time of Death and Rebirth. Here, France would become the Phoenix of the legends and achieve immortality. In fact, most of what politicians utter is mythology; politicians play on people's minds mostly with such mythological images as "Rebirth," "Golden Age," "Scapegoat." It is probably no exaggeration to argue that every politician (and, we may add, every company executive even) believes in Rebirth. Mythology is a mighty force, which moves governments and corporations. However, in the Western culture, it is not often admitted to be a fact of life, for reasons explained by Delahaye.

SOME CASES

Mythical Planning in the Middle East

Very often, planning, this effort to find new combinations, has a ritualistic character. It has a sense of holy communion, of transcendental meditation.

In the Middle East, one of the present authors participated in the work of planning one of the biggest scientific centers in the world. Housing complexes were actually being built; bills amounting to upwards of a million pounds came in almost daily. The offices abounded in colored, large-size papier-maché architects' models. There was really a feeling of go, and we all felt that we were at the pivotal point of a major event, one that can be experienced only once in a lifetime.

Natural conditions made the task difficult. The locality did not have any natural water resources. But expensively desalinated water could be piped in from a thousand miles away. Palm groves were planned and artificial ponds built, along which leading scholars and researchers, future Einsteins, could stroll, immersed in peripatetic discussions. It was planned to be both a great research center and a meeting place of the cutting edge of contemporary science. The physical part of the building activity took place at breathtaking speed.

Still, something was missing. All we were doing were houses, data bases, computer centers and audio-visual aids: in other words, more or less physical objects. But this kind of huge installation would have needed a scientific program to guide its research activities. If high-grade research was to be the end result, why were we building only houses and walls? What was the procedure for inviting people into them?

We did not know what was going to happen in block D, E, F, or G. The blocks were just built. We did not know where to put the humanists, where to put the philosophers or the physicists, where to put the architects, and what lines of research they were supposed to pursue. The center held futurology seminars, it is true, but their futurology was so far removed from our everyday work of building that it stood completely outside it. Planning went one way, and the actual building the other way. There was no connection between the two.

However, the project went forward, deadlines fell every day, and Western consultants built foundations for houses.

The physical appearance of the center was deemed extremely important, as were amenities of doubtful application, like a "swimming pool for nonswimmers."

In fact, the author has been in the same kind of situation twice. The other instance was in another Middle Eastern country. The deadlines for the contractors were quite strict, and the reason why anything happened was that the deadlines fell regularly, regardless of planning. Was this unplanned or misplanned work futile? We are inclined to think it was not.

Without the apocalyptic imagining and dreaming of the futurology seminars of the centers, there would *not* have been enough political will to pay the bills. However, the projects, with all their antics, could be justified by future research. Blocks D, E, F, and G could be utilized for the benefit of national research in some way not yet known. The costs of the gigantic project were also in proportion to the enormous state revenue during that period. The Research Centre would have its day at some future time. So the plan (or actually only a concept of doing things) was wrong and off key, but the end result was right, as in the case of the Sydney Opera House.

The staff meetings were illustrative examples of self-enhancing planning, or what we might call the mantra approach to planning. Philosophies criss-crossed over the conference table. Typically enough, the agendas were discussed beforehand at great length, but, during the discussions, they were laid aside. It was the feeling of forward thrust that mattered, the same feeling that the Chancellor of the Exchequer in Britain expressed at the start of the Concorde project: "Time is on the wing!"

The European state planning fad of the '70s consisted mainly of ego trips of this type. Many felt that a brighter future "beckoned with a golden finger" (a phrase bandied by the Concorde planners). They read a government departmental report, mimeographed on bad paper, and felt that they were Siegfrieds who were called upon to perform great deeds, such as building a state-owned factory. They did read facts, but they saw visions.

Criticism: All Planning Is Not Symbolic

Futurology, or long-range planning, seems to be prone to autocommunication. To state the truth, however, it must be acknowledged that there is much implemented, successful long-range planning. One example is the vast plan to renew the Finnish highway network in the '70s. Large-scale governmental planning could easily become autocommunicational, causing people later to say, "Thank God it was not implemented." In the case referred to, it gave a good infrastructure to the country.

Lee Iacocca's Chrysler success likewise stemmed from a plan that had very little of the symbolic about it, as told in his autobiography (*Iacocca* & Novak, 1984). Iacocca's book is admirably sober and free of symbolic expressions. Even the chapter on his methodology is clear-headed, without mythical overtones of "how we made it."

There is a strange discrepancy between Iacocca's book and his public performances. *Time* magazine's cover story of April 1, 1985, No. 13, portrays an "ebullient, passionate, volatile hipshooter" who gushes the choicest examples of American mythology. He is represented as a showman who in the end even wants to become President. A very different image from the one in the book. Which is the true one?

Further, we do not know yet whether his plans have really been successful. Iacocca has won a battle, but has he won the campaign? The Japanese are coming with undiminished vigor through their American subsidiaries.

Scientific Planning Methods

As one of the directors of Daimler-Benz, Edzard Reuter (1985) has remarked, the second, ego-enhancing code is often hidden in the garments of scientific methods like those of operations research. Charles E. Lindblom's (1959) by now classic study, "The Science of Muddling Through," describes this phenomenon. The planner might start by trying to list all related variables: full employment, reasonable business profit, etc. In planning to combat inflation, he would compare all policies in the light of the theory of prices. He would also consider strict central control and the abolition of all prices and markets on the one hand, and the elimination of all public controls on the other.

But this accumulation of more and more factors, and guarding against what is hard to foretell, are imaginary, as Lindblom notes. Intellectual capacities and sources of information are assumed that men do not possess. The gathering of too many unclear factors bears the seeds of disaster.

Trying to grasp the unknown, people in their quantitative zest add more variables. What is obtained is more variables, not the unknown.

Lindblom then suggests an "incremental planning" approach. This approach involves a method of successive limited comparisons and small adjustments to the present situation by so-called incremental planning.

Lindblom's incremental planning probably strikes gold, but it also overlooks an important human need, which autocommunication fulfills. He forgets hope and vision. Where does vision enter into incremental planning?

Taboo Aims in Organizations

Samuel Johnson wrote in his blunt manner that "Motives of action are unknown to men." At a time when nobody had yet spoken about organizational symbolism, Westerlund and Sjöstrand (1975) quite cogently classified some of the strangest kinds of organizational planning motives and hopes (p. 40). Here we find, in fact, the names of the autocommunicational devices that companies use to boost their hopes:

Type	Meaning
honorific Boy Scout aims	fictitious aims that credit the organization with qualities considered to be desirable by the environment
taboo aims	aims that one knows one has, but that one does not wish to, or should not, mention
stereotyped aims	based on norms for the way aims should look, regardless of the specific organization
existing aims	a composite picture of individuals', groups', and interested parties' endeavors in an organization (mixture of aims)
stated aims	e.g., stereotype aims instead of what is taboo or reality
repressed aims	aims that will not stand up when confronted with one's own valuations or one's own ego image
unconscious aims	one believes oneself to be working towards aim x, but in reality one works towards aim y

Is Even Budgetary Planning a Hype?

There are views even of budget planning as being futile. This is especially true of fiscal budgeting, but it appears also in business life (see Erik Dahmén, 1984). His analyses of prognostic failures are revealing. To hit the target, budgeting needs knowledge about more factors than anybody can command. Sometimes, the forecasters even vie among themselves to paint the brightest picture. Jan Wallander of Svenska Handelsbanken, a major Swedish bank, has written a pamphlet suggesting that even budgets should not be taken seriously at all, because the situation is bound to change in less than a year's time. Also Gunnar and Ulla Ehrlemark (1980) say in their illuminating book: "We have come to the conclusion that budgets cause more trouble than benefit."

Wallander's musings may be discarded by the people who are making day-to-day decisions, the executives. To think that even budgetary planning is a hype somehow seems to be against good taste and well-proven practices. It is like transforming the executive into a hopeless improviser, into a Hamlet whose doings have, in Shakespeare's words, "lost the name of action." But somebody should see the self-deception and hope element in all kinds of planning. Who? A scientific observer's position is different from an executive's.

Lotman's (1973) ideas on autocommunication provide us with the linguistic and communicational specifics or markers of wishful thinking and hope talk.

Hope Talk

That so much planning, even budgetary planning, is autocommunicational poses a problem: what to do with plans? Of course, they are not futile, but the contents of the planning ideology should be revised in the light of autocommunication. For the old teachers of planning heed Saint Paul's admonition: "Don't do as I do, but do as I say." Investors looking at ROI plans hope unconsciously that their money will come back, although the chances are it won't. What is this mixture of hope and built-in failure that seems to be the hallmark of planning?

At the core of the autocommunicational idea there seems to be the fact that autocommunicational planning, however far the outcome is from the original plan, gives new cues to the organization involved, helps it find new combinations.

East and West

On the basis of the foregoing, it ought to be more legitimate to accept the "new cues" aspect of planning, although it is a somewhat disconcerting idea. Our uneasiness about accepting ideas like planning as self-enhancement comes from the fact that we like to give planning "scientific" tasks it cannot perform. On the other hand, we do not hold in great esteem the values inherent in meditation, yet those values are present in autocommunicational planning. Even modern linguistics has mostly forgotten the language man speaks to himself. With this internal language, internal communication, he fabricates for himself hope and vision systems—and plans ultimately amount to hope and vision systems.

Eastern peoples traditionally had a better theoretical background while trying to reach for their visions; but in the West, teaching along similar lines are in disrepute, because we uphold our view of "hard-core" science.

Managerial sciences, having seen the shortcomings of planning, should be leading the way back to a combination of vision and good judgment. It is exactly management that has been among the first to reject the "superstition of management sciences." The thesis of Reuter (of Mercedes Benz) is that management and planning are, above all, good judgment and vision in daily dealings. He points out how much structural change in the market, for instance, is a matter of good guesswork, which no planning can replace.

Culturally, Lotman's theory reaches back towards the East. The visionary "second code" has an air of trying to reformulate a scientific basis for meditation and vision.

REFERENCES

Barnlund, D. C. (1971) A transactional model of communication." In L. L. Barker & R. J. Kibler (Eds.), *Speech communication behavior: Perspectives and principles*. Englewood Cliffs, NJ:Prentice-Hall.

Broms, H., & Gahmberg, H. (1981). *The mythology of the Chrysler crisis*. KODIKAS/CODE, Tuebingen, Germany: Guenther Narr Verlag.

Broms, H., & Gahmberg, H. (1982). *Mythology in management culture*. Helsinki, Finland: Publications of the Helsinki School of Economics, D-58.

Broms, H., & Gahmberg, H. (1983). Communication to self in organizations and cultures. *Administrative Science Quarterly*, Cornell Graduate School of Business and Public Administration, September.

Broms, H., & Gahmberg, H. (1987). *Semiotics of Management*. Helsinki: Helsinki School of Management.

Clausewitz, C., Von. (1976). *On war*. Princeton, NJ: Princeton University Press.

Dahmen, E. (1984). *Ekonomi i Omvandling*. Hfors, Finland: Finlands Bank.

Delahaye, Y. (1979). *Europe sous ies mots*. Paris: Payot.

Ehrlemark, G., & Ehrlemark, U. (1980). *Föreställningar och vanföreställningar om företag. Styrt, ostyrt och vanstyrt*. Lund, Sweden: Svenska Sivilekonomföreningen.

Hall, P. (1980). *Great planning disasters*. London: Weidenfeld and Nicholson.

Iacocca, L., & Novak, W. (1984). *Iacocca: An Autobiography*. Toronto, Canada: Bentam.

Iqbal, M. (n.d.). *The secrets of the self (Asrár-i-khudi). A philosophical poem*. [Transl. from the orig. Persian with introd. a. notes by R. A. Nicholson. 4 ed. Lahore 1950.]

Jakobson, R. (1972). Linguistik und Poetik." In H. Blumensath (Ed.), *Strukturalismus in der Literaturwissenschaft*. Köln:Kiepenheuer & Witsch.

Kuusi, O. (1984). *Miksi ja miten kommunikoida itselleen* (How and why to communicate with oneself). Paper read at the 4th Semiotic Conference of Semiotics in Finland. Helsinki, Oct. 1984.

Latouche, D. (1982). Paper presented for the XII World Congress of the International Political Science Association, August 9-14, Rio de Janeiro.

Lindbom, C. E. (1959). The science of muddling through. *Public Administration Review, 19*(2), 79-88.

Lotman, J. (1973). Ueber Zwei Kommunikationsmodelle in Kultursystem. Anonymous translation of "Trudy po znakovym sistemam." VI, Tartu.

Lotman, J. (1977). Two models of communication. In D. P. Lucid (Ed. and Trans.), *Soviet semiotics: An anthology*. Baltimore, MD: Johns Hopkins University Press.

Malaska, P. (1977). *Patterns of development in an organization*. Turku, Finland: Publications of the Turku School of Economics, A-5.

Mitroff, I.I., & Kilmann, R.H. (1976). On organizational stories: An approach to the design and analysis of organizations through myths and stories." In R.H. Kilmann (Eds.), *The management of organization design (Vol. 1)* New York: North Holland & Elsevier.

Oguibenine, B. (1979). Looking back on linguistic models of culture in Russian semiotics. *PTL: Journal for Descriptive Poetics and Theory of Literature, 4*, 91–118.

Pareto, V. (1968). *The rise and fall of the elites: An application of theoretical sociology*. (Intro. by Hans L. Zetterberg). Totowa, NJ: Bedminster Press.

Propp, V. (1958). *Morphology of the folktale*. Austin, TX: University of Texas Press (1929).

Reuter, E. (1985). Zwischen Management und Mythos. *Die Zeit, 13*, March 1985.

de Saussure, F. (1972). *Course in general linguistics*, (Trans. and annotated by R. Harris). London: Duckworth (originally published in 1916).

Thayer, L. (1968). *Communication and communication systems*. Homewood, IL: Irwin.

Waris, K. (1983). Statsbudgeten inte realistisk. *Ekonomiska Samfundets Tidskrift, 1*, 19–21.

Westerlund, G., & Sjöstrand, S.-E. (1979). *Organizational myths*. London and New York: Harper & Row.

Zolkiewski, S. (1979). Quelques problemes de sémiotique de la culture chez les auteurs est-Européens. In S. Chatman (Ed.), *A semiotic landscape*. The Hague: Mouton.

Author Index

Subject Index

Dependency, 112
Dialogue, vs. collective monologue, 122
Downward flows, 88
Dramaturgical skills, 55
Duty, 113 ff.

E
Educational failures (U. S.), 186
E. I. du Pont de Nemours Company,
  84 ff.
"Eloquence," as effective language use,
  58 ff.
Enactment, 4 ff.
Enhancement of experience, 60 ff.

F
Face-to-face interaction, 120–127
Form vs. content, 108 ff.
Forms of discourse, honorific/
  depreciatory, 113–114
Frame, 130 ff.
Functionalist approaches, 54

G
Group affiliation, 111 ff.
Group dynamics, & linguistic encoding,
  110–117

H
Haiku poetry, 119
Hand copying, 84–85
Hologram, 160
Honne, 140 ff.
Hope talk, 215

I
IBM, 172–173
Identity, 138 ff., 153 ff.
Illinois Central Railroad, 84 ff.
Image-making, 3
  as strategic function, 12–18
Imagery, and strategy, 12–18
  and change, 18
Images, 38
  as cognitive structures, 11 ff.
  managerial, 61
  of the organization, 22, 41
  organizational, 61
Imitation, role of, 144–145
Innovations, and organizational growth,
  87
  in record-keeping, 82 ff.

Interaction boundaries, 112–113
Interpretive approaches, characteristics of,
  48 ff.
  implications of, 46 ff.
Interpretive schemata, 7
ITT, 172–173

J
Japanese, management, 161–170
  management models, 132 ff.
  social systems, 173–176
  thinking, geometry of, 140–144
  thought, 145 ff.
Japanese culture, conceptual barriers to
  understanding, 137–152
  control mechanisms, 147
  diffuse calculus of belonging, 137–140
  distinctive influences, 156–159
  of organizational communication,
  136–181
  surface vs. deep, 147–148
Japanese vs. American thinking, 139–140,
  143–145, 147–148, 150
Jin, 159 ff.

K
Kami, 154
Kansas Democratic Party, 23 ff.
"Knowledge, sociology of," 4

L
Language, and culture, 107 ff.
  as mediation, 108 ff.
  managerial, 5 ff., 11 ff.
  role at work, 107 ff.
Language and judgment, 145
Lateral flows, 88 ff.
Leadership/followership, 107 ff., 130 ff.,
  170
Learning, organizational, 6 ff.
  individual, 6–7
Letter press, 85 ff.
Linguistic communication, two modes,
  205–207
  encoding, 110–117
"Linguistic gestalt," 122
"Loose" copies, 90–95

M
Man and nature, 156 ff.
  in Japanese thought, 159
Managerial "eloquence," 58 ff.